Contents

FORESTS   85

DESERTS 169

PRAIRIES 227

Introduction

I'm not exactly sure how the notion of the Rocky Mountain West drifted across half a continent to take hold of me, an eight-year-old boy, sitting in the corn fields of Indiana. Maybe it seeped from the musty pages of an old *Writers Project* tour guide, or poured out into the living room one Sunday night, when the "Wonderful World of Disney" was airing "Bear Country," or some such "True Life Adventure." But take hold it did. Two years later I got my first glimpse of the Colorado front range from the back seat of a '64 Impala, and I knew it was true love. I went home, sent in my subscription to *Rocky Mountain West* magazine, and announced to my parents that, if it was all the same to them, the Rockies was the place for me. Like my heroes—the trappers, explorers, naturalists, and wagon-train guides—I had come to a conclusion at the ripe age of ten similar to that of William Blake, 150 years earlier. "Great things are done," he said, "when men and mountains meet."

It was not until I had lived here for some time that I began to catch on to the fact that there was far more to be found in these Rocky Mountain states than just mountains. There were forests—great, wet cathedrals of ancient redcedars in the northwest corner of Montana, and lonely pockets of pinyon and juniper huddled in New Mexico along the old Santa Fe Trail. Deserts were here, too. I found windswept tablelands in Wyoming where wild horses still poured from the mouths of sagebrush draws, and ruts along the Texas border from the wheels of John Butterfield's stage. And perhaps most surprising of all, I found beautiful prairie—places where June grass and bluestem still rippled at the feet of wooden windmills, and where the great swells of land and sky held lean, fleet herds of pronghorn, and great clatters of southbound birds.

The majority of these walks are not meant to take you to any particular destination; indeed, many of the turnaround points are quite arbitrary. I've tried only to point you down the quietest, most gentle paths possible, introduce you to a few of the neighbors, and leave the rest to you and Mother Nature.

You'll find the trails here have been divided into four different ecosystems: mountain, forest, desert, and prairie. Each of these ecosystems has several clusters of from two to five walks, spread across as wide a geographical area as possible. This arrangement will allow you to explore the same environment in several different locations, while ensuring that there will be other walks fairly close to the one you're taking. You'll find a special locator map before each cluster; specific written directions are at the beginning of each individual trail.

A few of the walks we've included in the northern mountain and forest sections of the book will take you into grizzly bear country. Each of these has been specially marked. Far from scaring you away, these notations are simply to remind you to act in a way that will best allow you to enjoy the area, while leaving these magnificent creatures to their own business. One good way to avoid any contact with bears is to make sure that they are aware of your presence. Tying a decent bell onto your shorts or day pack so that it produces a sound ring with each step is an excellent precaution. If you do happen to see a bear, or any large mammal, *never* approach or make loud, startling noises. Take another route, and if that isn't possible, wait until the animal moves away on its own. The few small slices of the American West that have retained a significant portion of their former levels of wildness are precious, priceless gifts. The grizzly is a thrilling part of that wilderness—a measure of integrity that reflects not only the condition of the ecosystem but the condition and compassion of man himself.

"No one else looks out on the world so kindly and charitably as a pedestrian," said John Burroughs; "no one else gives and takes so much from the country as he passes through." May your saunters down these warm, brown paths convince you he was right.

WALKS OF
THE ROCKIES

MOUNTAINS

Although over half of the landscape of the Rocky Mountain states is composed of plains, plateaus, and deserts, it is the mountains we dream about most, the mountains we remember best. These soaring parapets of granite and gneiss, limestone and shale, form a world like no other on earth—a bold, astounding place, a sacred marriage of earth and sky. More than a few miners who came here in the nineteenth century looking for gold seemed unable to get enough of the Rockies, routinely selling out promising claims for the chance to roam even deeper into these dense forests, to make their way even farther along some icy braid of mountain water.

The geologic story of the Rockies is a complex one, not fully understood even today. While the oldest rocks in these states can be dated back more than 2 billion years—fully half as old as the earth itself—the rise of land that would become the Rockies we know today began much later, perhaps 50 to 60 million years ago. (These mountains are actually very young when compared to those of the eastern United States.) The ridge of Rocky Mountains through New Mexico, Colorado, Wyoming, and Montana is located in the center of a large tectonic plate, one of more than a dozen gargantuan land masses that encircle the globe. It is the ability of such plates to actually move, to drift across a broth of molten rock deep within the earth that, 200 million years ago, allowed the entire North American continent to break from Europe and drift 1,500 miles to the west. Weakness in the center of this plate allowed turmoils deep within the earth to cause great, slow uplifts, or *orogenies*, throughout the Rocky Mountain states. This was followed by a massive rise across a large portion of Colorado and New Mexico, accompanied in some regions by periods of intense volcanism.

Yet much of what we find most exciting about the high Rockies—the great rock amphitheaters, cobalt-colored lakes, and waterfalls making dramatic plunges into enormous, U-shaped valleys—are the result of the chilling scour of glacial ice. Over the past 2 million years there have been at least four periods when great sheets of ice ground their way out of the high country, where it often surrounded all but the highest peaks, carving the landscapes as effectively as hot metal scoops in a carton of ice cream. Small snow-field remnants of the last active glacial period, which ended roughly 20,000 years ago, still can be seen in many high folds of the Rocky Mountains.

More delicate though no less spectacular touches occurred thanks to the erosive power of wind and water. It was the incessant beating of raindrops, the splitting power of ice freezing and thawing between cracks in the rock surfaces, that gave many of the Rocky Mountain peaks their rugged, dramatic profiles—a sculpting process that continues to this day. It's important to remember that as the land uplifted, the streams and rivers rose also, giving them extraordinary strength. It was the "power of descent" that allowed the Colorado, the San Juan, and the Clarks Fork of the Yellowstone to create magnificent canyons. Inch by inch these rivers cut, exposing layer after layer of rock. As a result, today we are left with a canyon compendium of earth history that geologists can read as one might flip through the pages of a book.

By sending the landscape ever so slowly skyward, the forces that created the Rocky Mountains also determined what kind of plants (and therefore animals) would be able to live here. As you've undoubtedly noticed on your visits to the mountains, the air becomes colder the higher you go. Add to this the fact that cool air cannot hold as much moisture as warm air can, and you've got the key that unlocks a good portion of the Rocky Mountain climate mystery. Air coming in from the west will rise up the western flanks of the Rockies (after having already done the same above the Cascades or Sierras), losing most of its precipitation in the cold air of the high country—a fact that tends to make skiers very happy.

4

By the time it descends again over the eastern side of the range these air masses have very little moisture left to give. This is why there is a great belt of dry prairie running up the east side of each of the Rocky Mountain states. Such uplifts are also, incidentally, what cause the summer thunderstorms that are so common to the Rockies. Air lying next to the sun-warmed earth begins to rise in the early afternoon, invariably dropping its load of rain on surprised backpackers trekking the high mountain trails. (Be aware of this phenomenon, and that such thunderstorms often are accompanied by lightning, when you walk the mountain paths in this book.)

This well-regulated moisture-release system has created fairly predictable zones of vegetation. Depending on where you begin your trek up the mountains, you may pass first through a pinyon and juniper woodland, most often growing in lower areas that receive 10 to 20 inches of precipitation per year. Rabbitbrush, mountain mahogany, Mormon tea, and bunches of ricegrass and blue grass are typical companions. As you move up, the pinyon–juniper forest gives way to ponderosa or Douglas-fir, which in turn gives way to lodgepole pine and aspen. Finally there are the great, sweeping blankets of subalpine fir and Engelmann spruce, both battling their way up to the very limits of tree-growth, shrinking in the process to little more than ragged flag trees and creeping mats, their branches sheered by the raw, stinging fingers of the high country winds.

Above this line trees do not stray. Temperatures, usually averaging no more than 45 degrees Fahrenheit even in summer, create a growing season too short for trees to maintain their cells, let alone repair damage wrought by the winter winds that blow in excess of a hundred miles per hour. At this level you will find relatively few species of wildlife. White-crowned sparrows, horned larks, and brown-capped rosy finches nest in dwarf timber, grassy meadows, and along high cliffs. Elk and mule deer show up here and there to feed on the tundra grasses, while bighorn sheep can be seen dancing on dizzy stages that have been chiseled from the steep sides of the mountains. Coyotes, bobcats, and weasels meander through the rock gardens, and are gone. As winter is pulled across the landscape, all but the truly hardy drift down to the protection of the timber below. Plump yellow-bellied marmots

5

settle into their burrows for a long winter's nap, not to emerge again until the onset of the breeding season in the spring. Pikas, however, remain active throughout the winter, existing on larders of grass that were cut and dried on flat rocks during the previous summer. White-tailed ptarmigans are the sole bird to brave this long, bitter season, nestling into snow banks out of the wind, feeding on the tender buds of willow to survive.

The Rocky Mountains are not a forgiving landscape. Their storms can rise as if from beneath a magician's cape, turning a pleasant summer ramble into a frantic dance with spears of lightning. Autumn can dawn sunny and still, and by late morning be cloaked with great curtains of gray clouds bulging with ice and snow. Yet humans have always relished the mystery in these rocky folds. They came for the adventure, the thrills, or, as one refugee explorer from a well-to-do nineteenth-century family put it, for "freedom from conventionalities and a disregard of those social amenities to which I was accustomed." It was once said that the wild country of the Rocky Mountains never judged a person according to his or her past accomplishments or failures, but rather on the state of character at that particular moment. Indeed, to anyone standing atop the wind-scoured peaks for the first time, the Rockies could offer hardly anything *but* the present moment—a long, lovely eternity, stretching past the gentle curve of the far horizon.

Northwestern Montana

BLAINE MOUNTAIN

Distance: 4 miles
Location: From the town of Hungry Horse, head south on the West Reservoir Road (Forest Road 895). Then turn right near the Doris Boat Landing, on Forest Road 895A, and continue west for about 5 miles to Forest Road 1602. This leads to the trailhead in approximately 2 miles.
Note: Forest Road 1602 is a narrow, shrub-lined dirt road. While certainly driveable with most two-wheel drive vehicles, it may not suit the tastes of some readers. Another option is to park along the first 0.5 miles of route 1602 and simply walk the road. You still will have fantastic views, with fine opportunities to see wildlife.

At the time of this writing, a branch of Doris Creek, approximately 0.5 miles from the trailhead, had cut into the road to the point where small vehicles could no longer cross easily. Parking near this creek will add an extra mile to the walk, but it's a very pleasant mile, some of it along a tumbling mountain stream, with grand views of the high peaks of the Great Bear Wilderness to the east. If you have the time and patience to get to this location, you'll find the walk to be one of the finest available for sweeping views of the west Montana high country.

Near the beginning of the trail you'll be passing through lush gardens of cow parsnip, leafy aster, twinberry, alder, fireweed, and the fine, delicate purple hoods of the harebell. The harebell is quite common in Scotland, also known by the names "bluebell of Scotland" and "witches' thimble." This latter reference to witches, by the way, may give a clue to the origin of the name harebell, as well. In the Scottish Highlands, witches were once thought to be able to change into hares at will. Thus it was

7

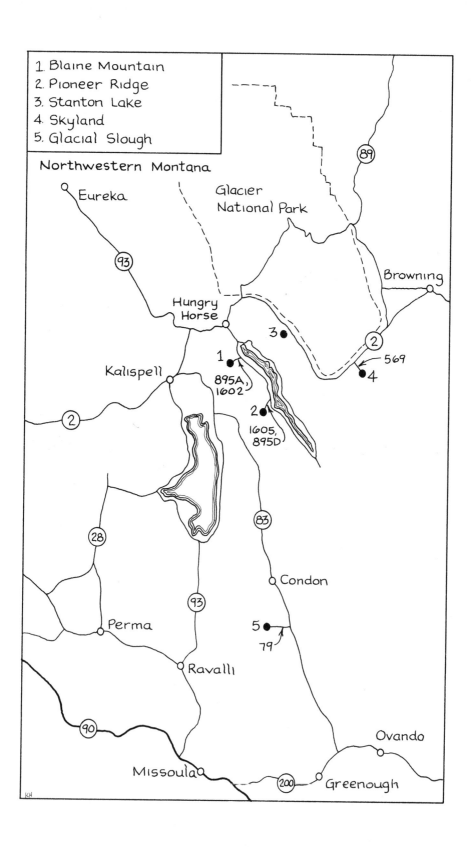

1. Blaine Mountain
2. Pioneer Ridge
3. Stanton Lake
4. Skyland
5. Glacial Slough

Northwestern Montana

89

Eureka

Glacier
National Park

93

Browning

Hungry
Horse

Kalispell

3

1

895A,
1602

2

569

4

2

1605,
895D

2

83

28

Condon

93

Perma

5

79

Ravalli

90

Ovando

Missoula

200

Greenough

KH

considered a very bad omen to have a hare cross your path as you were out walking the countryside. (Relax—the only bunny you may see on this walk is the mountain cottontail, and it really isn't a true hare at all.)

As the trail climbs gradually along a series of switchbacks, you'll get fantastic views of the Flathead Range to the east, between Hungry Horse Reservoir and Glacier National Park. These peaks, as well as the striking block formations of Glacier, were carved from a great slab of rock 1 billion years old, migrating to its present location from the west some 65 million years ago. It was this transported assemblage of Precambrian sedimentary rock that was eventually eroded by ice, rain, and snow to form the great drainage split known as the Continental Divide.

While the importance of conservationists' efforts to protect this wilderness cannot be overestimated, the truth is that most of these areas, in particular Glacier National Park, originally were

Peregrine Falcon

9

protected because they were not considered to be good for much else. The Hudson Bay Company's fur harvest had come and gone by the time the national park bill first came up in 1907, as had a minor mining boom along the Continental Divide. Promises of oil around the turn of the century were, thankfully, short-lived, and much of the park did not contain a great amount of profitable timber. In addition, some legislators were swayed by the argument that this area, as fine as any in Europe, could be used to grab a lucrative tourist trade that was spending too much time and money in the Alps of Switzerland. In 1909, on the third try, the bill to establish Glacier National Park was passed. Other wildernesses in the region followed much later, with the last of these, the Great Bear, created in 1974.

Interestingly, at the hearings for establishing Glacier National Park, one congressman objected to the whole idea, claiming that the area was so remote and inaccessible that it never could be exploited anyway. Less than 75 years later, in 1980, a report to Congress on the state of the national parks identified Glacier as the most beleaguered national park in the country, with 56 separate threats to its integrity, primarily from energy development proposals around its perimeter. Even with current protections, it will take a considerable effort to protect the wild essence of this region in the years ahead. The biggest problem is that national parks were established according to political rather than ecological boundaries. A grizzly bear wandering her territory has no way of knowing that she's just crossed the line into an area slated for mining development or summer homes. It would seem an easy solution to simply add buffer zones in the national forests that would help ensure that the needs be met of the wild residents of the region; unfortunately, the trend in forest management has been to yield to demands to develop the energy resources that lie within the forests.

Climbing higher, you'll find yourself in an increasingly thick quilt of high country sights and smells—a whiff of balsam fir mixed with moist soil, the sway of lavender wildflowers dancing in the afternoon winds. You can turn around at any point along this gradual climb, or follow the path a total of 2 miles to a quiet meadow where it meets the Alpine 7 trail. The Alpine 7 is a spectacular footpath, running along a high ridge just south of Columbia Falls into the beautiful Swan Range, east of Flathead Lake.

PIONEER RIDGE

Distance: 1.5 miles
Location: From the town of Hungry Horse, head south along
the west side of Hungry Horse Reservoir on Forest Road 895.
Just past Cayton Creek, turn right on Forest Road 1633/1605,
and follow the signs toward Goldie Creek. In 5.4 miles you'll
reach a T intersection with Forest Road 895D; turn right. The
road ends at the trailhead, about 8.5 miles from where you first
turned off the reservoir road. Our trail takes off to the right
(southwest).

This walk is very special in that it will allow you, after only a short
climb, to be literally "on top of the world." Pioneer Ridge is a
little-used high line of grassy hilltops, offering spectacular views of
Hungry Horse Reservoir and the Great Bear Wilderness to the east,
and the Swan and Mission Ranges to the south. To the west are the
rugged peaks of the Jewel Basin Hiking Area, lying between you
and the beautiful 200-square-mile Flathead Lake. Short of donning
a pack and getting down to some serious trail work, there may not
be a more expansive view in the area.

For the short term, you're in for some climbing, working

Hammond's Flycatcher

11

your way up a grassy ridge for about 0.25 mile to the intersection with the Pioneer Ridge Trail. The trail becomes faint in some places, but if you simply remember to keep heading up along the obvious flank of the hill, you'll reach the top in fine shape. On the last stretch of the climb, look carefully to your left and you'll spot a fire tower on the next knoll. Though no longer manned, for years this lookout served as an effective early warning system for spotting wildfires brewing in the vast expanses of the Flathead National Forest. Before the advent of air surveillance, forest lookouts saved thousands of national forest acres each year. During World War II, women were routinely recruited for this duty right out of high school. Comfortable with the solitary nature of the job, they have made up the majority of the lookout force since then. Interestingly, with the cost of airplane patrols rising and forest budgets falling, the popularity of the lookout may yet rebound.

Once on top of Pioneer Ridge, take a left and head southeast along a series of grassy, windswept alpine hummocks, turning around and heading back when the notion strikes you.

Besides a large collection of beargrass tufts, you should see fine gardens of lupine, paintbrush, pink spirea, and asters, all folded into a spotty conifer forest. You'll notice that some of the plants on this high ridge, while familiar, are growing in stunted form. In fact, one of the most important survival adaptations of alpine plants is to restrict the size of their growth shoots. Hugging the ground helps them to remain out of the worst of the weather. Also, since the growing season is shorter at high elevations, there is a distinct advantage to putting precious sun energy into the development of flowers instead of stems. (The grasses are more normal in size; their narrow leaves and protected reproductive parts are not as likely to be damaged by the roaring mountain winds.)

The grassy ridge you'll be walking along here supports a surprising population of small rodents, which means that hunting birds, like Swainson's hawks, are often seen cruising these alpine byways looking for dinner. These fine fliers migrate from Montana in great flocks each autumn, finally setting up winter housekeeping 12,000 to 15,000 miles to the south, in Argentina. Also no strangers

Lupine

to this wild place are golden eagles, who in this area make most of their meals out of the available supply of pocket gophers, voles, and rabbits. A short distance off the exposed ridges you may see rosy finches, mountain bluebirds, Clark's nutcrackers, and Steller's jays. You may recognize both of the latter birds by their loud calls, as well as by their brazen tendency to steal food from picnic areas throughout the forests of the Rockies.

Mountain Bluebird

STANTON LAKE

Distance: 2.5 miles

Location: Located on the south side of U.S. Highway 2, 0.25 mile west of mile marker 170. A sign is next to the turnoff that reads Stanton Lake Trail 146. Because there is only a small parking area at the trailhead, you may want to park along the power-line corridor next to U.S. Highway 2 and walk the extra 50 yards to the trail.

Special Note: This is bear country: please take appropriate precautions.

Just as an old adage warns us not to judge books by their covers, we must be careful of shunning trails because of what happens in the first few steps. If you haven't guessed, I'm talking about a climb at the beginning of the Stanton Lake trail. Standing at the bottom looking up, you may be tempted to scrap this walk entirely, or at least sit down in the path and hope for a lift from a southbound mountain goat. In fact, the toughest section of the walk is over rather quickly, and virtually all climbing will have come to an end before a half mile of trail has passed beneath your feet. If you need more convincing, there's some beautiful plant life to study during rest stops, and the view at the end of the walk is a treasure like few you'll ever see.

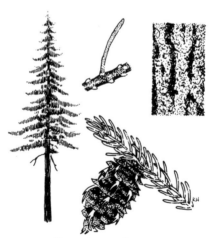

Douglas-fir

If you've spent much time in other forests of the Rocky Mountain states, you may be surprised at how incredibly lush this corner of the Rockies is. Fir, spruce, birch, and larches grow thick here, while the open ground is covered with thick green carpets of bracken fern, fireweed, thimbleberry, cow parsnip, red twinberry, and false Solomon's seal. To the native people of this region these wild gardens were pantries, medicine cabinets, and general stores all rolled into one. Thimbleberries, as well as the young shoots and leaves of the fireweed (so named for its ability to colonize burned areas), made very tasty eating, while cow parsnip and the sap of the western larch had significant medicinal values. Sewing thread could be obtained from the stringy outer layers of larch tree roots, and birch bark provided an excellent covering for canoes. Despite this bounty, most of us shudder to think how much time and energy it took to harvest and prepare each of these plants so that they could be used to sustain everyday life. However, is it any more amazing to consider how much time we spend today making money, only to trade it in for food and shelter that was once free?

In 0.5 mile the trail flattens out onto a bench with beautiful views to the left and slightly behind you of the majestic mountains in the southern tip of Glacier National Park. The landscape of the Glacier region is truly spectacular—a great storyboard of geologic history. Here one can see thick, multicolored layers of rocks that are at least a billion years old. This congregation of stone formed a block nearly 2 miles thick, and actually migrated here from the

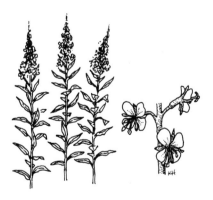

Fireweed

15

west over what is known as an overthrust belt. During the ice ages, tremendous rivers of glacial ice, some thousands of feet thick, carved the peaks into a collage of horns, cirques, and long, straight valleys. In fact, the stream you hear below (Stanton Creek) actually gets its start at the foot of a remnant glacier 8 miles to the southwest.

A hundred yards after entering the Great Bear Wilderness, you'll come to an open spot along the trail that offers a wonderful view to the southwest of Great Northern Mountain and Mount Grant, 8,705 feet, and 8,790 feet high, respectively. Near here you'll also get your first good glimpse of Stanton Lake. Shortly after this view spot, the trail will begin to make a descent, most of which is much more gradual than the fast climb you made at the beginning of the walk.

The outlet stream of Stanton Lake is a wide, meandering ribbon of crystal framed on either side by the dark green of fir trees—the classic hiker's fantasy of an alpine wonderland. Just after crossing a small wooden footpath over a wet area, you'll come to a path on the left in the middle of an incredibly lush garden of cow parsnip, ferns, fireweed, and paintbrush. This small path will take you to the north shore of the lake, where a few old logs serve as perfect perches on which to enjoy the view.

Sitting here, gazing down this long blue line of mountain water, it's easy to imagine that time has hardly budged since great fur trappers like Thomas Fitzpatrick and David Jackson plied the streams of this region during the 1820s looking for beaver. Reading the diaries of these early explorers one gets the sense that it was the adventure just as much as the promise of riches that kept them roaming the wilds season after season.

SKYLAND

Distance: 4 miles
Location: From U.S. Highway 2, just east of mile marker 195, head south on Forest Road 569 for 3.9 miles. Here you'll see a sign on the left side of the road for trail 382 to Elk Calf Mountain. Our walk takes off about 20 yards past this on the other side of the road. You can park 0.75 mile farther at a wide place on the right.
Note: The first mile of this trail can be muddy; wear appropriate shoes.
Special Note: This is bear country; please take appropriate precautions.

After a steep but very short climb, this trail heads northwest along a high bench, offering fine glimpses of Elkcalf and Flattop Mountains to the northeast, near the Continental Divide. Although much of this trail meanders through a rather sheltered plant community, there is a very definite "wilderness" here, borne of the thick fir forests that mark the high, lonesome country of the Rockies. This is the land of grizzly and black bears, elk, deer, and moose; here are the twitters and squawks of Steller's jays and Clark's nutcrackers, and the silent wings of golden eagles soaring on the mountain winds.

Along the first mile of trail you'll be in gardens of subalpine fir, queencup lily, twinberry, Canada violets, thimbleberry, and

Clark's Nutcracker

17

asters, as well as the beautiful yellow columbine. This latter flower derives its name from the Latin word for "dove," since the bloom somewhat resembles a cluster of five doves, their heads formed by the bloom's trailing spurs.

This walk does have some climbing sections, but these are often relieved by flat or brief downhill stretches. At just under a mile the path tops a small knoll and then continues on a faint roadway. Just past this point a trail takes off to the left, heading into a northern arm of the Great Bear Wilderness; we'll keep to the right. From here you'll notice the forest becoming a bit less congested. Alder thickets and the 7-foot-tall rustyleaf menziesia give way to open areas dotted with the plants more common to soils somewhat better drained. The tufts of thin, needle-shaped grass you see along the path belong to beargrass. This is the same plant that produces very large clusters of beautiful white flowers on a green stalk 2 to 3 feet tall. Beargrass sends up this large tuft of blooms only once every 4 to 7 years, so in any given season there will be only a portion of the plants actually flowering. While the grassy base may look like it would provide good forage, running one through your hand will give you an idea of how very tough these leaves really are. In fact, with the exception of the Rocky Mountain goat, very few animals will eat them. Northwest Indians

Beargrass

used the dried leaves to weave very durable clothing and baskets; hence the plant's common name "basket grass."

About 1.3 miles into the walk, along a climbing section of trail, you'll pass a beautiful collection of wildflowers on the right, set against a grand view of both the mountains to the northeast along the Continental Divide as well as the Blacktail Hills in the southern reaches of Glacier National Park. Besides lupine, paintbrush, beargrass, and stonecrop, in June and early July there will be the delicate three-petaled flowers of the mariposa lily. This plant has a bulb-shaped root that tastes a great deal like a potato. The Indians used it widely as a food source, as did thousands of very hungry Mormon settlers in Utah, who were so thankful for its presence in those early years that they ended up making it the Utah state flower.

It's often been written that the area before you, in particular the rugged mountainscape of Glacier National Park, was land that was avoided even by the Indians. This simply is not so. The Blackfoot in particular regarded many sites in these mountains as sources of great spiritual power and not only used them regularly for religious ceremonies but lost a number of their best warriors defending the place from intruders.

At 2 miles you'll reach our turnaround point—a flat section of trail with a sweeping view of the high country to the north and east. As you look north into the peaks of Glacier, the trees before you are subalpine fir, certainly the most abundant fir in the American West. Their tall green spires lend a bold, dramatic beauty to the Rocky Mountain high country, marking one of the last belts of protective vegetation before reaching the wind-blasted rock above timberline. At the base of a couple of these firs you can see small semicircles of young, shrubby-looking trees. When branches of the subalpine fir are held down by heavy winter snows, they will often take root, thus creating these clusters of small growths sometimes referred to as "snowmats." The other tree near to you (primarily behind you) on this perch is the lodgepole pine—the only type of pine in the area to bear its needles in clusters of two.

Sitting atop a high, wild slice of mountain such as this one seems to somehow shorten the span between present time and the days when Blackfoot warriors roamed these rocky folds. The Black-

Subalpine Fir

foot drifted into this country in the early part of the seventeenth century, during their famous "dog days," when great packs of dogs carried their meager possessions across the land, following the seasons of the buffalo. Comparing them to other tribes of the region, one writer called them "the most independent and happy people." For most of the nineteenth century they were able to remain surprisingly strong and confident, taking the best of European culture—horses, guns, metal arrow points—and adding it to their traditional life. Only when they were forced off this rugged, windswept land, which was the true source of their power and inspiration, did their bold, unfettered spirits begin to wane.

GLACIAL SLOUGH

Distance: 3 miles

Location: From State Highway 83, roughly 20 miles north of Seeley Lake, turn west on Forest Road 79, at the sign for Lindbergh Lake. (This turn is just north of mile marker 34.) Continue west on Forest Road 79, staying right at the first fork in the road. In 3.7 miles you'll reach a signed junction; take a right, following 79 toward Bunyon Lake. The trailhead will be just under 0.5 mile from the junction, where the road makes a sharp horseshoe turn to the left. Park in the large grassy area adjacent to the trail.

This walk begins with a long, gentle meander through a quiet forest draped with black tree lichen. This stringy, eerie looking plant, which, with the right amount of moisture hangs in many conifer forests in profusion, was once an important source of food for area Indian peoples. Usually baked with either wild onion or the bulbs of camas lilies, the concoction has a slightly sweet flavor, and looks far better in the pot than it does in the rough.

During the first 0.5 mile of the walk you'll also pass lots of needle-shaped grass tufts, a few of which may have sprouted tall green stems with beautiful white flower clusters. These represent the two stages of beargrass, certainly one of the most common and frequently photographed plants of northwest Montana. Only once every 4 to 7 years will the tufts actually produce blooms. Also along the right side of the trail is a healthy collection of buffaloberry. These beautiful red berries were a favorite food of both settlers and Indians; members of the Flathead tribe made a solution from the bark that was quite effective as a relief for sore eyes.

Shortly after crossing a road, the trail descends a small incline to join a hollow that has the appearance of having been furnished by an entirely different decorator. While the ground was vegetated only sparsely a short distance before, here there is suddenly a riot of green plants, including grasses, false hellebore, twinberry, and the lovely wavy-edged, arrow-shaped leaves of pathfinder.

If you've been wondering why this walk was placed in the mountain section of the book, suddenly coming out onto the glacial slough at 1.5 miles will satisfy your curiosity. Here a large, crys-

21

White-tailed Deer

Mule Deer

talline pool of water (Glacier Creek) flows through an immense depression, or glacial slough, its cool water nursing a lush pocket of deep green sedges and canary grass. To the southwest, a striking pair of mountain peaks—Lindy and Daughter of the Sun Mountain—rise from the southern reaches of the Mission Mountains Wilderness. At your feet are tiny blooms of elephant heads, peppering the shoreline with delicate spatters of lavender.

This entire section of the Swan River Valley was covered with ice 15,000 years ago as great glaciers pushed slowly southward from British Columbia. About 10,000 years ago the climate moderated and the ice began to melt. The depressions that had been scoured from the earth—some deep, and some, like this one, shallow—began to fill with millions of gallons of melt water. It is, in fact, thanks to this glacial scouring that the Swan River Valley has so many beautiful natural lakes.

Additional tongues of ice protruding from the mouths of nearby mountain valleys hung on longer. When they did melt, the large accumulations of sediment they carried in their icy fingers (glacial till) were left to accumulate in large mounds. One such deposit, known as a glacial moraine, is located along the shore of Lindbergh Lake, less than 2 miles to the southeast of where you now stand.

It's hard to imagine that just one hundred centuries ago this valley was little more than a long line of mud, sand, and gravel. Inch by inch, life gained a toehold on the land. Mosses slowly turned to grasses, which turned to shrubs, which finally made way for mature conifer forests. In our brief life span, it's easy to forget that this ecosystem, indeed the entire earth, is a melting pot of change—a dance between the forces of nature that sometimes leads to creation, sometimes to destruction, but never comes to rest.

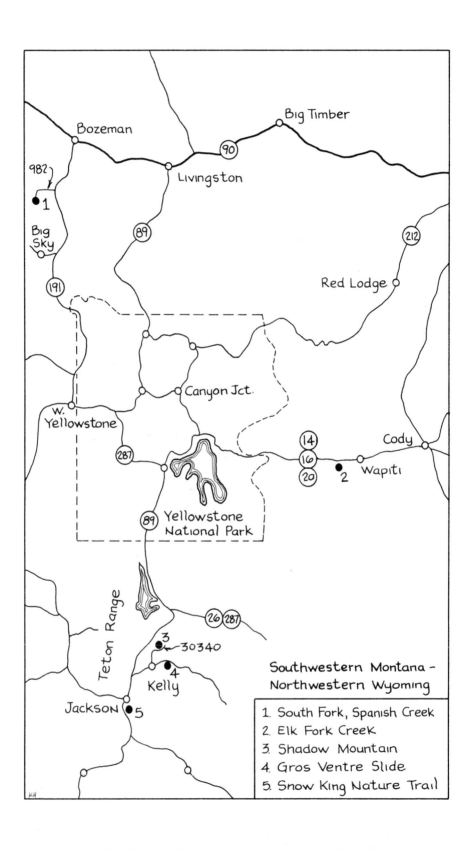

Bozeman

Big Timber

90

Livingston

982

● 1

Big
Sky

89

191

Red Lodge

212

Canyon Jct.

W.
Yellowstone

Cody

14

16

● 2 Wapiti

287

20

89 Yellowstone
National Park

Teton Range

26 287

3
● —30340

● 4
Kelly

Jackson ● 5

Southwestern Montana –
Northwestern Wyoming

1. South Fork, Spanish Creek
2. Elk Fork Creek
3. Shadow Mountain
4. Gros Ventre Slide
5. Snow King Nature Trail

KH

Southwestern Montana–
Northwestern Wyoming

SOUTH FORK, SPANISH CREEK

Distance: 2.5 miles
Location: From U.S. Highway 191, south of Bozeman, Montana, head west on Spanish Creek Road (Forest Road 982). This road is approximately 1.5 miles south of mile marker 70. The trailhead is located at the end of Spanish Creek Road, 9.5 miles from U.S. Highway 191. The last 4 miles are paved.

The trailhead of this walk is so beautiful that you may find yourself intoxicated by the grandeur of the place before taking a single step down the trail. The delightful stream before you comes laughing out of a high country thick with great stands of timber, fringed for much of its northward flow by olive green willows, and to the distant south, by the great granite domes of the Spanish Peaks. This mountainscape is home for an amazing variety of wildlife, including bighorn sheep, Rocky Mountain goat, black bear, mountain lion, elk, and mule deer. From an ecological point of view, the land before you is considered to be part of the Greater Yellowstone Ecosystem—one of only two large, relatively intact environments left in the Rocky Mountains.

The peaks visible at the head of the South Fork of Spanish Creek are part of the Madison Range, a name first given by Lewis and Clark to the beautiful river that runs west of here along U.S. Highway 287. The Madison they refer to is James Madison, who at the time was serving as secretary of state. After Lewis and Clark passed from this country on their return to the East in 1806, the Madison country remained fairly untouched by outsiders until half a century later, when gold strikes at the town of Bannack brought

Bighorn Sheep

hopeful prospectors pouring through these valleys like ants to a picnic.

Bannack went on to become Montana's first territorial capital in 1864, although such status was hardly a guarantee of future stability. As soon as other rumors began of eastern gold strikes, the fickle citizens of Bannack hit the trail to start life anew at the infamous Virginia City, just 35 air miles to the east. (Ten thousand people streamed into Virginia City in a single year!) As it turned out, Virginia City lay beside the largest collection of placer gold in the Rocky Mountains. In fact, of the $65 million in minerals that Montana produced in the 1860s, nearly half of that came from this area. Nevertheless, Virginia City proved no more successful than the others at holding its citizenry, especially when rumors started to fly of "even better finds" to the north.

After crossing the South Fork of Spanish Creek near the trailhead, turn left, following the footpath upstream through a beautiful forest of lodgepole pine, Engelmann spruce, and blue spruce. You'll find that there is a certain smell to the riparian environments of the central and northern Rockies, a luscious blend of willow and conifers, stirred by slight breezes laden with whiffs of damp earth and wildflowers from the nearby meadows.

At 0.5 mile you'll enter the Spanish Peaks unit of the Lee Metcalf Wilderness. This unit contains more than 50,000 acres of land, nearly all of which is perfect for anyone seeking aimless wanderings up and down nameless folds of rock, sky, and water. After passing a side trail on the left (stay right), the path will climb up on a small bench overlooking the stream as it courses through a maze of willow-lined passages.

The generic scientific name assigned to the class of plants known as willows is *salix*, combination of "sal," meaning near, and "lis," meaning water. In North America there are more than 150 species of willow, 29 of which occur in Montana. The inner bark of willow contains an acid related to common aspirin, and has been used in similar fashion as a healing compound for headache and fever for more than 300 years. In addition, many Montana Indian peoples have used willow preparations to stop cuts from bleeding, as well as to treat various ailments of the stomach and upper intestine. For centuries the willow has served as building material

Mountain Goat

for making animal traps, snowshoes, baskets, drum and sweat lodge frames, and fish traps. Indeed, it would be hard to think of a plant with a longer or more variant history of human use.

About 0.3 mile after the previously mentioned fork in the path, a side trail once again joins the main footpath. This is our turnaround point. For a bit of variety, take the other fork back, passing through the thick, lush willow environment that you were looking down upon just a few minutes earlier. Incidentally, such streamside vegetation, especially when combined with good nearby timber, is a favorite environment of the mighty moose. These grand animals, which should always be given a wide berth, can stand more than 6 feet tall at the shoulder and weigh over 1,200 pounds! The rather bizarre looking posture of this animal is due largely to the construction of its rear legs. They are formed in a way that allows the moose to pull the lower portion of its legs straight up. While this may sound like a strange attribute to have, you'd understand the advantages immediately if you spent much of your day up to your kneecaps in sticky mud.

ELK FORK CREEK

Distance: 3 miles
Location: Trail takes off from the south end of Elk Fork Campground, which is located on the south side of the Cody–Yellowstone Highway, just east of mile marker 22. The campground is also approximately 1 mile west of the Wapiti Ranger Station.

Besides offering healthy doses of mountain scenery, this trail, along with the two Shoshone National Forest walks just west of here, offers a bit of interesting history. The Shoshone National Forest was the first national forest in the United States. It was created by congressional mandate in 1907, after having been known for sixteen years as the Yellowstone Park Timberland Reserve. The Wapiti Ranger Station, just 1 mile east of here, served as the first ranger station. ("Wapiti" is the name that

Algonquin Indians gave to the elk; the literal translation of the word is "light colored.")

The life of the first forest rangers was certainly colorful, if not downright exciting. During the early years rangers received little direction from Washington other than to "manage the resource." A new guardian of the nation's forests might find himself building a trail during the day, pulling a rancher's wagon out of the mud before supper, and coming to blows with a gang of timber thieves in the evening—finally bedding down under a sheet of wagon canvas about the time that summer twilight sank into a black sky shot full of stars. His tireless efforts earned him a salary of about $25 a week.

Standing at the trailhead for this walk, you'll see a road going off to the right and a trail going up a small hill to the left. We'll stick to the trail, which makes a flat, beautiful meander along the grass-covered hills that rise gently above the eastern flank of Elk Fork Creek. The first part of the walk is through healthy stands of sage and paintbrush. These two plants occur together for a reason. More often than not, paintbrush sticks its tendrils into the roots of other nearby plants, in this case the sagebrush, thereby stealing nutrients for its own survival. Another common resident you'll see in this area is rabbitbrush, a thin-leaved plant with soft golden flower heads. While rabbitbrush is an important food source for deer, rabbit, and elk, the fact that it grows on nutrient-poor soil has made it an important index for assessing the condition of the land. Widespread growth of rabbitbrush often is an indication that the land has been overgrazed.

Some of the finest features of this walk are the dramatic rock formations visible on the other side of Elk Fork Creek. Dry, windswept shoulders give way to fantastic spires of eroded volcanic conglomerate rock. These rocks erupted from the depths of the earth more than 30 million years ago, spewing through a series of volcanic vents that were common to so much of the Yellowstone Country. The pinnacle effect you see here is the result of ice and rain eroding the fairly soft rock along large vertical cracks. The strangest formations of all are the tall, lone spires topped by large capstones. The hard capstone actually protects the rock column beneath from the eroding effects of the weather. The resulting spires—graceful, though somewhat bizarre-looking balancing acts—are referred to by geologists as *hoodoos*.

Far ahead of you are equally dramatic views of huge, flat-top mountains, some composed of 300-million-year-old rock that actually slid to this point along a great fault, 40 to 50 million years ago. Up the canyon you can see the various east–west drainages that have been carved into the landscape by patient, relentless fingers of water stroking the face of the land.

A short way into the walk the trail forks. Follow the left branch, which will fork again into several smaller paths. Your goal is simply to wind around the small wooded draw and head back out again to the bench overlooking Elk Fork. Common in this draw are huddles of Rocky Mountain juniper, a hardy, beautiful tree sporting dull blue "fruits." This was an extremely sacred tree to many Indian tribes of the Rockies. The sweet-smelling incense it produced when burned, for example, was used in many purification ceremonies. Interestingly, this particular use of the juniper was common in cultures totally removed from each other, from the Pueblo people of the southwestern United States, to early nomads in the far reaches of China. American Indians also used the wood to construct excellent bows, and teas made from the boughs and branches were consumed regularly to relieve colds and flu.

As you continue up the canyon, at about 1.1 miles look once again to the other side of the creek and notice how, in many places, tree growth is limited completely to the deep draws that running water has cut into the side of the mountain. In this arid country, such draws are often the only places where rain or snowmelt concentrates in sufficient amounts to support tree growth. The far richer slice of life visible along the creek corridor below—from fine stands of cottonwood to pockets of tall meadow grass—is an even more dramatic example of the difference that soil moisture can make on the face of the western landscape.

Of course, changes in vegetation due to water availability also bring changes in the kinds of animals and birds that frequent the area. This stream corridor below you is rich enough to support a wide range of wildlife including moose. Those who sit for a while and scan the cottonwood groves or willows that fringe the creek stand a good chance of seeing one of these great creatures.

About 1.5 miles into the walk you'll reach our turnaround point, opposite a fine collection of eroded volcanic rock pinnacles on the other side of Elk Fork Creek.

SHADOW MOUNTAIN

Distance: 1.2 miles

Location: Take U.S. Highway 89/191 north out of Jackson, Wyoming, for 7 miles, to the Gros Ventre Road, and turn right. Continue through Kelly. Several miles north of Kelly you'll pass an intersection with Antelope Flats Road. Continue straight, turning left 1.6 miles past this intersection, following a National Park Service sign pointing toward Bridger–Teton National Forest. Continue for 0.7 mile from this point and make a right turn, heading up a hill through a grove of aspen. The trailhead is on this road, 3.7 miles from that last right turn. (You'll join a fence at 2.7 miles. Past this fence the road continues to climb, eventually reaching a level section with a small road turning off to the right; the trail takes off to the west, opposite this side road.)

Far below these soft green shoulders, through a thin veil of trees, is the long, green reach of Antelope Flats. At the far edge, a twist of cottonwoods can be seen cradling the Snake River as it tumbles southward to meet the Gros Ventre and the Hoback. But rising abruptly past the Snake, almost shouting through the blue Wyoming sky, is the one truly unforgettable part of this high country scene—the Tetons themselves. The views along this walk, mostly across a lovely patchwork of forest and meadow, are sparkling, even mesmerizing. It is as if you've suddenly entered the beating heart of the Rocky Mountains. There is a whisper of wonder on the wind here, a prickly, giddy feeling for the sheer magnificence of this mountain spectacle.

Shadow Mountain supports a healthy collection of aspen, the beautiful white-barked deciduous tree with leaves that flutter in the slightest puff of air; hence its common name "quaking aspen." One famous myth says the leaves of this tree began to tremble the day that an aspen was chosen to make the cross of Christ. The more observable explanation, useful but rather colorless, is that the leaves twist due to the fact that they have a flat stem at the point where they attach to the leaf.

Into the walk 0.2 mile the trail passes a meadow filled with yarrow, larkspur, balsamroot, showy goldeneye, and the tall spikes of green-leaved gentian. A thick, green curtain of Douglas-fir and subalpine fir rises to the left. The bark of the subalpine fir (the tree with a spire-shaped crown and needles curving upward in tight bunches) is eaten often by deer and elk. Look for nibbled patches along the trunks of these trees. From here the trail slopes gently downward through a young forest of fir, spruce, lodgepole, and limber pine, soon coming out on a bench that affords spectacular views of 26,000-acre Jackson Lake, far to the northwest. This long, sweeping valley was scoured into its present shape by a river of ice nearly 2,000 feet thick, creeping out of the Absaroka and Wind River ranges, southbound to what is now the state of Idaho.

Continue for a short distance, reaching our turnaround point in 0.5 mile, at a stretch of trail descending through a delightful meadow. Grand Teton Peak, with an elevation of 13,770 feet, looms straight ahead. I can tell you from personal experience that this is a particularly fine place to assume the prone position in these thick mats of lupine and showy goldeneye. For some reason it seems good for the soul to lie back occasionally and grab a mouse-eye view of worlds peppered with wildflowers, capped by puffs of summer cloud.

GROS VENTRE SLIDE

Distance: 0.8 mile
Location: Head north out of Jackson, Wyoming, on U.S. Highway 89/191 for approximately 7 miles to the Gros Ventre Road, and turn right. The Gros Ventre Road turns right 1.2 miles north of Kelly toward Slide Lake. Our walk begins at the Gros Ventre Slide overlook, on the right side of the road, 4.8 miles after this turn.

A wet June morning, 1925: The early songs of the wrens and tanagers have come and gone; only the raucous calls of magpies and Steller's jays can be heard with any regularity. The Gros Ventre

River tumbles eastward out of the Red Hills toward its rendezvous with the Snake, as it has done for countless mornings before. And then, without warning, an event of catastrophic proportions occurs. From a point 9,000 feet up on a high ridge south of the river, an enormous slab of earth, a mile long and over a third of a mile wide, tears loose from its mountain moorings and comes rolling toward the river—a frightening tidal wave of rock and timber. So much momentum is packed into these 15 million cubic tons of shale and sandstone rubble that it buries the river completely, screams over the road where you now stand, and continues to roll a short distance up the north side of the red rock valley wall. In less than three minutes, the calamity is over.

As a result of the river blockage, the lake to your left (Lower Slide Lake) begins to form, rising quickly against the earthen dam. But less than two years later, in May of 1927, this dam gives out. A great wall of water races down the channel toward the town of Kelly, 6 river miles downstream. A forest ranger sees what is happening, and makes a frantic call to warn the people below. Some refuse to listen; six people drown.

And so went the tale of the Gros Ventre Slide, one of the largest observed earth movements in the world. That this slice of mountain country was unstable was hardly news to the people who lived in the region. A smaller, slower slide blocked the Gros Ventre River channel several miles upstream years before, creating Upper Slide Lake. Land and mud slides in several of the nearby drainages also were common, which made the proposition of building a road up the Gros Ventre River a chancy project at best.

There are several theories as to what actually caused the Gros Ventre Slide. One attributes the soil instability here to a slow but steady melt of glacial ice still buried deep in the ground. The melt water saturates the earth, slowly loosening the unstable rock foundations until the ground gives way. Another theory says that these mountains are still settling, and as sheets of soft rock, such as gypsum, dissolve in the presence of ground moisture, the landscape collapses. Unlike the Gros Ventre Slide, most of the time these collapses are slow, quiet events. Whatever the reason, viewing the remains of events like the Gros Ventre Slide, with its great rubble piles and tilted timber, or Quake Lake on the northwest corner of Yellowstone, should dispel any notions you may have had about the landscapes of the Rockies being unchanging, static environments.

In its present state, the Gros Ventre Slide Nature Trail is not so much a loop as a single path with two spikes taking off of it. Begin to the left of the overlook through a sparse forest of limber and lodgepole pine surrounded by thick mats of fireweed and buffaloberry. Buffaloberry, which is somewhat bitter when eaten in its present form, was nevertheless an important food source to many Rocky Mountain Native American cultures. The fruit was collected by women in late summer, usually by beating the bushes soundly with a stick. Many of the berries were then dried in the sun to be used over the long winter. A foamy treat known in Montana as "Indian ice cream" was made by placing a few berries in a little water and then beating them with a stirring device until they reached a pink froth.

About 0.2 mile into the walk the trail will fork; continue right and proceed up a huge jumble of rubble, much of which hardly looks 60 days old but is 60 years old. The giant slabs of sedimentary rock on this rise give a good clue to the formation of the Gros Ventre Range. For millions of years this area was an ancient seabed, where ocean debris filtered down through the

Yellow-bellied Marmot

millenniums to form layers of sediment that would eventually harden into rock. Much later pressures inside the earth thrust these beds of rock upward to form mountains, which were then sculpted into their present shape by glaciers, as well as the incessant rush of wind and weather.

Continue along these slabs past black elderberry and dwarf juniper onto a bench lush with purple fireweed bloom and the tattered yellow heads of groundsel. From here the trail descends over a maze of sedimentary rock down to the shore of Slide Lake, a quiet, peaceful stretch of water framed to the east by the beautiful russet flanks of the Red Hills.

Return along the same path to the far side of the debris, back to the point where you encountered a fork in the nature trail. Turn right and again wind through a sparse forest sprinkled with buffaloberry and dwarf juniper. Notice the tilted trees, still growing after having slid here 60 years ago from their original home, high on the mountain to the south! Turn around at a lovely overlook of Slide Lake, and return to the parking area the way you came.

SNOW KING NATURE TRAIL

Distance: 0.75 mile
Location: The chairlift to the trailhead is located on the south end of Jackson, Wyoming, at the Snow King Ski Resort. Park near the corner of Snow King and Cache streets. The cost for the chairlift to the top is $4, and the hours of operation are typically 11 A.M. to 6 P.M. June through September.

Although a few hearty walkers may feel that riding a chairlift up Snow King will rob them of that special sense of accomplishment that comes from plodding up 1,500 vertical feet under their own power, most will consider it a fine way to climb mountains. The cruise up the north face is over meadows bursting with lupine, yarrow, buckwheat, an occasional sticky geranium and, in late July and August, bright lavender fireweed blooms flying from atop great huddles of tall green stalks. There are two stories as to how fire-weed got its name. One says that the blooms resemble flames, and the other, more commonly accepted notion is that the name comes from the plant's ability to colonize areas that have been burned or otherwise disturbed. (The plant spreads quickly from a network of underground stems.) Bear, deer, and elk find fireweed to be quite tasty, as do some people, who boil and eat the young leaves and shoots.

When you reach the top, take a few minutes to visit one of the two observation platforms on either side of the chairlift. The one on the right, near the snack shop, has an interpretive sign that will help you identify the distant peaks, but the one on the left, being slightly quieter, may be more appropriate for mental drifters.

And this is definitely a view to drift with. To the north the Tetons seem to literally explode from the earth, grey horns of granite ripping through the sky like mythical ramparts guarding the brink of the world. To the Snake Indian people they were known as the "hoary-headed Fathers." To the northeast, just outside of Jackson, Flat Creek meanders through the National Elk Refuge, a seasonal home for thousands of elk who pour down from the sur-rounding drainages each year, prodded by the cold sting of winter.

Because so much of the elk's traditional wintering range has been lost to development, the animals who concentrate here must be given supplemental feed during a portion of their stay. Part of the cost for this food (perhaps $250,000 a year) is actually earned by the elk themselves. Males shed their antlers each year while on the refuge. Area Boy Scouts collect these under a special use permit and then sell them at a rather famous auction held each May at the Jackson town square. People come from around the world to pur-chase these antlers, both for making crafts and for grinding them into various health mixtures. By the time the last ring of the auctioneer's gavel is heard, $30,000 to $50,000 may have been collected. The Boy Scouts use most of these earnings to buy feed in the form of alfalfa pellets, which is then donated to the elk refuge.

Looking along the base of the Tetons (in Grand Teton National Park) you can see a ribbon of cottonwoods marking the course of the beautiful Snake River. From here the river continues

American Elk

south for about 30 miles through thick glacial deposits, then turns west to do a fast dance through the magnificent Snake River Canyon before entering Idaho at Palisades Reservoir. At one time or another the Snake River Valley (often referred to as the "Mad River") was used as a highway, hunting ground, or meeting place by nearly every trapper worth his beaver pelts. Over your right shoulder is the western fringe of the Gros Ventre Wilderness.

The Snow King Nature Trail begins directly across from the chairlift unloading ramp; be sure to pick up a trail guide near the start of the walk. The path begins in an open area sprinkled with yarrow, scarlet gilia, lupine, buckwheat, and big sagebrush. By the way, sagebrush (or wormwood) is not the same "sage" used for seasoning meats, as anyone who has tried it could certainly verify. In the Rockies, the type of sage used for seasoning is a small annual plant, actually a member of the mint family. Nevertheless, sagebrush has been ingested by humans for centuries, often in the form of a hot tea taken for an upset stomach, or to induce sweating during fever. This tea, which tastes incredibly bad, has been shown to be of some help in relieving painful menstruation.

The trail meanders along a meadow sprinkled with balsamroot and showy goldeneye, fringed to the north by fir and pine. At the outermost point in the loop, another trail leaves the nature path heading west. Follow this path out past wind-clipped limber pines to a promontory affording fine views to the south. The Snake River is 1,500 feet below, writhing toward its rendezvous with the Hoback River, named for mountain man John Hoback.

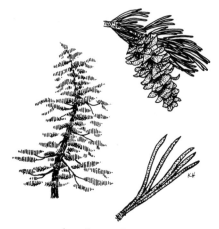

Limber Pine

Balsamroot

Southwestern Colorado

AMPHITHEATER

Distance: 1 mile
Location: Head south out of Ouray on U.S. Highway 550 for 1.1 miles, where you'll see a road taking off to the left toward Amphitheater Campground. Continue through the campground to the end of the road; our trail takes off from here toward the south.

This is a short, relatively quick walk offering double scoops of the same magnificent mountain scenery that has cradled the roadway for so much of your trip into Ouray. Ouray was named after the great Chief Ouray of the Ute Indians. Hardly had the ink dried on the treaty that guaranteed the Utes nearly the entire western quarter of Colorado when prospectors began to flood into this area in their thirsty search for silver and gold. To head off the growing risk of a clash, in 1873 the peaceful Utes were convinced to sell about 4 million acres of this most mountainous part of the region to the government, which would then open it to mineral exploration. The surrounding valleys, however, were to be left alone.

Alas, only a few years later a tidal wave of white protest, much of it beginning here in Ouray, began to crest. By the end of the 1870s, the roar of "The Utes Must Go!" had reached across the entire state. A writer for the Denver *Times* brashly declared, "He who gets in the way of [the Western Empire] will be crushed." And so Ouray and his people were crushed, if not physically, then in spirit, and sent off to live out their days on a Utah reservation.

After running through a beautiful open forest for approximately 75 yards, the trail comes out on an open bench sporting clumps of Gambel oak, with views both of Ouray and the great swell of mountains that rise from its western flanks. The mining

41

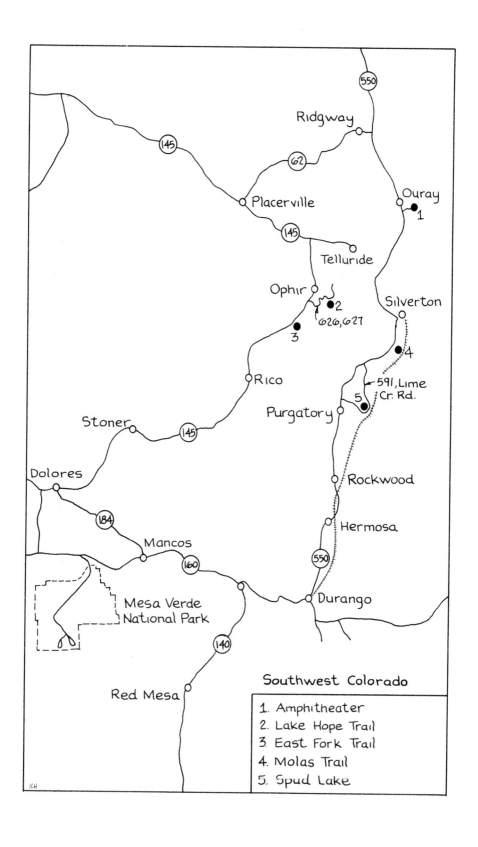

Ridgway

Ouray
●1

550

145

62

Placerville

145

Telluride

Ophir

●2
← 626,627

Silverton

●3

●4

591,Lime
Cr. Rd.

Rico

Purgatory

5
●

Stoner

145

Dolores

184

Rockwood

Mancos

Hermosa

160

550

Mesa Verde
National Park

Durango

140

Red Mesa

Southwest Colorado

1. Amphitheater
2. Lake Hope Trail
3. East Fork Trail
4. Molas Trail
5. Spud Lake

camp of Ouray, like its neighbors Telluride and Silverton, sprang from fervent hopes of the riches to be found here. In these parts, however, becoming anything more than a tumble of shacks and shanties required capital investment, and a lot of it—both to build a transportation system (second in importance only to the minerals themselves) and to get at the valuable ore, which, in the San Juans, was most often buried deep within the earth.

To this end mining camps did everything in their power to attract money. Pamphlets and newspapers, locally the *Ouray Times* and the *Solid Muldoon*, painted incredibly rosy pictures of the amount of wealth that lay here for the taking. Local accomplishments and attractions, be it a new brass band or a toll road, were lavished with praise, while it was left to rival papers in the nearby towns to point out murders, horse thefts, and so forth, which of course they wasted absolutely no time in doing. Thousands of maps were distributed that showed roads to the wealthiest mines, and rich ore samples were sent on cross-country displays in hopes of catching the attention of potential investors. (In the case of Ouray all of this was not without merit; the district produced more than $125 million in silver, gold, copper, lead, and zinc.)

A short distance along this bench, you'll intersect another path running east–west. Turn left here, and proceed for about 75 yards up a steep section of trail. (This short stretch is much steeper than is typical for this book, but in these mountains there is usually no where to go but up!) To your right along this stretch is a magnificent view of the Amphitheater, a sweeping cirque of ancient gray volcanic deposits known as San Juan Tuff.

The path turns slowly to the north and in 0.1 mile heads back east again. Shortly after turning east you'll see a small spur trail taking off to the left to a fine perch overlooking the Ouray Valley and Sister and Twin peaks. This is our turnaround. The massive collection of summits and ridge lines visible from this point are a complex collection of "redbeds," made of sand and muds deposited 200 million years ago by streams running off the high Uncompahgre Plateau, as well as volcanic intrusions and thick layers of limestone laid down by ancient seas. Wind, ice, and water continue to split these highlands into bits and pieces that are then

43

carried off by the braid of streams running to the north. It stretches the mind almost past eternity to think of this mountainscape being torn down grain by grain, year after year, turning it once again into a flat, featureless plain.

LAKE HOPE TRAIL

Distance: 2 miles

Location: From Colorado State Highway 145, about 12 miles south of Telluride, turn southeast on the entrance road to Trout Lake. Follow along and then past the east side of Trout Lake for just under 2 miles to a fork, where you'll turn left up a hill. Continue to climb on this road for a couple of miles to the signed trailhead, which takes off from the right side of a sharp horseshoe turn to the left. The round trip distance to Lake Hope itself, which involves a long, steep climb, is about 5 miles.

While the trail up to Lake Hope itself—a cobalt-colored jewel set in a field of precipitous rock—is beyond the easy walking nature of this book, the first mile of the pathway offers spectacular mountain vistas, as well as vast, blushing gardens of alpine wildflowers. The road up to the trailhead after leaving the Trout Lake basin does have enough potholes to keep you honest. In most years, however, the route isn't anything that a passenger car can't negotiate. Early morning is an especially fine time to walk and photograph along this trail, as summer sunlight pours like warm honey across the face of this tumbling mountainscape.

The first section of trail traverses a fine subalpine fir forest, offering occasional glimpses through the trees of sheer white waterfalls running off the high ridges near Sheep and San Miguel mountains. At 0.25 mile you'll cross a shallow stream basin where you'll see a wide swath of uprooted conifers, many trees broken several feet above the ground, like so many match sticks snapped between a giant's fingers. This is testimony to the enormous power of the avalanche, a frequent occurrence in the mountains of southwest Colorado.

A short way into the walk you'll see a large, rust-colored mountain to the east of the trail. This is Vermillion Peak, and it gets its strange coloration from the fact that igneous gases once poured up through the earth along cracks in the mountain, oxidizing the iron in the rock. It was this oxidation process that gave the mountain its brilliant color. This peak is slowly being eroded by wind, water, and ice. Far in the future, assuming there are no further uplifts here, Vermillion Peak will crumble into a featureless plain.

At just over 0.3 mile the forest on the right will open up, offering great views of Lizard Head and the peak of massive 14,246-foot Mount Wilson off to the northwest. Many of the smooth, U-shaped valleys in this region were sculpted by the slow grind of glacial ice. Glaciers did not, however, cover the jagged upper tips and ridge lines of the peaks you now see, which poked above the frigid landscape like islands in a frozen sea. (Those mountain tops that remained above the ice are known as "nanataks.") The land here is a tortured blend of various rocks—feldspars, sedimentary slabs, and multicolored, highly eroded volcanics, such as San Juan Tuff, which is really made up of tightly compressed cinders and ash. It was this tuff, in fact, that came sliding down on a sheet of slippery shale to block the Lake Fork of the San Miguel River, creating magnificent Trout Lake in the process.

As you walk along a section of the trail about 0.5 mile in, keep an eye out for what many have called the most beautiful alpine wildflower in the world, the blue columbine, state flower of Colorado. This flower was once picked in enormous quantities to adorn the households and restaurants of early mining towns—so much so that in many regions the flower soon became scarce. Eventually, legislation was passed prohibiting its harvest.

Make your way slowly along this relatively flat section of path, through gardens overflowing with bluebells, twinberries, paintbrush, clover, and cow parsnip. On your left will be enormous scree slopes, which are slices of mountainside covered with small rocks that have been broken down by constant freezing and thawing. Our turnaround is in 1 mile, at a point where the trail makes crossings of several small snow-melt streams. Just to the left are two

45

Columbine

waterfalls, dripping like lacy white veils over the gray lips of volcanic rock. Still more wildflowers can be found here, their feet planted in moist alpine soil, their heads basking in a wash of mountain sunshine. Besides those species mentioned earlier, look for scattered bouquets of delphinium, marsh marigolds, and sticky geraniums.

EAST FORK TRAIL

Distance: 2.2 miles
Location: The trail takes off along road 204, which leaves from the south side of Colorado State Highway 145, 2 miles west of Lizard Head Pass and 0.6 mile west of mile marker 58. (There's an east-facing sign right across from where the walk begins that gives the elevation of Lizard Head Peak. This peak is the abrupt spire located just to the north.)

In all of southwest Colorado there are few walks that offer easy access to such incredible mountain beauty as the East Fork Trail. You'll be traversing a plateau of rolling, open meadow lands fringed with spruce and fir—a vast, parklike setting which, when rimmed

46

with precipitous rocky peaks, is downright dazzling in its unabashed beauty.

After taking a right at a fork just 40 to 50 yards from the highway, the road will continue to climb moderately through a meadow peppered with alpine wildflowers. In 0.3 mile you'll reach a sheep cabin perched on a grassy bench. (Please respect the privacy of the owners by not touching or molesting this property in any way.) From this point the path forks again, with the right branch being the most obvious. You'll want to take the fainter route to the left, through a large, moist, grassy meadow filled with cinquefoil, bistort, buttercup, and tall huddles of false hellebore. (If you have any doubts, the proper route heads 180 degrees away from Lizard Head Peak, which is the spire-shaped mountain directly to the north.) Watch your step, as the meadow may be wet.

About halfway through this meadow you'll spot the remains of a small pond on the right side of the trail. Now little more than a high country puddle, this body of water was once much larger. As happens to most ponds, it is in the final throes of succession. The additional moisture around the edge of the pond provides opportunities for a plethora of green plants to set up shop that could never survive otherwise. Each season these shoreline plants, as well as those that are able to live in open water, die off and sink to the bottom. The edges of this pond have been filled in slowly but surely, shrinking the size of the open water. One day there will be no pond at all—just a slight depression filled with the same kinds of grasses and wildflowers that grow in the surrounding park.

From this meadow the trail climbs in small tiers for 0.5 mile to a signed intersection with the East Fork Trail. Almost from the moment you set foot on this trail, fantastic views begin to open up to the west and south, like a grand curtain being slowly drawn open to reveal an alpine paradise. The first rush of scenery will be off to your right past a small grove of aspen. Far below this high perch toward the southwest is the Dolores River, tracing a graceful, shimmering arc at the feet of immense, broad-shouldered mountains. Just out of sight around the far reaches of the river is the tiny hamlet of Rico.

In the 1870s, Rico was one of four major mining towns, along with Ouray, Silverton, and Lake City, to end up riding a long, wild rollercoaster of boom, bust, and boom again. It's important to remember that inexpensive mining with rockers or gold pans, which provided some easy, often fantastic pickings in the California gold fields, did not produce nearly such satisfying results in the San Juans. By the late 1870s, men working in this area had come to realize that the real riches of these mountains—gold, and especially silver—could be retrieved only by "hard-rock" mining, which involved sinking shafts into the earth along quartz veins. But making money the hard-rock way meant having money in the first place, since drills, rails, mining cars, and timbers all had to be purchased before operations could begin in earnest. In the San Juans, then, a miner was most often tied to a company. Few poor men ever trailed their burros down to a creek, returning a few days later with saddlebags filled with gold.

When the Rico Argentine Mining Company closed its doors in the mid-1960s, many people thought it was the bust that would finally break Rico's back. By the mid-1980s, only about fifty residents were left. Today, however, there are a few new, fledgling signs of life here—hopeful shop owners trying to eke out a living from passersby who are more interested in looking for rushes of scenery than rushes of silver and gold.

As you continue along this steep bench with the sound of the Dolores River far below, views begin to open up to the south, toward a great forested basin capped by cool granite peaks. Still further on, as the steep bench begins to flatten and the ridge line to your left melts away, even more mountains become visible to the east. Standing in this great alpine park thick with grass and royal blue harebells, it would be hard to imagine a more magnificent mountain setting. To the north is 14,246-foot Mount Wilson and the fat gray finger of Lizard Head. To the east lies Grizzly Peak, to the south Hermosa Peak and Bolam Pass, and to the west the Dolores River, flying down the high country on its way to meet the mighty Colorado.

Our turnaround occurs 0.25 mile after getting on the East Fork Trail, at a point where the path crosses a small lip of land and begins a gentle descent into a shallow ravine. You can, however, continue southward along an equally gentle, equally spectacular stretch of trail.

MOLAS TRAIL

Distance: 3 miles

Location: The parking area is located along the east side of U.S. Highway 550, approximately 1.5 miles north of Molas Pass, and 6 miles south of the town of Silverton. There is a sign at the highway turnoff for both Molas Lake and Molas Trail. The main dirt road continues past the parking area, descending northeast to Molas Lake. Our walk, however, begins adjacent to the highway along a small, rutted dirt road that heads south from the west end of the parking lot.

This is truly a high country delight. For much of the walk the trail flows gently downward through a rolling, open parkland thick with grass, willow, and wildflowers, occasionally brushing elbows with dark green pockets of spruce and fir, and soft, milk-white stands of aspen. Lending grandeur to the scene are the mighty Grenadier Range to the northeast, and the aptly named Needle Mountains to the southeast, soaring into the sky in a magnificent chain of parapets and sheer, granite ridge lines.

Besides the fine collections of yarrow, asters, and harebells growing in these high meadows, you'll see an abundance of willow along this route—testimony to the fact that you are indeed in the high west, where deep, lingering snows mean an abundance of moisture to support such plant life. In very high alpine meadows, the various vegetation patterns can be used to determine a great deal about the climate. Thick, shiny dark mats of sedge and rush grasses, for instance, usually grow in sheltered depressions where the snow lingers for much of the year. Willow, in contrast, can flourish only in habitats with more prolonged periods of exposure to the sun.

Willow has been used for centuries for the relief of headaches and the treatment of inflamed joints. In addition, boiling the bark in water results in an excellent antiseptic that can be applied externally to infected cuts or lacerations. Native Americans of this area once used the supple twigs of the plant to make collecting baskets. The willow is still important to the furry and feathered residents that make their homes in the San Juan high country. Leaves are considered a tasty browse by mule deer, while beavers have an outright passion for the bark. Hidden beneath thick mats of willow leaves can be found the nests of white-crowned sparrows, who each year wing their way to San Juans from as far away as Mexico. Besides offering superb hiding places for nests, temperatures beneath a willow mat are typically several degrees warmer than that of the air above, making the hatching of the sparrows' small, spotted blue eggs a surer bet in this chilly environment.

A short distance down the road the Molas Trail takes off to the right, curves in a wide horseshoe turn to the left with views of privately owned Molas Lake, finally heading southeast again toward the beautiful Needle Mountains. This entire open area resembles a crumpled blanket laced with depressions, one of the most obvious containing Molas Lake. This type of land form is known as a *karst*, which is an ancient limestone bed that has been dissolved slowly into a tapestry of sinks and basins. The smooth, gentle roll of many of the surrounding hills is the result of careful sculpting by an immense blanket of ice that covered all but the highest peaks here during the Pleistocene Ice Age.

In 0.5 mile the trail reaches a small rocky perch above a shallow valley. At the bottom is a cold, clear stream, dancing quietly toward the Animas River. Stealing the scene in the background is mighty Mount Garfield, just over 13,000 feet high. From this point the trail descends fairly sharply for a couple of hundred feet, and then follows a fine open area fringed with timber for nearly 0.75 mile. This stretch offers superb walking, nothing to distract you but puffs of scarlet, lemon and lavender blooms scattered across the meadows, huddles of conifer spires poking at the sky, and the outstretched wings of red-tailed hawks hanging on the summer breeze.

At 1.3 miles the path suddenly enters a fine spruce–fir forest—a good place to watch for pygmy owls, nuthatches, and northern three-toed woodpeckers. Before long you'll pass a small sign on the left advising against cutting trail switchbacks. Forty or fifty yards past this sign keep an eye out to the right, near a small cluster of aspen, for a spur trail up a short incline. It is the perch at the top of this trail that forms our turnaround point.

The vantage point from here is pure mountain fantasy—a quilt of soaring, rugged mountains that form the western flanks of the rugged Weminuche Wilderness. From their skyscraping summits, which were all that was visible above the massive sheet of ice that once covered this area, the high country takes a long, dizzy plunge to the banks of the Animas River, visible 1,000 feet below where you now stand.

Along the Animas you'll be able to barely make out the line of tracks belonging to the Durango and Silverton Narrow Gauge Railroad, the longest continuously operated steam line in the United States. It is now a meticulously restored passenger line. Originally established by the Denver and Rio Grande to serve the mines of Silverton, the spur was completed in July 1882 after a Herculean effort (much of it during midwinter!) to punch the line through the tortuous twist of canyons and rugged mountain folds that mark much of the route. Since the fate of most mining camps was tied firmly to the reins of the iron horse, Silverton could not have been happier that the effort to link it to Durango was successful. Largely as a result, by the middle of the decade this oldest of the San Juan mining camps was producing a cool million dollars a year in precious minerals.

SPUD LAKE

Distance: 2.2 miles

Location: From U.S. Highway 550, approximately 15 miles south of Silverton, head east on the signed Lime Creek Road. Continue for 3.5 miles until you see a large lily pond on the right. The parking area and trailhead for Spud Lake is just past this pond on the left.

There is something special about Potato Lake, known by its close friends simply as Spud Lake. It's an inviting place—a soft, sparkling destination set in an ancient braid of mountain rock and fringed by a truly pleasant medley of aspen, spruce, and willow. Even before you set foot on this trail you may feel a tug from the large, lovely lily pond located along the south edge of the entrance road. Water lilies produce long, sinewy root stalks that twist through the depths of their host pond or lake like spaghetti. Beautiful yellow flowers are visible through much of the summer, perched on the tops of hearty green leaf pads that can grow thick enough to actually insulate a body of water from the heating effects of the sun. Seeds of the yellow pond lily can be collected and roasted (as was commonly done by Rocky Mountain Indian peoples), producing a food that tastes remarkably like popcorn.

The first stretch of the Spud Lake walk is through a fine grove of aspen, the occasional brief climbs made easier when done to the musical accompaniment of black-capped chickadees, yellow warblers, and red-shafted flickers. Besides providing homes for many types of birds, the buds, bark, and leaves of the aspen provide food for a variety of local animal life, including deer, elk, beaver, grouse, and even snowshoe hares. They also provide humankind with stunning beauty each autumn, the green of summer seeping away into a wash of brilliant gold, flashing like Caesar's coins in the early October sun. Incidentally, the delightful ceaseless quiver of these leaves (the common name of the tree is actually "quaking" aspen) is due to flat, supple leaf stalks that yield to the slightest breeze.

After walking 0.3 mile you'll catch fine glimpses to the northwest of a strikingly handsome peak known as Engineer Mountain. This great uplift, an easily recognizable landmark from various points around the region, is a massive block of sedimentary and hardened volcanic rock sitting on a layered bed of sandstone, limestone, and shale. These lower layers were laid down during repeated intrusions of ocean water. In fact, fossils of the shellfish that lived in these ancient seas can be found in abundance in the limestone layers of this and other nearby mountains. How strange they seem here, stranded high and dry in a cold world of soaring, wind-scored rock—far, far away from the warm seawater that nurtured them 300 million years ago.

At 0.75 mile the path will skirt a fine pocket of willows— always a sign that water is not far away—and then proceed past a tumble of granite talus (large, loose rocks), providing a fine home for a couple of indomitable pikas, sometimes called rock rabbits. These tailless bundles of energy, looking rather like guinea pigs, are most famous for their practice of harvesting grasses and laying them to dry on a rock in the sun, gathering them later into neat little bundles that are then stored as a winter food source. Although the pika's small size and gray coloring make it hard to spot, chances are you'll hear its shrill "eeek eeek" ringing out from beneath the cover of a nearby rock pile. Despite its low profile, these tiny farmers occasionally end up as dinner for hungry coyotes and hawks.

At just over 1 mile the trail passes a couple of old beaver ponds, the fringes of the second one sporting a small crop of scouring rush, or horsetail. This primitive plant consists of dark green, segmented stems, and derives one of its common names from the silica in its stem that, when dried, is an excellent substance for polishing wood, metal, and even certain types of stone. Scouring rush was used often by pioneer women to clean metal pots and pans.

Just past these small ponds is Spud Lake, flanked on the north by Potato Hill, and on the east by the beautifully rugged West Needle Mountains—a glittering, ancient massif of feldspar, quartz, and other metamorphic ingredients squeezed into existence through the heat and pressures of a restless earth. There's something about this lake that welcomes you, making you feel like a local as soon as you arrive. Though a fairly popular spot with Durango residents for fishing and picnicking, I recommend nothing more than a long, lazy soak in the Colorado sunshine, listening to tongues of waves softly licking the shoreline rocks.

Pika

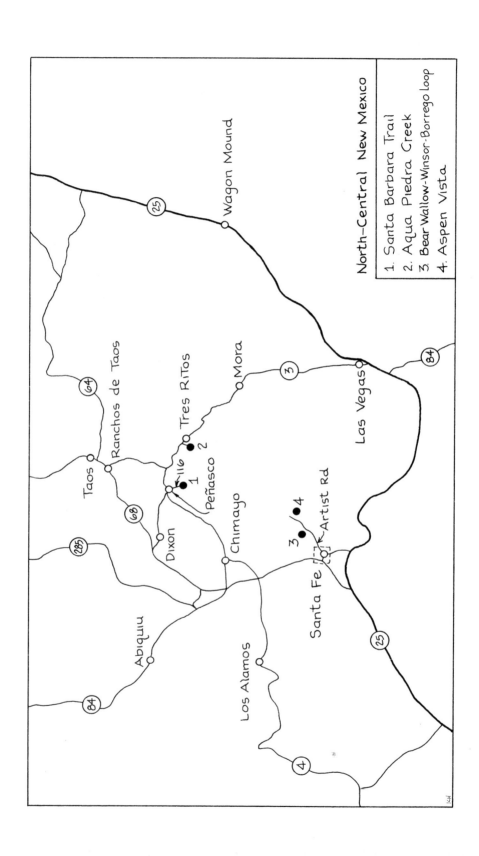

North-Central New Mexico

1. Santa Barbara Trail
2. Aqua Piedra Creek
3. Bear Wallow-Winsor-Borrego Loop
4. Aspen Vista

North–Central New Mexico

SANTA BARBARA TRAIL

Distance: 4.4 miles
Location: Head south along the small village road at the intersection of New Mexico State Highway 75 and New Mexico State Highway 73, near Penasco. South of this intersection 1.5 miles, Forest Road 116 will take off to the left. Follow 116 southward 4.6 miles, reaching the trailhead adjacent to the campground. There is a large parking area on the left before you actually reach the campground. Park here; our trail (no. 24) takes off opposite this parking area.

These spectacular mountains, running south out of Colorado along the eastern flank of the Rio Grande River Valley, have been important to European man for nearly 300 years. It was their tendency to give birth to a collection of cool streams and rivulets that allowed early Spaniards to settle at their feet, shaping a string of tiny corn, fruit, and grazing communities that still exist today. The name of this range is the Sangre de Cristo, or "Blood of Christ." The most common explanation for this somewhat imposing title is that during sunset the mountains tend to turn a beautiful rusty red color, a phenomenon also known as alpenglow. But many historians tag this name that originated in the early 1800s to a group of zealous Christ-conscious people known as the Penitentes. In fact, Penitente Peak is one of the more lovely of the region's mountains, located a dozen miles northeast of the capital city of Santa Fe.

Up the trail 0.2 mile the path will drop down from its perch above Santa Barbara Campground into a lovely quilt of mountain forest. On the left is an open meadow dotted with asters, harebells, paintbrush, groundsel, and a fine mat of grasses, while the slope on the right sports fine growths of Engelmann spruce, dwarf juniper,

55

white fir, and Rocky Mountain maple. The fir and spruce of this latter collection form what is known as the climax forest, a shade-tolerant mixture of conifers that are beginning to replace the smattering of milky-white aspen you see here today.

As you walk through this stretch of forest, keep your ears and eyes out for mountain chickadees, olive-sided flycatchers, mountain bluebirds, pine siskins, gray-headed juncos, and also the ruby-crowned kinglets that feed on the tips of the conifer branches. Keep in mind that even if you're not able to get clear views of these common birds (often a problem in a conifer forest) you usually can make some good guesses as to their identity by watching their feeding behaviors. Kinglets, as we've noted, are able to feed on the ends of conifer branches due to their small size. Olive-sided flycatchers, in contrast, will catch their meals of winged insects from the tops of the pines and not the lower branches. If you don't hear the unmistakable "chick-a-dee dee dee," you might recognize a mountain chickadee from its tendency to flit through the tree looking for insects with amazing speed, often hanging upside down in the process.

The beautiful Rio Santa Barbara will join you about 0.45 mile into the walk. (This stream, which drains the high Sangre de Cristo to the south, takes its name from the Santa Barbara Land Grant which was ceded by the King of Spain to forty-two petitioners in 1796. Much of the private land in New Mexico was obtained in just this way, with many grants still intact.) After joining Rio Santa Barbara you'll find the pathway lined with thimbleberries, ferns, and an occasional clump of creeping Oregon grape. This latter plant, especially beautiful when its leaves turn red in autumn, actually grows from a long, sinewy stem running just beneath the ground; hence its species name *repens*, which means "creeping." Many Indian peoples made a beautiful yellow dye from Oregon grape, commonly used for coloring both baskets and clothing.

You'll also see a good collection of willow growing streamside on the left. This was yet another extremely valuable plant to those who lived close to the land long ago, using the inner bark to treat fevers and headaches, and the branches for construction and creating willow mats. This is also one of the favorite foods of that

56

Mountain Chickadee

Olive-sided Flycatcher

spectacular engineer, the beaver. In fact, at just over 0.5 mile you'll spot the remnants of an old willow branch beaver dam still holding back water. These flooded areas create environments that are perfect for the growth of more willow.

After walking 1.2 miles you'll reach the border of the Pecos Wilderness, a quarter-million-acre jewel of thickly cloaked mountains dotted with braids of cool mountain streams and shimmering blue lakes. Shortly after entering the wilderness you'll cross the Rio Santa Barbara on a footbridge, entering an even lusher forest corridor, replete with moss-covered rocks and logs, harebells, strawberries, and dogbane. The whole feeling changes here, becoming more wild, as if the border of the wilderness was a gateway of sorts. There is an untrammeled, rugged beauty to this stretch of trail. The stream channel is framed suddenly by towering scarps of sedimentary rock. Giant spruce lie toppled across the watercourse, ever so slowly turning back to soil by the rains and snows of the high country, the nutrients held now in its trunk to be used one day for yet another organism.

At 2.2 miles you'll reach the junction of the West Fork Trail. Continue past this intersection on the right fork for about 50 yards. Here you'll find a lovely meadow framed to the east by a ribbon of towering fir and spruce, and beyond that is a sheer, soaring ridge of mountain that absolutely sings of the Sangre de

False Hellebore

Cristo high country. In summer this meadow will be dotted with the white flower clusters of yarrow, the green spikes of false hellebore, and the lavender petals of harebells. The stream can be reached by crossing this meadow, descending through a grove of young aspen suckers, and making your way down to yet another low bench perhaps 100 yards from the West Fork Trail. This stream bank is a wonderful spot, thick with the sound of chickadees and laughing water, with spruce and fir clinging to the sheer rock faces high above. It is a southern Rocky Mountain collage of the highest, most unforgettable order.

AGUA PIEDRA CREEK

Distance: 2.2 miles
Location: From New Mexico State Highway 3, west of Tres Ritos, turn south on the dirt road 0.1 mile west of mile marker 51. Just after crossing the bridge over the Rio Pueblo River, turn left and follow the road through a series of high meadows until you come to a horse corral on the right. Park here. The walk continues southward on the same road.

It has been nearly 450 years since Hernando de Alvarado, an officer under the infamous Spanish explorer Francisco Coronado, pushed into this part of New Mexico on his tireless search for the fabled Quivera. At the time, Quivera was used to denote a region of immense wealth lying somewhere north of Mexico. This was basically an extension of the Spaniards' earlier fantasies about seven golden cities, which in the end turned out to be no more than a cluster of Zuni Indian pueblos located in what is now the state of Arizona. It was south of here about 40 miles near the town of Pecos that Alvarado met an Indian who he dubbed "El Turco," or "the Turk," for his distinctive facial features. El Turco assured Alvarado that such a region of riches did in fact exist, but far to the northeast of where he was searching. After a bitter winter spent near present day Bernalillo, Coronado himself took command of the expedition with El Turco as guide, confident that he was at last on the brink of finding fortune. As it turned out, El Turco's story was a ruse,

59

likely dreamed up to lure the oppressive Spaniards away from the
pueblo villages. After two months of aimless wandering through
the empty Kansas prairie, Coronado caught on. El Turco was
ordered put to death and the Spaniards returned to their New
Mexico headquarters. By the following spring the natives had
grown truly restless and Coronado decided it was time to head back
to Mexico.

Thanks to short bursts of tenacious resistance by the Pueblo
Indians, more than 150 years passed before the Spaniards were able
to establish safe, permanent settlements in New Mexico. To meet
the needs of the settlers that were pouring in from the south, a land
grant system was developed. Tracts of varying size were granted
either to individuals or groups by the King of Spain, a process
conducted by his regional governors. On this road you'll be walking
through the old Santa Barbara Grant, made to a group of petitioners
in 1796. In the same year, far to the east, John Adams and Thomas
Jefferson would take on the jobs of president and vice-president of
the United States.

This walk begins in a fine forest, a few clumps of mature
aspen lending lovely shimmers of light green to the darker, wilder
complexion of spruce and fir. Then in 0.25 mile you'll find yourself
rubbing elbows with Agua Piedra (rocky water) Creek, along which
a completely different array of life is found. Here on these cool,
moist banks are a few water birch, as well as healthy stands of
willow, alder, and mountain maple. The seeds of these latter two
plants are an important food source for birds, a particularly delightful chorus of which usually can be heard along this drainage in the
early morning hours. Splashes of yellow, purple, and pale lavender
can be found here in the monkeyflowers, harebells, and sticky
geraniums that dot the stream banks. Sticky geraniums are a favorite food of the mule deer that make this forest home.

A small meadow on the right just past your first stream
crossing is a particularly good place to watch mule deer graze during
late evening. Although the number of points on a male deer's
antlers (antlers are shed each year) are not an exact indicator of how
old the animal is, in the early years they can serve as a good guide.
Born in June or July, males will show no antlers their first fall. By
the second autumn of their lives, two short points may be visible,

and by the third, some will show three or even four very light points. For many of the following years, however, the deer may continue to show only those four points, though much more prominently than when they first appeared.

Into the walk 0.5 mile you'll see a collection of aspen growing leaves only at their very tops, like a cluster of frizzled brushes that have been dipped in green paint and stood on their handles. This fairly common phenomenon speaks of the aspens' need for direct sunlight, a preference that eventually will cause them to be replaced by the more shade-tolerant spruce and fir trees growing nearby.

In just over 0.8 mile you'll come to a fork in the road at the northern edge of a fuel wood-cutting area. Follow the right branch, which will double back along Agua Piedra Creek, now thick with maples, thimbleberries, and wild roses. Through the trees you can catch glimpses of a high line of forested mountains to the north, spiked by Gallegos and La Cueva Peaks. The term *La Cueva* (Spanish for "the cave") refers to a region southeast of here pocked with shallow caves. An ancient legend says that it was from the mouths of these caves that the Keres-speaking Indian cultures, dating back to the fourteenth century, first entered this world.

Soon the roadway veers away from the stream toward our turnaround point in a huddle of aspen sprouting from a thick, lush carpet of bracken. The underground root stems of bracken spread over large areas, a single plant giving rise to several leaf systems. In early autumn, after the first major frost, they will turn a beautiful shade of pale salmon-orange. In large bracken communities like this one, the effect is absolutely magical—a collection of fairy feather-dusters standing at attention, ready to whisk away the aspen leaves that in a matter of weeks will begin raining down on them in shimmering showers of gold.

BEAR WALLOW–WINSOR–
BORREGO LOOP

Distance: 4 miles
Location: From Sante Fe, head east on Artist Road, which becomes Hyde Park Road near the outskirts of town. The trailhead parking area is located just over 8 miles from town on the north side of the road opposite mile marker 8. Watch for the highway sign marking Borrego Trail.

Although this loop trail can be on the busy side, especially on summer weekends, it traverses such an enchanting slice of New Mexico mountainscape that it would be a real shame to be in the area and not loose your feet in its cool, green quilt of conifers. While pinyon and juniper were the norm as you made your way out of Santa Fe, the mountains here are draped with white fir, ponderosa, aspen, and Douglas-fir. The earth is no longer sand-colored but a rich dark chocolate, nursing a surprising variety of flowers and shrubs. There are small huddles of raspberries, elderberries, and strawberries. Oregon grape, kinnikinick, and an occasional Gambel oak hug the drier ground next to the loud red shouts of scarlet gilia. The leaves of Rocky Mountain maple and box elder whisper in the shaded, moist canyons; snowberry, sticky geranium, and baneberry listen nearby.

Why this sudden richness when hardly a stone's throw away the strings of life are pulled by a much more Spartan hand? For one thing, there is more moisture here than in Santa Fe. Also, temperatures are lower. But these two factors, one tightly bound to the other, both depend on a common master—the mountains themselves. When air systems being pushed across the landscape reach the high country, there is nowhere for them to go but up. As they climb, they enter cooler and cooler temperatures—roughly 3 degrees Fahrenheit cooler for every 1,000 feet they ascend. Cool air cannot hold as much moisture in it as warm air can, so as air rises and cools, some of the moisture it contains has to be released in the form of rain and snow. There are many days when you can stand in a sunny New Mexico desert and watch afternoon clouds form like magic over nearby mountain peaks.

In simple terms, more moisture leads to more bacterial

activity in the soil, which means more nutrients to feed more plants. But even in a mountain garden like this one you'll find that plants have evolved into fairly specific niches, comprised of complicated combinations of soil, sunlight, and so forth. An aspen forest eventually loses the race to firs and spruce simply because the latter trees can reproduce well in shade, whereas the aspen cannot. Scarlet gilias grow in open, gravelly areas, but sticky geraniums don't. Ponderosa and Gambel oak do well on dry exposed ground, which is why you often see them together, but Rocky Mountain maple and box elder wouldn't think of setting up shop there.

As you walk, stop and study the great diversity of plant communities that you see here. Notice the effects of added sunlight where the trees have been cut for the trail, how stream bottoms compare to south-facing slopes, what plants do well on gravelly or sandy soil compared to those on the acidic floor of the pine forest. Besides being beautiful to behold, you'll find this mountain forest to be an incredible slice of evolution—a design of incalculable proportions.

In 0.5 mile you'll reach the first fork, where the Borrego Trail joins the Bear Wallow. Head left here, following the Bear Wallow on a beautiful, gentle descent to Big Tesuque Creek. Creamy white aspen trunks seem to almost glow in the deep greens of the spruce–fir forest. Strawberries and an occasional baneberry line the path, with lavender asters and harebells nodding in the breeze. This latter plant shows a remarkable adaptability. In moist conditions it grows quite tall and sports numerous beautiful blue bell-shaped flowers. Yet if a harebell seed's fate is to end up on a drier, south-facing patch of ground, it just makes the best of it by reducing height and leaf size, and keeping the blooms to only one or two.

You'll reach Big Tesuque Creek 1.5 miles from the trailhead. (Tesuque is a corruption of a Tewa Indian word roughly meaning "spotted dry place." The name refers to the location of Tewa Pueblo north of Santa Fe, where in places the creek sinks into the sand and then reappears again. Up here in the mountains, however, Big Tesuque runs strong and free.) Immediately after crossing the creek you'll take a right onto the Winsor trail. From

63

here the path is pretty much all uphill, so plan to take your time and enjoy the sights along the way.

There are several raspberry plants along this stretch of the walk as well as thimbleberries, mullein, Oregon grape and, in late summer and early fall, the strikingly beautiful blooms of the Hooker evening primrose. This latter plant produces a beautiful, large yellow blossom that typically blooms in the evening and withers away by the afternoon of the following day. The plant produces an element that has long been used in the treatment of asthma.

After about 1 mile of walking upstream along Big Tesuque Creek you'll come to a trail junction marked by two wooden posts which may (or may not) have signs on them. You'll want to turn right here toward a crossing of Big Tesuque. This is the Borrego Trail, which as late as the 1930s was a primary route for trailing sheep to market in Santa Fe from settlements to the north. Some of the large aspen you'll pass on this part of the walk still bear inscriptions of the shepherds who routinely made this trek. This region is woven with one of the most engaging historical fabrics to be found anywhere in the United States. Santa Fe itself was established by Pedro de Peralta in 1609, just two weeks after the fledgling colony of Jamestown was established in Virginia. (Albuquerque was still a hundred years away.) Santa Fe was considered a villa (a larger version of a pueblo), established by the acting provincial governor. There was no ownership of land; each person was allotted a house lot and enough acreage for a small farm, all by favor of the king. Lands immediately surrounding the villa were considered common areas.

It was more than two centuries following Santa Fe's founding, after a troubled Spain finally relinquished the lands that would become an independent Mexico, that traders began pouring into the region from the edge of the American frontier with tools, shoes, fabrics, and woolens—much to the delight of Santa Fe residents. It was one of these commercial wagon trains, rolling over what would become the famous Santa Fe Trail, that brought a sixteen-year-old boy named Kit Carson to Santa Fe in 1826.

Again, the majority of your walk along the Borrego Trail is indeed a climb, so slow down your pace and really enjoy this beautiful forest community. Steller's jays, mountain chickadees, hermit thrushes, and western tanagers will be cheering you on.

ASPEN VISTA

Distance: 1.6 miles
Location: From Santa Fe, head east on Artist Road, which becomes Hyde Park Road near the outskirts of town. We'll be walking along the dirt road that takes off from Aspen Vista picnic area, located on your right, just past mile marker 13. This is actually a service road leading in 6 miles to a microwave station at the top of Tesuque Peak; a sign at the beginning of the gated road reads "Not for Public Use." This does not, however, pertain to people on foot.

The name of the picnic area from which this walk leaves aptly describes the walk itself—aspen and more aspen. To meander along this road at virtually any time of the year will leave you with a new appreciation for this most widely distributed of all North American trees. To walk it in late September or early October, when these trembling leaves are shimmering like gold coins in the autumn sun, will leave you breathless. Before you actually set out, stop for a moment at the picnic area vista point. On a clear day you can see one mountain ridge after another falling away in soft green walls, broken in the distance by a large valley, backed by yet another line of mountains so far away that they almost seem painted on the distant sky.

The *quaking* in the name quaking aspen refers to the leaves, which you'll almost never find completely at rest. A flattened, slightly twisted stem near the point where it joins the leaf is the cause of this trembling, though other more colorful explanations abound. One of these says that aspen wood was used for the cross of Christ, which caused all aspen around the world to begin trembling.

Aspen is what is known as a *pioneer* tree, meaning that it is among the first plants to reclaim land that has been disturbed by fire, logging, or even avalanches. Aspen produce what are essentially clones from common underground root stems or suckers. These suckers usually are not damaged by whatever disturbance has moved through the area, which leaves them ready and waiting to send up a new batch of trees as quickly as possible. (This tendency to produce many trees off a common root stem is why in the fall you'll often see distinct blocks of aspen turning the same color at the same rate.) Aspen, however, like most of pioneer species, are very intolerant of shade. With no further disruptions of the normal growth cycle (which doesn't often happen), aspen is eventually replaced by the spruce–fir forest, a few of which you'll see poking their dark green branches up among this sea of soft white trunks.

During the first stretch of this roadway you'll be in a very young aspen forest. But by 0.5 mile into the walk you will have entered a grove of young adults (thirty- to forty-year-olds)—the age at which an aspen grove becomes truly a place of wonder. Here the lower trunks of the trees are smooth and leafless. They begin growing in more open patterns, looking like thin towers of porcelain rising out of a rich, green carpet of grass. There is a strange, eerie complexion to such a woodland, a deep, haunting beauty that stretches on and on, ultimately melting away into a wall of summer shadows. It can produce a real feeling of fantasy in a dose much larger than most of us are used to experiencing.

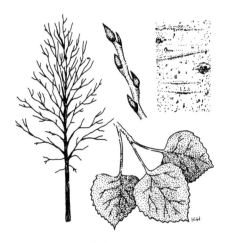

Aspen

Aspen are not the only resident you'll see here. Watch for the large, maplelike leaves of thimbleberries growing along the road, as well as Bebb willows and Rocky Mountain maple. Yarrow, harebells, and asters are also in good supply, as are occasional splashes of scarlet gilia, growing in the drier, more open areas along the road.

You'll reach the North Fork of Tesuque Creek in just 0.8 mile. This fine little stream makes a sprightly, laughing tumble through the aspen, giving rise to an even greater array of moisture-loving wildflowers. Small paths can be found on either side of the road that meander along the creek into fine pockets of hushed forest, each one perfect for snuggling up with a good, long daydream.

Yarrow

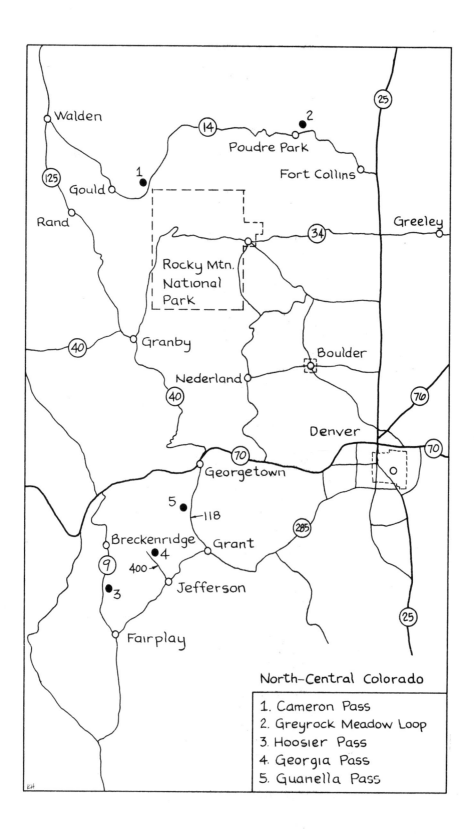

Walden

(14)

2

Poudre Park

(25)

(125)

Gould

1

Fort Collins

Rand

(34)

Greeley

Rocky Mtn.
National
Park

(40)

Granby

Boulder

Nederland

(40)

(76)

Denver

(70)

Georgetown

(70)

5

118

(285)

Breckenridge

Grant

(9)

400

4

Jefferson

3

(25)

Fairplay

North–Central Colorado

1. Cameron Pass
2. Greyrock Meadow Loop
3. Hoosier Pass
4. Georgia Pass
5. Guanella Pass

KH

North–Central Colorado

CAMERON PASS

Distance: 0.7 mile
Location: Cameron Pass is located on Colorado State Highway 14, just south of Joe Wright Reservoir, at the northeast corner of Rocky Mountain National Park. Park at the picnic/parking area located at the top of the pass on the west side of the road. Our trail is on the faint roadway that takes off behind the picnic tables to the north.

This is no more than a hiccup of a hike—a short, uphill puff through a classic slice of Rocky Mountain spruce–fir, or subalpine forest. It will do fine for weary road travelers in the mood for a nice, cool shower of high country.

The abrupt peak and valley landscape that surrounds you here can be thought of as a series of vegetative bands stacked one on top of the other, commonly referred to as "life zones." This term refers to the fact that as you climb you pass through rather specific zones of vegetation. From a plant species point of view, walking or driving up through these belts has much the same effect as if you were to go north in latitude. In fact, to take a trip from the low plains lying to the east, near Boulder, to the tops of these highest mountain peaks, would be the equivalent of having traveled into the Arctic, nearly 2,000 miles to the north.

In this area the subalpine zone lies roughly between 9,000 and 11,000 feet, and is dominated by Engelmann spruce and subalpine fir. You also may see lodgepole at this height, the young stands sometimes growing so thick that no sunlight can penetrate their canopies, leaving the ground devoid of plants, as well as the animals that would eat them.

Our walk begins on a faint roadway on the north side of the

parking area, and climbs steadily upward into thicker and thicker forest. The turnaround point is reached in just 0.35 mile, past a lovely mat of twinflower, at a small stream tumbling down the mountain where it will join forces first with Wright Creek, and then with the Cache la Poudre River. At times this forest is as quiet as a wing stroke. And at other times the magic of this hush is abruptly broken by the scolding buzz of the chickaree, a small tree squirrel that ranges from the intermountain states of the West all the way to the East Coast. These little nut harvesters are extremely territorial, and they feel quite justified in chattering regular sermons to you about the evils of trespassing.

In a healthy conifer environment like this one, where there are chickarees, the beautiful, cinnamon-and-sugar colored marten cannot be far behind. Martens have a look similar to that of a weasel, and are among the greatest acrobats in all the natural world. Their trapeze is the weave of branches that form the tree canopy, where they hunt and chase prey across great distances with incredible grace and speed, never once needing to place a paw on the ground. In winter they grow fine, thick leggings of fur to protect them from the cold. It's hard to see these animals, not necessarily because they are shy, but because they tend to conduct their most serious business after darkness has rolled across the forest.

Englemann Spruce

Though the timber hides much of the distant views here, you are actually in one of the region's more rugged mountainscapes. Those who feel particularly ambitious can make the rather steep climb up along this small stream to a high ridge line. From here you'll have fine views of the Never Summer Mountains and the high country of the Neota Wilderness to the east, adjacent to Rocky Mountain National Park. Also visible higher up are the Nokhu Crags, which lie just a couple of miles south of Cameron Pass. These abrupt ramparts are composed of layers of shale, sculpted by cold glacial fingers that advanced and retreated into the mountains of this region many times over the past 2 million years. Each session with the ice artist peeled away additional layers of surface rock, leaving the remarkably rugged collection of ridge lines, headwalls, and parapets that we call the Nokhu Crags. Appropriately, Nokhu is a somewhat condensed version of an Arapaho Indian phrase meaning "eagle's nest."

GREYROCK MEADOW LOOP

Distance: 6.5 miles
Location: This trail is located on Colorado State Highway 14, approximately 17 miles west of Fort Collins. Although the trail begins by crossing a footbridge over the Cache la Poudre River, the parking area for the walk is located on top of a hill on the south side of the highway. The turnoff for this parking area is 0.5 mile west of mile marker 114.

When writing about the footpaths of Colorado, it seems almost irreverent not to include one good, hearty plod up a mountain. This 6.5 mile trek, while gaining 2,000 feet in elevation, is by no means as rugged as many in this region. Give these wooded, bird-filled ravines, these warm, brown hills of grass, and the rugged, soaring vistas the slow, deliberate attention they deserve, and you should be able to handle this day walk just fine. A particularly appealing aspect of this trail is that it is an especially good one to take in early spring or late autumn, when most other mountain trails are locked in winter white.

The walk begins with a crossing of the beautiful Cache la Poudre River. This rather ponderous name is French for "Hide the Powder," a title bestowed on it by a group of rendezvous-bound trappers who, caught by an autumn snowstorm, had to bury their gunpowder as well as several other items and return for them the following spring. Rising in the cold high country along Trail Ridge Road in Rocky Mountain National Park, the Cache la Poudre flows through increasingly arid country on its way to the South Platte River.

Once you are over the river, continue west through fine clumps of dry land vegetation, including narrowleaf yucca and an occasional plains prickly pear. Like nearly every other plant you see here, from ponderosa to ricegrass to snakeweed to juniper, these plants were used by the Native Americans that once made these hills home. Both were sources of food—the young shoots of the yucca and the fruit or "tuna" of the prickly pear. The white, curling fibers of yucca leaves served as sewing thread, while whatever needles were necessary could be found in the sharp tips.

The Indians of Colorado were as overwhelmed as any native people in the nation when European-style progress rolled westward. By the 1860s, sweeping the Indian onto reservations and gaining title to his lands was a territorial obsession. Papers in the state routinely lambasted military leaders who seemed reluctant to make war against the natives. (After the gruesome 1864 Sand Creek Massacre, in which soldiers under the command of a former minister launched a surprise attack that killed 200 Cheyennes, mostly women and children huddled under a white surrender flag, one paper reported that the state's soldiers had "again covered themselves with glory.") With precious careers on the line, it became more and more common for high-ranking officials to resort to outright deadly assault to convince constituents that they were serious. In fact, the scalps of Indians often were put on public display, sometimes as intermission entertainment at local theaters, to reinforce the notion that Colorado territory was under strong, heroic leadership.

Continue climbing gently along the trail (this section was constructed by the Civilian Conservation Corps) to a junction in 0.6

mile. Here we'll stay to the left, although those who are only interested in getting to Greyrock Mountain can cut their distance (though their effort!) by taking a right. The next 1.5 mile of pathway will require the most effort. Stop often among the open stands of ponderosa or in the shade of junipers huddled in the washes. At the 2-mile mark you will cross a high ridge, offering spectacular views up Cache la Poudre River, and to the south, toward Rocky Mountain National Park. This prospect offers a truly magnificent view of young mountains that have been uplifted fully for only the past 5 to 7 million years. Instead of the dense cloak of spruce–fir forest that blankets the higher slopes, here the land is covered in thin layers of grass and ragged groves of ponderosa. Buff-colored sedimentary rocks line the ridge lines and canyon headwalls, some forming strange, fierce shapes, looking haggard and parched when held against a cloudless western sky.

The path continues to climb more gently toward the east, finally reaching a small perch that offers long, long views across the western fringes of the Great Plains. From here you'll descend into Greyrock Meadow, a beautiful tapestry of rock and grass, with Greyrock Mountain rising on its granite pedestal to the east. Your last climb will be up the west flank of Greyrock Mountain to a crossing point south of the actual summit. Just past this you'll meet up with the Greyrock Mountain Trail. Turn right and start the

Yellow-rumped Warbler

long, steep descent back toward your starting point along the Cache la Poudre.

The trip down is through a wonderful wooded canyon, which much of the time is thoroughly washed in the echoes of bird song. Look and listen for jays, Say's phoebes, warbling vireos, western bluebirds, orange-crowned warblers, green-tailed towhees, and dark-eyed juncos, among others.

HOOSIER PASS

Distance: 0.8 mile
Location: This trail is located approximately 10 miles north of Fairplay on Colorado Route 9. Park at the pass parking area located on the west side of the road. Our walk begins across the highway near a series of cross-country ski trails on a road climbing to the east.

Hoosier Pass is along the Continental Divide with an elevation of 11,542 feet. It derives its name from a group of Indiana men (Hoosiers) who worked a placer-gold operation not far from here. Indeed, armed with a history book and map, it doesn't take long to realize that you are absolutely surrounded by towns, creeks, gulches, mountains, and lakes that bear the fanciful names bestowed on them by a group of hardy, hopeful gold mining men. The town of Fairplay, just to the south, was named by a group of miners who discovered gold there after having been snubbed in their attempts to work other diggings nearby. Tarryall Creek, 6 miles to the east, supposedly got its title from a posse who "tarried" long enough in pursuit of Ute Indians to dig and find gold. Lost Lake, Mosquito Pass, Gold Basin, and Georgia Pass were named after the troubles, dreams, and fondest memories of the men who came here looking for gold to make those long, back-breaking days and cold mountain nights worthwhile.

Begin this walk by crossing over to the east side of the highway and climbing up to a road that takes off up a hill from the base of a cross-country ski trail complex. (The large rock and concrete flume visible on your left once carried water for hydraulic mining operations.) The walk up is a steady climb, and the high altitude will require that you take your time and breathe in as much of this spruce- and fir-spiked air as you possibly can. In 0.25 mile the path begins to level off, arriving 0.15 mile further at a small, flat plateau dotted with needle and mutton grasses, false buckwheat, and spike trisetum. Also here in summer are several beautiful alpine wildflowers, including harebells, shrubby cinquefoil, globe gilia, bistort, false dandelion, and death camus.

Hoosier Pass is rapidly becoming one of the most famous botanical sites in the entire state. The unusual east—west alignment of this mountain, as well as its particular elevation and soil composition, have allowed some extremely rare plants to flourish here. One 2-inch tall species with white blossoms, known as braya, is not found anywhere else in the world; another, armeria, has been found only at this site, on the Arctic tundra, and in Siberia. The vegetation at Hoosier Pass is actually an amazingly diverse botanical melting pot, supporting species found from the Andes to central Asia. A few plants form links with vegetation that existed 70 million years ago!

Just before reaching our turnaround point at this open, grassy area, you'll see one or two examples of *flagging* adjacent to the road. This is the phenomenon where conifers sport branches only on the lee side of their trunks, the ones facing into the wind having been pruned away by its cold, scouring fingers.

The view to the south from this knoll is a spectacular one. Far below, you can see the South Platte River complex running to the south, framed on all sides by thick stands of willow, a band of silvery braids gleaming in the morning sunlight like a maze of walkways paved with diamonds. Rising abruptly to the southwest is the line of weather-beaten mountains comprising the aptly named Windy Ridge. This is the heart of the Bristlecone Pine Scenic Area, a 3-mile-long slice of high country devoted to the tree with the singular distinction of being the oldest living thing on earth. To the south 10 miles is the old mining town of Fairplay, which at one time was rather notorious for the wild, unruly behavior of its residents.

One of the most interesting tales about Fairplay concerns a miner named Rupert Sherwood and his trusty burro companion, Prunes. Though dogs may be considered man's best friend today, for nineteenth-century miners nothing could beat a good burro, or, as they frequently were dubbed, "mountain canaries"—a title that refers to their tendency to let out in a chorus of high-pitched braying whenever the mood strikes. In Prunes, Rupert Sherwood had much more than he actually expected when he laid down his $10 for the stout little animal in 1879. Not only did Prunes routinely carry his weight in ore but Rupert was able to send Prunes down the mountain all by himself to the general store. The storekeeper would remove the shopping list that he carried, fill the order, and off Prunes would go back up the mountain to his master, his packs full of supplies. Over the years, Prunes and Rupert became somewhat of a legend throughout this part of Colorado.

The mountain mining life was a hard one, but these two best friends didn't seem any worse for the wear. Prunes died in 1930, at the ripe old age of sixty-three. He's buried on Front Street in downtown Fairplay, with an elaborate tombstone and bronze plaque marking the spot. Rupert passed on at eighty-one; true to his last wish, the townspeople buried his ashes next to the monument of his faithful companion.

GEORGIA PASS

Distance: 2 miles
Location: From U.S. Highway 285, in the town of Jefferson, head north, following signs for Michigan Creek Campground. Continue past the campground, climbing until you reach the top of Georgia Pass. Park here. From the pass you'll see two roads. One descends to Breckenridge; the other (Forest Road 268) climbs toward Glacier Ridge. Our walk begins along this latter route.

If you've come to the Colorado Rockies for the views, here is one walk that most certainly will not disappoint you. This particular line of high peaks and ridges—just one wave in a sea of such dramatic mountainscapes—happens to form that great spine of the American West, the Continental Divide. Drops of rain or snowmelt falling to your left (north) are destined to return to the Pacific Ocean, while those on your right (south) are bound for the Gulf of Mexico. Standing here at Georgia Pass, it seems hard to dispute Colorado's claim of having the highest mean elevation of any state in the country. More than 1,000 of her peaks scrape these powder blue skies at over 10,000 feet above sea level; 54 of them come in at over 14,000 feet.

As you make the steady climb up Forest Road 268, you will see a slow but steady transition in the forest that fills these high country nooks and crannies. Engelmann spruce, for instance, grows 25 to 30 feet tall near the beginning of your walk, but as you make your way up onto the higher, more northerly exposed ridges, some rather strange changes take place in the shape of these trees. Besides their becoming smaller, you'll notice a peculiar phenomena known as *flagging*, which refers to

White-tailed Ptarmigan

77

trees sporting branches only on one side of their trunks. The bitter blasts of wind that roar across this high ridge, often nearing 100 miles per hour, prune away those branches on the windward side, leaving only the lee growth intact. On even more exposed sites the spruce may grow in such dwarfed versions that they resemble shrubs more than they do trees. These wind-scoured mats of vegetation, in this area typically consisting of either Engelmann spruce or subalpine fir, are known as *krummholz*, a German word that translates roughly into "elfin timber." The Colorado Rockies krummholz belt characteristically occurs on exposed ridges in areas where monthly average temperatures rarely exceed 50 degrees. Since the growing season may be as short as seven weeks, the trees grow at an incredibly slow rate. Though they appear small, these spruce mats may be well over a hundred years old. (Bristlecone pines, which are even more famous champions of the high altitude tough life, have been found to be a thousand years old and only to measure a few inches in diameter.)

Just over 0.6 mile into the walk you'll come to an intersection on a flat, high plateau, covered with cushion plants and, for a few weeks each summer, the brilliantly colored forbs that mark the alpine tundra. Here we'll turn right onto a small road heading south. Because the alpine tundra is incredibly fragile, it's very important that you stay on established roads and trails. A tin can lying over a patch of tundra plants can kill them in less than a month; their return can take a quarter of a century. Recent studies conducted in Rocky Mountain National Park have reconfirmed the delicate nature of these ecosystems, having identified several types of tundra plant communities that, if disturbed, may take as long as a thousand years to recover.

As you proceed southward, notice on your left the remains of a hanging glacial snow field—a cold, white remnant of the last ice age when all but the highest peaks around you were covered with thick slabs of grinding ice. Ahead of you, becoming more expansive the further you go, are fantastic views of South Park, an extensive intermontane valley, much of which rests on beds of 200- to 400-million-year-old sedimentary rock. South Park has figured prominently in the exciting comings and goings of Colo-

rado. Through these fields of high grass tramped many a hopeful
miner, some bound for Blue River, some for Breckenridge, and,
by 1860, a great many for the infamous California Gulch located
to the west along the upper reaches of the Arkansas River. This
famous valley reportedly got its name when a veteran of the
California gold rush named Abraham Lee dipped a gold pan into
a small stream here and declared "Boys, all California is in this
here pan!" Well, maybe not all of California, but the discovery
did earn this small group of Georgia boys more than $50,000 in
the first three weeks of digging. The summer of 1860 was barely
half over before eight thousand people had crammed their way
into California Gulch.

Just four years later, South Park was the scene of an intense
manhunt for a gang of Confederate bandits led by brothers Jim and
John Reynolds. Each time this gang would pick off a stage passing
through South Park, they presented their victims with the grand lie
that they were breaking ground for a force of Texas rangers on their
way to destroy Denver. With a good share of the populace already
fearful that Southerners were banding together with disgruntled
Indians to overthrow the region (such alliances were attempted
occasionally), this particular story spread like wildfire, causing near
panic in the towns up and down the front range. The locals were
not amused by such shenanigans and all of the captured gang
members eventually ended up with a bullet in them; one was even
decapitated, with his head preserved and put on display in the
nearby town of Fairplay.

The road curves around toward the west again, making a
short climb at 1.2 miles onto another high plateau. At 1.4 miles it
turns south onto a spur of land, overlooking the drainage that
you drove up on your way to Georgia Pass. Along this stretch of
ground is a recent addition to the Colorado Trail—a tremendous
recreational effort to link Durango to Denver with 470 miles of
footpath. From this point you should be able to see a small
pathway that follows along a series of cairns (small piles of rocks)
to the north. If you spot it, you can follow it northward until it
rejoins Forest Road 268, a short distance east of where you
parked. If you can't spot it from the road, however, don't aim-
lessly comb the tundra looking for it; just turn around and return

79

the way you came. This is too fragile an environment for engaging in cross-country rambling.

GUANELLA PASS

Distance: 3.5 miles
Location: The trail is 12 miles south of Georgetown, on the Guanella Pass Road (Forest Road 118). The pass also can be reached from the south by taking the Guanella Pass Road north from U.S. Highway 285, northeast of Kenosha Pass.

The high path to Square Top Lakes lies 6 miles or so east of the Continental Divide, and offers fine opportunities to at least begin to taste the powerful yet extremely delicate fringes of the alpine tundra. Like the Arctic tundra, with which it shares many traits, this is a place of contrasts. Due to the thinner atmosphere here, the sun beats down with three times the intensity of that in lower elevations; reflected off a snowfield, it can actually blind a man. In the winter, bitter winds howl across these smooth slopes at 100 miles per hour, whipping snow into strange patterns, dumping it into protected pockets until it forms blankets 20 feet thick, while in more exposed places the rock surfaces are scoured completely clean.

Marsh Marigold

Such extreme conditions have not, however, left this high valley devoid of life. Besides the beautiful mountain mosaic of willow growing here, there is no shortage of bunch grass, Rocky Mountain sedge, tufted hairgrass, alpine avens, haircap moss, buttercups, marsh marigolds, and Parry's clover. To really see how packed with life these high gardens can be often requires getting down on your stomach with your nose in the mat. Alpine plants grow small and close to the ground to escape the drying and damaging effects of the wind. Also, when you face a growing season of 12 to 16 weeks, it makes little sense to waste your time producing stems.

The view to the southwest along this stretch of Continental Divide is a fine one, the forested western flanks of Geneva and Arrowhead Peaks tumbling southward into the Platte River Mountains. It was along another fork of the Platte River, south of this high perch where you now stand, that twenty-seven-year-old Zebulon Pike headed west in late November of 1807, in his search for the headwaters of the Red River. Pike already had been beaten back by snow during an attempt to climb the high peak that would one day bear his name, but still he pressed on at this frightfully late date, his horses so weary that many had to be abandoned, food running so low that it was only the most amazing stroke of hunting fortune that kept Pike and his men from total starvation. Yet Pike, driven by an intense desire to have his own place in the explorer's hall of fame, pressed on through the increasingly bitter days of early winter, eventually clambering back out onto the plains via the Royal Gorge of the Arkansas River. He was now more confused about the real source of the Red River than before. (It was on some unknown high peak west of here that Pike claimed to have seen the headwaters of the Yellowstone, which in fact rises several hundred miles to the north. This mistake undoubtedly caused more than a little confusion for some trappers, who then would have expected to find New Mexico just a short trek from the Tetons.)

In 0.4 mile you'll reach a fork; stay to the left. The thick huddle of willows growing on the hillsides at 0.5 mile into the walk have done much to prevent soil erosion here—especially important

White-crowned Sparrow

in light of the questionable practice of allowing cattle to graze in the area. These willow thickets are also the home for white-crowned sparrows who migrate to this high landscape each year from as far south as Mexico. This delightful little bird sometimes can be heard singing even at night. Willow thickets not only protect the birds from predators but actually tend to hold in heat so that their eggs will stand a better chance of hatching in this cold environment.

There are a few steep sections about 1 mile in. At this high elevation where there is less oxygen you should pause often to avoid getting overly tired or developing a headache. There is plenty of scenery to ponder, from Duck Lake 1 mile to the south, glimmering like a sapphire in the midday sun, to the long tumble of high ridge lines fading into a fine blue haze 70 to 80 miles distant.

After topping a small crest at 1.5 miles, you only have to make a gentle descent and then an easy, arcing climb to arrive at the lower of the two Square Top Lakes, named after the large block-shaped peak located immediately to the west. The stream you followed on the last stretch of the walk begins in this rugged lake basin, tumbling through a wonderful wildflower-strewn corridor into Duck Lake, ultimately bound for the North Fork of the South Platte River. For the adventurous among you, there is another lake just above this one, similar in size, at the base of the sheer scree slope visible to the northwest. Such lakes often are frozen into July, with water temperatures rarely soaring above 50 degrees Fahrenheit at any time of the year. The barren, rocky parameters of the lake mean that very little organic food is available to feed these waters. Consequently, few life forms can be found here; only deep, clear, steel-blue waters—a tranquil, rock-rimmed jewel of the high divide.

FORESTS

One cannot speak of forests in the Rocky Mountain states without talking about mountains as well. The rise of the Rockies, and later the Cascades and Sierras, altered the climate in profound ways that would change the face of the landscape across much of the continent. These soaring peaks forced storm systems upward, where, in the cooler air they dumped their moisture on the flanks of the mountains, often leaving lands to the east high and dry. Whereas the forest belt once stretched across the entire northern reach of the United States in one long melting pot of deciduous trees and conifers, the drying effect of the Rockies helped split it into two parts, divided by a great sea of grass. Many areas of the West that were warm enough to support trees now lacked the moisture they required. In contrast, the higher reaches that did receive sufficient moisture for tree growth were too cool for deciduous trees to survive.

Much of the mountain West, therefore, would become a land ruled by conifers—a dizzy plunge of landscape blanketed with thick quilts of spruce, fir, juniper, and pine. Everything about conifers—which were among the first plants to colonize the earth— fits well into the climate parameters of the Rocky Mountains. By keeping their leaves (needles) year-round, these trees have the option of growing during warm spells of winter and spring, when the moisture content in the mountains is at its peak. Special waxy coatings on the needles keep water loss at a minimum, while the sticky resin that they produce freezes at temperatures far below that of water. Even the shape of conifers is appropriate to this environment. Their spirelike appearance, a phenomenon espe-

87

cially pronounced in species that grow at high altitudes, are perfect for shedding heavy snows. In addition, most conifers have slender, flexible branches that can "give" beneath the weight of ice and snow.

Just as lower, drier areas of the Rocky Mountain states are not suitable growing sites for most trees, there are upper limits to timber growth as well. These are the frigid, howling places that beat normally stately trees into cowering mats, which instead of rising upright, crawl on their knees across forlorn reaches of the high country. Growth in such places is extremely slow; a 500-year-old tree may measure only 2 inches across.

Given these two extremes, then, you'll find that most of the timber of this region grows in a distinct belt, neither too high and cold nor too low and dry. Because moisture and cold tend to increase as you go north, this timber belt tends to become lower as you move in that direction. In the central Rockies, it lies roughly between 5,000 and 11,000 feet.

While each of the four Rocky Mountain states covered in this book has its own special blend of forest, there are certainly great overlappings. Douglas-fir, for example, which is found at relatively low elevations in northwest Montana, also can be found in the peaks of central New Mexico. Ponderosa pine peppers many of the dry slopes along the entire Rocky Mountain range. This mixing is the result of the Rockies forming a nearly continuous north–south high line over which species can migrate easily into other appropriate regions. Spruce and fir species typically poured out of the Canadian boreal forest, while the long-needle pines worked their way up from Mexico.

There are, of course, exceptions to the conifer monopoly in the Rocky Mountains. Gambel oak, for instance, is especially common throughout the drier slopes of the southern range, while a great many stream banks support alder, mountain maple, and red-osier dogwood. But perhaps the most noticeable exception of all is the aspen, a member of the willow family and the most widely distributed tree on the North American continent. To see this tree set fire to an entire mountainside each autumn with a blanket of gold is one of the most unforgettable experiences in the West. Similarly appealing is the sight of milky white aspen trunks, flying soft, shimmering green canopies against a deep blue wash of summer sky.

New aspen often sprout from the root stems of existing trees, creating large clone groups. This tendency is a decided advantage to a tree whose existence depends heavily on exposure to light. When new clearings are created in the forest by fire, disease, or avalanche, the aspen can send up a new crop of trees from the undamaged root system, virtually guaranteeing themselves a place in the sun. However, it is precisely because of their love for sun that, barring a disturbance of some kind, the aspen is ultimately doomed to be replaced by shade-tolerant conifers.

Certainly the forests of the Rocky Mountain states do not live by trees alone. There are literally thousands of species of flowers, ferns, grasses, and shrubs here. Succulent berries splash the trails with reds, purples, and even whites. Wildflowers with names as delightful as their blooms—shooting stars, monkeyflowers, yellow bells, and paintbrush—turn cool stream banks and sun-drenched rips in the forest canopy into splendid gardens of color. Like the trees themselves, the plants that spread along the floor of the forest have a certain range of tastes that must be met in order for them to survive. Some, like the paintbrush, are amazingly adaptable, perfectly able to "sponge" off the nutrients in the root systems of other plants over a wide variety of settings and exposures. Others, like marsh marigold, are limited to rather narrowly defined environments.

As you might have guessed, it is much the same for the birds and mammals of the forests. For example, you will typically spot golden-crowned kinglets, mountain chickadees, gray jays, pine grosbeaks, and Williamson's sapsuckers only in conifer forests. Birds such as redstarts, northern orioles, and warbling vireos, in contrast, are much more likely to be seen in deciduous woods. Some feathered residents of the Rocky Mountain states can switch between deciduous and coniferous forest at will, even ranging into grassland or desert areas, whereas others are so specialized that they will feed and nest only in particular parts of a certain type of tree! Some have developed physical traits that complement the environment. Crossbills, for instance, have bills that are perfectly suited to opening pine cones to retrieve the nuts. Seen in this way, evolution is much less a vicious survival of the fittest than an attempt by each species to minimize competition by becoming particularly adept in a specific niche.

Animals survive using a similar strategy. It is the amazing acrobatic ability of the marten that allows it to catch squirrels in the tops of tree canopies. The porcupine has developed a strong, easily manipulated tail to balance itself while stripping a bark dinner from the trunks of ponderosa pine. Deer mice, which live along grassy edges of the forest, suffer enormous casualties in the clutches of hawks and coyotes. Their survival as a species depends almost entirely on their ability to reproduce, the adult female going through continuous 23- to 30-day gestation periods during the warm months of the year.

While many animals are specialists of sorts, it is not hard to see that the niches in which they and the plants they depend on operate are replete with overlappings. It is a marvelously complex web of life, each strand being dependent on many others. This systems lesson, where the whole is seen as more than just the sum of its parts, is just now beginning to sink in. Scientists hardly have begun to trace all of the intricate crossings and anchor points of a Rocky Mountain forest, let alone its place in the large web of the world. While our technology has given us new tools to understand these worlds, it also has allowed us to impact them to a degree that was absolutely unimaginable just a century ago.

Today we are still bound to promoting the preservation ethic as a purely pragmatic philosophy. No worthy ecologist fails to mention the fact that we may yet discover myriad forest plants that have valuable medical applications, or that the destruction of forest cover might severely deplete our groundwater supplies. I can't help but wonder, though, if we will ever grow up to accept the idea that the forest is valuable in and of itself—that beyond the nurturing and sustenance it offers to us, it represents a sacred life song that deserves to be sung whether or not the music ever falls upon human ears.

Northwestern Montana

ROSS CREEK

Distance: 2.4 miles

Location: Proceed on Montana State Highway 56, about 18.5 miles south of the junction with U.S. Highway 2. Turn off Montana State Highway 56 between mile markers 16 and 17, and head west for 4 miles, following signs for Ross Creek Cedars.

Note: Trailers are not allowed beyond a point roughly 0.75 mile west of Highway 56. Those with trailers may want to park them just east of this point, or leave them near Bad Medicine Campground, 1 mile to the north.

It would be hard to think of another pocket of forest anywhere in the Rocky Mountain states that offers the sense of mystery and enchantment of these thousand-year-old redcedars. Here it's possible to feel wonderfully close to a faraway era when Kootenai Indians passed through these great groves, bound for clearings that sported shrubs heavy with juicy berries, or crept on hide moccasins through the grassy fringes of lower Ross Creek, looking for white-tail deer.

To find a collection of western redcedars this old in this region of the country is rare, most having been lost long ago to fire or to the teeth of the loggers' saws. It's astounding to consider that some of these trees were just starting life when Peter the Hermit was busy leading the peasants on the first crusade to the Holy Land.

Another fairly common tree you'll see here is the western hemlock. But while hemlocks may grow in profusion in wet soils like these, the redcedars have the edge when it comes to drier environments, as they are better able to absorb water from the surrounding soil. As you walk this trail, you may find it interesting

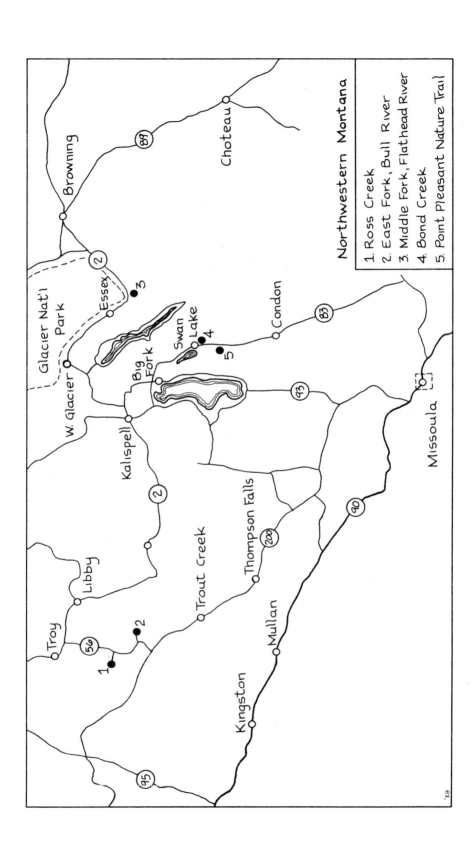

Northwestern Montana

1. Ross Creek
2. East Fork, Bull River
3. Middle Fork, Flathead River
4. Bond Creek
5. Point Pleasant Nature Trail

to study the growth patterns that occur in different kinds of habitats. How do sunny sites compare to shady ones, or rocky sites to those with thicker layers of soil? Part of the path we'll be following is along the Ross Creek Nature Trail, a very pleasant loop walk that has several interpretive signs to help you identify a few of the plants you'll see along the way.

Near the beginning of the nature trail, an interpretive sign mentions that the path you're now walking is actually part of an old pack trail, once used by miners and prospectors. As in much of the Rocky Mountain West, the 1860s and 1870s saw swarms of determined men sweeping through the valleys of the Cabinet Mountains looking for silver and gold. Strangely, many who did stumble across fairly promising sites sold their claims and moved on before they really could be developed, a fact that gave rise to the notion that it was as much the roaming as the lure of riches that pushed these independents from one wild slice of mountainscape to the next.

While there were a few small, mildly successful placer operations in the Cabinets, the closest thing to a bonanza in the immediate area occurred near the turn of the twentieth century about 13 miles east of here at Snowshoe Mine. Before the ore wagons stopped rolling, this mine produced over a million dollars worth of silver, gold, and lead. Some descendants of these early Montana miners can be found today in the nearby towns of Libby and Troy.

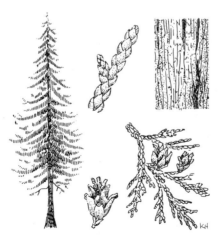

Western Redcedar

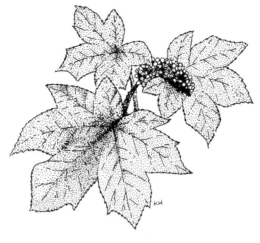

Devil's Club

Besides towering redcedars and hemlocks, as you walk through this forest you'll see Engelmann spruce, mountain maple, western white pine, and grand fir, not to mention a ground rich with queencup, wild ginger, violets, showy devils club, and trillium. The trillium's beautiful three-petaled white flower is considered by many outdoor lovers to be the first assurance that spring has really arrived. One species of this plant (ovatum) was widely used by Indian peoples to ease pain during childbirth; hence one of the plant's other names, "birthroot." Trillium roots are firmly anchored in a myth that claims they produce a wonderful love potion.

A short distance past a wooden bridge crossing Ross Creek you'll come to a fork in the nature trail. Take the right branch, and watch for trail 142, which also takes off to the right. We'll follow this more rugged, far less-used path for about 0.75 mile, meandering through grand redcedar stands and lush pockets of ground cover, finally joining up with the Middle Fork of Ross Creek.

About 0.25 mile after leaving the nature trail, notice the plethora of exposed tree roots woven across the dirt path. Many of the trees in this forest actually have very shallow roots, a fact that comes as somewhat of a surprise, considering how much weight they have to support. But the soil here is not particularly rich; instead, the trees of these environments have evolved the tech-

94

nique of gathering their nutrients from the constant supply of plant material decaying on the forest floor.

Just before our turnaround point, beside the Middle Fork of Ross Creek, you'll pass through an open area that supports an amazing collection of ground plants. Compare the growth here to that present beneath the canopy of the nearby forest. For every plant you see, including the great trees themselves, survival is largely a matter of finding a place in the sun. The strategies that some plants have developed to get the jump on openings in the forest canopy is remarkable. Many conifers, for example, have cones that will open only to release their seeds if exposed to intense heat. This way, when a fire comes through and "clears the competition," they will get a significant jump on colonizing the newly opened sun space.

When you reach the nature trail again on your return trip, take a right to complete the loop. Really slow down in this forest, smell its smells, listen to the bird song, and throw back your head and note the overwhelming enormity of these great trees. It's hard not to agree with the famous explorer David Thompson, who was struck with the difference between the great forests of western Montana and the smaller trees that grew a week's ride away on the eastern slope of the Continental Divide. "There we were men," he wrote in the early 1800s, "but on the west side we were pigmies."

EAST FORK, BULL RIVER

Distance: 3.25 miles

Location: From Montana State Highway 56, head east for 4.5 miles on Forest Road 407. A sign along the highway reads "East Fork Bull River." This turnoff of Montana State Highway 56 is about 8 miles north of the junction with Montana State Highway 200. The trail we'll be following is the one to St. Paul Lake.

The East Fork of the Bull River begins its westward roll from beneath the shadows of St. Paul Peak, high in the Cabinet Mountains Wilderness. (Some say that these mountains got the name

95

"Cabinet" from a steamboat by the same name that operated on the Clarks Fork river during the 1860s.)

Driving to the trailhead on Forest Road 407 will offer you a tempting glimpse into the rugged beauty of this mountain range. These vertical walls and serrated ridgelines are a definite contrast to the more gentle, rounded peaks visible elsewhere in this part of Montana. When glaciers inched their way southward out of Canada 75,000 to 100,000 years ago, most of the mountains, such as the Purcells north of Libby, were covered completely by ice. But the taller peaks in the more southerly Cabinets stayed above the level of advancing ice. Here they stood as grand sentinels through the long, relentless winters, their faces splitting into rugged ridges and headwalls under the pounding of the weather, while great rivers of glacial ice carved U-shaped valleys at their feet.

After a few short climbs during the first 0.25 mile of trail, the pathway along the Bull River's East Fork becomes a gentle, relaxing meander through a quiet, soothing forest of old-growth redcedar, hemlock, fir, and spruce. Because of the abundant moisture here, and therefore the increased decay, much of the path lies on a soft, plush surface that is an absolute delight to walk on. After 0.25 mile you'll begin a slow amble along a forested bench perhaps 40 feet above the East Fork valley bottom. From this slightly elevated perch you can look down into an absolutely magical interplay of light and shadow, where shafts of sun seem to float down for soft landings on rich green carpets of bracken fern and thimbleberry leaves.

While walking this stretch of trail, you may notice that you can't begin to compare in lushness much of the forest ground immediately surrounding you with that visible below. These dramatic differences are the result of several conditions, a key one being sunlight. Since many species of trees cannot grow well if their roots are submerged in water, a saturated bottom land adjacent to a stream usually will not be as heavily forested as the surrounding hillsides. Fewer trees means a more open tree canopy, which means more sunlight will reach the floor of the forest to support the growth of ground plants.

You'll see a particularly striking example of how a rip in the forest canopy can affect ground cover at 1 mile into the walk. Here

Thimbleberry

Bracken Fern

the trail suddenly emerges into a large opening thick with fireweed, thimbleberry, cow parsnip, ferns, and paintbrush. After 30 yards the path ducks back into a thick conifer forest with almost no ground cover, and finally into a more open forest supporting a modest growth of wild ginger, violets, bracken fern, and false Solomon's seal. While you may tend to view a forest as a fairly stable environment, a simple event like a large tree blowing over in a windstorm can have a profound effect on what plant life will grow there. This in turn influences the number of grazing and browsing animals such as deer and elk found in the area.

Approximately 1.6 miles into the walk, just past another open area, the trail will come very close to the East Fork of Bull River. This is our turnaround spot. Plan to spend some time here, watching this lovely stream fast-dancing through what best can be described as a great cathedral of old-growth redcedars, many of which have been guarding this lush pocket of wilderness for over 400 years. For those who wish to keep walking, it's slightly less than 2.5 miles to the beautiful St. Paul Lake, high in the Cabinet Mountains Wilderness.

If you haven't noticed them already, on the way back to the trailhead look for fairly large triangular holes that have been cut in several of the trees lining the trail. These are trap sites used against

Marten

martens, a beautiful weasellike creature that spends much of its time hunting squirrels in the conifers. Typically a small log is set against the trunk, with it's upper point placed in the opening that has been carved in the side of the tree. A baited trap is inserted, luring the unsuspecting marten up the pole and into its steel jaws. This method of trapping results in a slow, cruel death to the marten, not to mention causing totally unnecessary destruction to the tree. If you see such trap sites in the national forests, report them to the Forest Service as soon as possible.

MIDDLE FORK, FLATHEAD RIVER

Distance: 1 mile
Location: The trail is off U.S. Highway 2, at mile marker 185, about 5 miles southeast of Essex. The parking area is located on the south side of the highway next to Bear Creek. Our walk begins by crossing Bear Creek on a wooden bridge, approximately 50 yards west of the parking area.
Special Note: This is bear country; please take appropriate precautions.

The Middle Fork of the Flathead River begins in the womb of one of the largest, wildest mountainscapes to be found anywhere in the continental United States. Near its birthplace along the high peaks of the Continental Divide it is little more than an icy finger of snowmelt. But as it makes its way to the northwest it quickly gathers heart, dancing through the Bob Marshall and Great Bear wildernesses, then along the southern border of Glacier National Park, finally joining its equally dazzling sisters—the north and south forks of the Flathead—near the town of West Glacier. Fortunately, large sections of each of the three forks of the Flathead have been designated by Congress as National Wild and Scenic Rivers, a special type of protection that will keep their spirits from ever dissolving into the slack waters of a reservoir.

The term *Flathead* refers to a great Indian nation whose homeland once stretched across much of western Montana. There are two accepted stories as to the naming of these Indians. The first, and perhaps most popular, puts responsibility for the title in the laps of Lewis and Clark, who apparently heard secondhand stories that the Indians used special cradle boards to flatten the heads of their infants. Many past and present tribal members, however, deny that their people ever engaged in this practice. The other version claims that the name was given by nineteenth-century trappers and missionaries because these people made their homes along the "flat head" of the South Fork.

As you cross Bear Creek on the wooden bridge just west of the parking area, take a look at the tall western larch trees to the south, towering above the rest of the forest canopy like feathered lances piercing a cloak of tattered green satin. The first 0.25 mile of the trail will take you through the shady heart of this forest, the ground dressed in a rich collection of thimbleberry, queen's cup, and lichen. Here too you'll spot birch, easily recognized by its lovely thin layers of light-colored bark. Several northwest Indian tribes used birch bark as a sort of drawing paper, and occasionally so did the famous Western artist Charles M. Russell.

After a short climb the path will turn south to parallel the Middle Fork of the Flathead River, which for the time being will remain out of sight. Here you'll enter a rather thick, homogeneous forest of lodgepole pines, their otherwise somber mood broken by

Queen's Cup

the profusion of thimbleberry, a ground plant with large, maplelike leaves. You'll also see a few tall spikes of beargrass, their bundles of white flowers resting on tall green stems like tiny puffs of cloud.

The lodgepole pines growing so thick along this stretch of trail are actually the most common pine of the region. They are quick to get things growing on a site that has been disturbed by fire or logging. (This area was in fact burned many years ago.) Lewis and Clark were probably the first to give these trees the name lodgepole, a title given them after the intrepid explorers noticed that many Indian tribes were using young trees of this species as framing poles for their lodges.

In 0.5 mile the trail will make a sharp horseshoe turn to the left. At this turn you'll see a very faint path continuing on to the south. Trail crews may have blocked off this southbound path with a small pile of logs, since a short distance from here a rockslide has made it impassable. But if you walk this faint trail for about 80 yards, you'll come to an open area that offers sweeping views of the Middle Fork of the Flathead River. (Our turnaround is located beside an old wooden pole, the last remnant of a telephone system that once led to a Forest Service ranger station a short way up the river.) The U-shaped valley visible from this fine perch was formed during the last ice age when mighty glaciers ground northward, rounding the sharp edges of these rocky landscapes.

To the south lies the Great Bear Wilderness, which is drained by the Middle Fork of the Flathead. The region is a stunning collection of vast fir forests, glacier-scoured valleys, and singing mountain water, not to mention the great bear herself—the grizzly—for which the wilderness was named. This federally protected area, when combined with the Bob Marshall Wilderness to the south and Glacier National Park to the north, is a virtual masterpiece of unspoiled nature—one of the only ecosystems in the Rocky Mountains still containing significant populations of the birds and mammals that made their homes here a century ago. Here at the lush green feet of Spruce Point and Java and Vinegar mountains is a rare opportunity to experience wilderness on a grand scale—a last chance to touch the very spirits that gave form and color to those first visions of the American West.

BOND CREEK

Distance: 3.5 miles

Location: The trail heads east off State Highway 83, just south of mile marker 70, near the town of Swan Lake. A sign along the highway identifies the Bond Creek Trail. There is enough parking here for a couple of cars, but make sure you don't block the dirt road running past the trailhead.

The walk to Bond Creek is a gentle, soothing meander through the forest—the perfect trek for anyone wishing to lose themselves in a thick, green cloak of solitude. Here you'll find rich carpets of wildflowers, grasses, and berry shrubs, along with a pleasant sprinkling of paper birches and mountain maples. This latter tree forms the northernmost maple on the continent, extending from here all the way up through western Canada to southeast Alaska. Stop for a moment and look at the tips of the branches on the mountain maple. More than likely you'll see places where a hungry white-tailed deer has made a meal on the soft, hairless leaves.

The sheer variety and density of plant life in this forest is far different than that found on the other side of the Continental Divide 40 miles east of here. This comes down to a matter of moisture. Great storm clouds from the Pacific Ocean routinely roll into Montana, herded like sheep by the prevailing westerly winds. When these storms finally reach the Rocky Mountains, there is nowhere for them to go but up. And, the higher up you go, the cooler the temperature becomes. Since cool air cannot hold as much moisture as warm air, any cloud working its way up the peaks will end up dumping most of its moisture before it can get across the high line of the Continental Divide. The forest you are walking through right now may receive 7 to 10 inches more precipitation each year than regions immediately to the east.

It will be hard to miss the lacy strings of dark-colored lichen hanging from the branches of the conifers surrounding much of this walk. This is known as black tree lichen, and was a common source of food for Flathead, Nez Percé, and Kootenai Indians. It was usually soaked in water first, and then baked in fire pits for one to two days. Far from being survival food, it was considered quite delicious. In fact, Indian people continue to prepare black tree lichen today.

If you are here during midsummer, at 0.75 mile into the walk you'll see an abundance of small, golden flowers lining the pathway. These are an introduced species of clover, perhaps first brought into the area on some hiker's shoe or pants leg. In the same area, look for a shrub that has oval-shaped olive green leaves with small brown spots on the underside, and attractive reddish orange berries. This is buffaloberry, relished by Indians and early settlers alike. When mixed with water and beat with a stick to which grass fronds had been tied, it foamed into a tasty concoction known as Indian ice cream. These plants still provide many a meal for the occasional black bear, as well as for a host of birds.

You'll find this stretch of trail a good place to spot (or at least hear) several of the common feathered residents of this low-lying woodland. Look for hermit thrushes and dark-eyed juncos foraging on the ground and in the lower branches of the shrubs, while crossbills, evening grosbeaks, and the beautiful yellow body and red head of the western tanager may be seen flitting through the more open stands of conifers.

At about 1.25 miles into the walk you'll reach a junction where the trail forms a T intersection with a faint roadway. Here you'll turn left and pick up the trail again in about 25 yards. Shortly after this intersection is a gradual descent into the Bond Creek drainage, sporting a great variety of plant life along the way. Just before this descent, keep an eye out for the prickly leafed ground cover known as Oregon grape. The plant's purple berries, which

Western Tanager

follow beautiful clusters of yellow flowers, are enjoyed by humans as well as wildlife, the former using them for everything from jelly to wine.

Pay particularly close attention to the stretch of trail about 1.5 miles into the walk that occurs after the previously described descent and just after crossing a small stream. On both sides of the path the forest suddenly has become somber, so thick with middle-aged conifers that no light can penetrate beneath the canopy. Consequently, the ground is almost void of vegetation. But where trees have been cleared for the trail, sunlight pours in like honey, giving rise to a virtual garden of bracken fern, thimbleberry, twinflower, and pathfinder. There is no better place to get an idea of what a little sunshine can do.

The turnaround point is at Bond Creek, which you'll reach in about 1.7 miles. This beautiful little watercourse empties into Swan Lake after a delightful run down the mountains high in the northern reaches of the Swan Range. The path you've been on continues along the creek for 4.5 miles to Bond Lake, turns north to Trinkus Lake, and finally joins the beautiful ridge-running trail known as the Alpine 7, roughly 7.5 miles from our parking spot along State Highway 83. Those who elect to continue on will not regret a single step.

POINT PLEASANT NATURE TRAIL

Distance: 0.6 mile

Location: Turn off State Highway 83, just south of mile marker 64. If you are traveling from the south, you'll see a small wooden sign on the east side of the road that reads "Point Pleasant Campground." From the north, however, there is no sign. The campground road heads west from the highway for a short distance, then makes a sharp left turn before reaching the trailhead. (The trailhead is just before the campground.)

Although only slightly over a half mile in length, this trail, developed by the Montana Department of State Lands for the Swan River State Forest, serves as a wonderful introduction to the plethora of plants that grow on the moist western flanks of the Rocky Mountains. A small interpretive brochure can be picked up at the beginning of the walk, which should then be deposited at the end of the trail in the box provided. Rather than duplicate what the Department of Forestry already has covered, we'll take a closer look at some of the plants along the trail that have been merely identified with signs.

Before we discuss plants, though, be sure not to miss interpretive stop 1, a collection of nesting cavities in an old larch snag that has a family of flying squirrels living in it, at least for the time being. Flying squirrels should really be called gliding squirrels, since they use the two large folds of skin between their front and back legs to glide from the branch of one tree to the trunk of another. Nonetheless, the grace they exhibit while soaring through the air—controlling their flight paths carefully with tail and skin flaps—is quite remarkable.

These handsome animals mate during late winter and have litters of 2 to 5 young during the spring. Flying squirrels are quite common in the forests of northwestern Montana, but because their airborne missions to round up pine nuts are almost always conducted under the cloak of darkness, they are seldom seen by people.

About 0.1 mile into the walk you'll come to a sign identi-

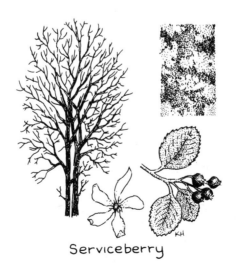

Serviceberry

fying lodgepole pine. Try to become familiar with the look of this tree, since it is one of the most widespread pines in the area. It is the only one that bears its needles in bundles of two. Besides using the straight trunks of young lodgepoles to support their tipis, some Indian people chewed the sap or sweet inner bark, and used the pitch in the treatment of burns and minor skin irritations.

The trail continues to wind through a fine forest, dominated by grand old-growth stands of western larch. While this tree is used for little besides lumber today, Flathead Indians of the area used to gather a sweet syrup from the larch, while Nez Percé tribes drank a tea made from the tree's bark to help cure colds and coughs. If you're here late in the fall you'll notice that the needles of the larches have turned gold, perhaps causing you to wonder whether or not they are the victims of some terrible insect invasion. In fact, unlike other conifers, each autumn the needles of the larch actually lose their green color and drop off.

Near interpretive stop number 12 you'll see a small sign identifying Oregon grape. While you may be familiar with the use of this plant in jams and jellies, throughout history it has had enough health uses to fill a medicine chest. Flathead people, for example, used root potions of the Oregon grape to prepare everything from antiseptics and contraceptives to treatments for syphilis and gonorrhea! Early settlers made a tea from the roots that was widely used for kidney problems. (If you're confused as to which of the plants around this sign is the Oregon grape, simply look for a

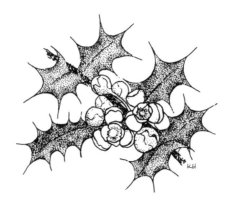

Oregon Grape

creeping ground plant with dull green leaves 2 to 3 inches long, each of which sports small spines on the tips, giving them a look somewhat like a holly.)

The overlook of the Swan River, stop 16, is truly a beautiful one. It may, however, leave you somewhat melancholy about how overtimbered this area has become, a process that began almost from the time settlers first moved into the area during the latter part of the nineteenth century. What a magical sight it must have been to see this clear, meandering watercourse flowing through endless stands of giant western larch trees, white swans floating in the morning mist like the dream painting of a druid priest. Whatever money was earned from the taking of trees in this once-sacred valley, it is difficult to imagine that it was enough.

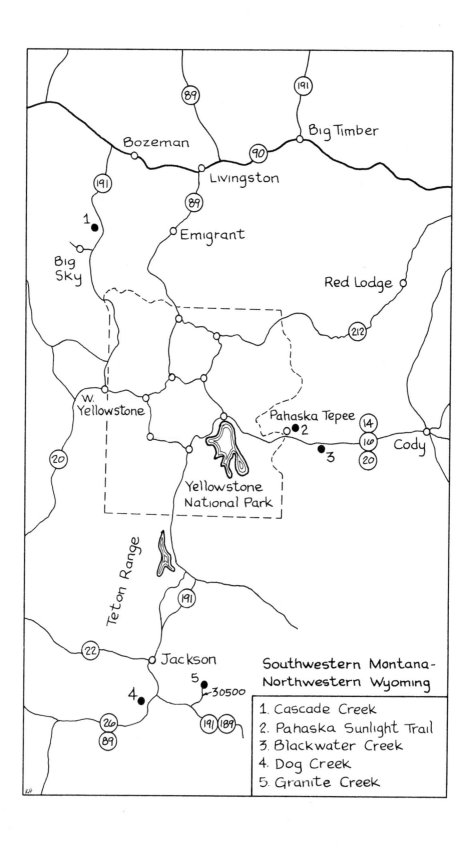

Southwestern Montana-
Northwestern Wyoming

1. Cascade Creek
2. Pahaska Sunlight Trail
3. Blackwater Creek
4. Dog Creek
5. Granite Creek

Southwestern Montana–
Northwestern Wyoming

CASCADE CREEK

Distance: 6 miles (round-trip to Lava Lake)
Location: Proceed to U.S. Highway 191, between Bozeman
and West Yellowstone, Montana. The turnoff is located on the
west side of the highway, 0.3 to 0.4 mile north of mile marker
61, and just north of a bridge crossing the Gallatin River.
Follow this small roadway 100 yards or so to the signed trailhead on the right.

Before you take your first steps up this forest trail, turn around for
a moment and enjoy the beautiful river running to the east. The
Gallatin was named in 1905 by Captain William Clark (of the
famous Lewis and Clark expedition) for Albert Gallatin, then the
secretary of the treasury. To the Indians of the region, however,
much of the watercourse was known as the Valley of Flowers, a
name that walkers along Cascade Creek also will find appropriate.
Besides finding favor with the likes of John Colter and Jim Bridger,
the stretch of the Gallatin to the north of here was most impressive
to those who came with an eye toward feeding cattle. "Such a
wealth of grass I had never before seen," wrote one early visitor.
"Silence reigned everywhere, broken only by the startled bird,
antelope or deer, many of which I disturbed as I came upon them
unawares, hidden as they were by the tall, waving grass." The
Gallatin Valley was to many as close to a high country paradise as
they ever would ever see.

There is no getting around the fact that this trail is an uphill
affair. The grades are quite variable, however, with short huff-
and-puff sections broken up nicely by climbs of a much more

mellow nature. What's more, there is no shortage of beautiful scenery along the way. The walk makes a nice all-day affair, ideally broken up by a long, lazy lunch on the cool green shores of Lava Lake.

The path begins in a classic lodgepole pine forest, a tree whose name refers to the fact that many Indian tribes of the region used this species to build their tipis. A typical tipi, or lodge, required 25 to 30 poles, each one approximately 20 to 25 feet in length. The lodgepole is the dominant tree from this point south, where it forms endless blankets of dull green across the broad, wild shoulders of Yellowstone. (Some historians have suggested that it was the dominance of this commercially worthless tree that enabled Yellowstone National Park to be established in the face of a strong nineteenth-century timber lobby.) The lodgepole is, in fact, one of the most widely distributed conifers in North America, and the only pine growing naturally in both Mexico and Alaska. As you walk through this forest, keep ears and eyes peeled for brown creepers, pine grosbeaks, Steller's jays, pine siskins, calliope hummingbirds, and hairy woodpeckers.

You'll become partners with Cascade Creek at a point about 0.3 mile up the trail. This is a beautiful, frothing flow of water that supports an incredibly rich variety of plant life. During the first part of your walk notice how much more lush the stream bottom is compared to that of the forest floor to your right. Besides having more water nearby, plants growing along streamsides tend to have more sunlight available to them, since few Rocky Mountain conifers (and perhaps least of all lodgepoles) grow very well with their feet planted in saturated soil.

Lining the trail at 0.5 miles will be white clover, spirea, and lots of beautiful thimbleberries at just over 0.75 mile, with their distinctive maplelike leaves and beautiful white flowers. This plant derives its name from the delicious red, thimble-shaped fruit it produces, which is an important food source for many birds and mammals.

At 1.5 to 1.7 miles into the walk, keep your eye on the foaming waters of Cascade Creek. Here you'll find several large rocks in the stream that are sporting wonderful islands of lush moss and plant life on their flat upper surfaces. This is a wonderful

Lodgepole Pine

Pine Siskin

attestation to the fact that a little water can speed up greatly the rate at which plants break down solid rock into new soil. From here on, largely because you've gained elevation, you'll notice a much different kind of forest than what you left behind along the Gallatin River. At higher elevations the air is cooler, meaning that it cannot hold as much moisture. Clouds routinely rise from the lowlands and drop their liquid cargo up on these high mountain flanks, giving rise to thick huddles of grasses and wildflowers, as well as Engelmann spruce and Douglas-fir.

By the time you cross Cascade Creek at 2.4 miles, the land will have exploded into a rush of life—willow, cow parsnip, columbine, wild rose, fireweed, and sticky geranium—each lending splashes of lavender, scarlet, lemon, or cream to the rich green carpets that grow at the feet of the great trees.

Lava Lake is a geologic splendor, carved out of ancient Precambrian "basement" rock, 2,500 million years old. The peaks before you are part of the eastern fringe of the Spanish Peaks Mountains that rise dramatically from the larger Madison Range to the west. The northern shore of the lake is lined with thickets of willow, rose, and mats of dwarf juniper. When combined with the sight of rugged peaks tumbling down to these cold blue waters, it becomes a place all too hard to leave.

Wild Rose

PAHASKA SUNLIGHT TRAIL

Distance: 2.5 miles

Location: The walk is on the north side of the Cody–Yellowstone Highway, approximately 2.5 miles east of Yellowstone National Park. The turnoff, which is marked by a sign reading "Pahaska Sunlight Trail," takes off to the north, just east of a bridge crossing the North Fork of the Shoshone River. The trailhead lies 0.2 mile down this road, on the right. (Sleeping Giant Winter Sports Area lies just to the west of the highway turnoff.)

Special Note: This is bear country; please take appropriate precautions.

A century ago, the beautiful North Fork of the Shoshone River that you'll be meandering along for this entire walk was known by the not-so-beautiful Indian name of Stinkingwater. It was at the headwaters of this river, little more than a one-day walk from here, that one of the more dramatic events took place in the epic tale of Chief Joseph's flight for Canada.

In 1863, the United States handed a treaty to the peaceful Nez Percé Indians of eastern Oregon and Washington, calling on them to give up nearly all of their Wallowa Mountain homeland so it could be opened for exploration by the rush of gold miners scouring the mountain West. Chief Joseph, representing a band of about 700 Nez Percé, mostly women, children, and old men, refused to sign the treaty, insisting (quite correctly) that rights to the land still belonged to them. Unfortunately, most whites in the area thought otherwise.

Several miners repeatedly harassed the band, finally engaging a few Nez Percé braves in a skirmish during the summer of 1877. Cries went out quickly to the U.S. Cavalry, calling on the boys in U.S. blue to come in and take care of the Nez Percé problem once and for all. But the Nez Percé refused to fight. Instead, Chief Joseph rounded up his people and approximately 2,000 horses, and set out on a twisted, 1,700-mile run through some of the most rugged country in the West, bound for the free turf of Canada.

On urgent request from General Howard, who was hot on Chief Joseph's trail as he headed east toward the Yellowstone country, the War Department dispatched General Sturgis and about 360 men to intercept the Nez Percé a short distance north of where you now stand. Smelling a trap, Joseph sent a small band of braves riding ahead pulling brush behind them, raising such a dust that Sturgis couldn't help but think that the distant commotion was made by the entire band. As he doggedly pursued the decoy, Joseph and his people doubled back and escaped northward through a wild maze of narrow canyons thick with timber.

Chief Joseph and his people eventually were caught by the cavalry almost within sight of the Canadian border. Thinking they already had reached their destination, Joseph had called a rest for his tired people, most of whom had been marching day and night. Despite surrender terms guaranteeing that the Nez Percé would reside on a reservation in their Northwest homeland, the government gave in to pressures from settlers to send them elsewhere. Tired, their spirits broken, more than two hundred perished in a matter of months. It was a sad, sad ending to one of the most unfortunate tales of the Indian campaigns.

This walk will take you into the thick of a mature mountain forest, composed primarily of Douglas-fir and blue and Engelmann spruce, with a lush understory dappled with lavender splashes of sticky geranium, lupine, and harebell. In 0.6 mile you'll reach the southern boundary of the Absaroka Wilderness. Absaroka, or more correctly Absarokee, is a combination of Hidatsa Indian words that formed the original name of the people we now know as the Crow. "Absa" means large-billed bird, and "rokee" is best translated as offspring or children. European explorers combined this description with the sign language used to describe these people—a flapping of arms—to arrive at the name "Crow."

There is a certain wild feeling to this place, as there is with so much of the greater Yellowstone ecosystem. The woods are mature, the river clean and strong. This is the only national forest in the entire state of Wyoming that contains elk, mule, and white-tailed deer, grizzly and black bear, bighorn sheep, mountain goat, antelope, moose, and mountain lion. As we have been all too slow to learn, it is not one single species of plant or animal but the diversity of life forms that marks the healthy ecosystem. You are

Sticky Geranium

fortunate to be standing in one of the finest in the continental United States.

At about 1.1 miles into the walk, just past a point that offers a grand view up the Shoshone, you'll find a small group of aspen to the left of the footpath. These lovely trees often sprout off of a single root stem, producing an entire grove of clone trees. (This is why you'll often see large groups of aspen turning the same color in the fall at precisely the same time.) Early trappers would scan the mountainsides looking for groves of aspen, knowing that their sweet bark was a favorite food of the beaver.

Our turnaround point is at about 1.25 miles, along a bench overlooking a lush slice of meadow that frames the North Fork of the Shoshone. If you feel like a dose of real tranquility, walk down into this park and sit by the river for a while. Between the sound of your own slow breathing and the laughter of mountain water, you may hear the hooves of Nez Percé horses echoing up the canyon, the whisper of moccasins rushing northward toward the Canadian border.

Black Bear

Grizzly Bear

BLACKWATER CREEK

Distance: 3.8 miles
Location: The walk leaves from the Blackwater Pond Picnic Ground, east of Yellowstone National Park on the Yellowstone–Cody Highway. This picnic ground is located on the south side of the highway, 0.5 mile west of the Rex Hale Campground. Park in the lot provided; the walk takes off on a bridge across the North Fork of the Shoshone River.
Special Note: This is bear country; please take appropriate precautions.

Even if you don't get very far up the walking road, this riverside picnic ground, complete with a lovely little rush-lined pond, is certainly worth a stop on your roll to or from Yellowstone Park. The landscape is a beautiful mix of wet and dry. Cool streams flow beneath thick blankets of mature conifers, many perched precariously on the high, sun-baked shoulders of volcanic rock laid down in the hot, steaming world of 40 million years ago. Some of the thick volcanic gravels surrounding this picnic area contain petrified trees.

This region is especially rich with wildlife. Moose routinely amble along the North Fork of the Shoshone on early morning browsing forays. As evening shadows begin to roll across the landscape, deer will begin drifting along the grassy fringes of the conifer forest. Elk and black bear are also quite common. Although this can be a harsh land during winter, there seems little doubt that it was an important place to the countless generations of Indian people who once hunted here. In fact, just north of the highway is a cave that archeologists have determined was occupied off and on from 7280 B.C. to A.D. 1580—a span of almost 9,000 years! This shelter is known as Mummy Cave, so named for the mummified body of a man that was found here who is thought to have lived in the latter part of the seventh century.

Begin your walk by crossing the North Fork of the Shoshone River on a wooden bridge. You may notice that this stretch of valley is defined by a rather narrow V shape instead of the broader U shape common to many of the surrounding canyon systems. More rounded features are the result of massive glaciers grinding their way down the valleys during the last ice age. This stretch of the Shoshone, however, saw no such activity.

117

After crossing the Shoshone, Blackwater Lodge will be on your left, and shortly afterward you'll pass through a National Forest Service gate. From here the dirt road makes a sharp huff-and-puff climb for about 0.25 mile, after which it continues to rise along Blackwater Creek at a far more gentle rate. By 0.3 mile into the walk you'll be wrapped in a beautiful forest environment—tall, thick conifers with dwarf juniper, buckwheat, and balsamroot gathered at their feet, broken here and there by patches of grass and clusters of aspen. The balsamroot you see here was a popular source of food for many native peoples of this region. The inner portion of young flower stems were eaten frequently, as were the seeds, which are very similar in taste to those of the sunflower. A few tribes ate the woody roots, which is an almost impossible proposition unless they are first baked in a hot fire pit for several days. The arrow-shaped leaves of this plant were quite effective as a poultice for treating burns. If you leave the road occasionally and wander over to lovely Blackwater Creek, most of the summer you'll be treated to lovely mats of mountain wildflowers.

By the time you go 0.75 mile you'll catch several glimpses of Coxcomb Mountain to the south. This is part of a long, wild finger of land that protrudes northward out of the Washakie Wilderness. (Washakie was the name of a great chief of the Shoshone Indians.) This is a massive, broad-shouldered country, where the edges of flat-topped volcanic plateaus make dizzy plunges into untrammeled mazes of stone and pine. The rugged nature of this land is often reflected in the names of the region's peaks: Sleeping Giant, Citadel, Giant Castle, and Fortress mountains, to name a few.

Both the lushness and age of the forest continue to increase as you climb southward. Old, stately Engelmann spruce and Douglas-fir are joined by ponderosa and blue spruce, as well as a mat of thimbleberry, harebells, and wild rose. Our turnaround point is at 1.9 miles, at a point where the road ends and the footpath portion of the Blackwater Fire Memorial Trail begins. This trail eventually climbs up to the high, windswept shoulders of Clayton Mountain. It traverses a battleground of sorts, the site of a heroic fight against a forest fire that raged through this country half a century ago—a fire as tragic as any that has burned through the forests of the Rocky Mountains.

Blue Spruce

The fighting men, a combination of forest service employees and a hearty band of young Civilian Conservation Corps workers from Company 1811, first hit the line of the Blackwater burn on August 20, 1937. The forest was hot and dry, and it didn't take long to realize that a major fire was close at hand. Then, on August 21, an unexpected windstorm roared across the land, suddenly whipping the flames up the forested gulches and flanks of Clayton Mountain, where a number of firefighters were furiously cutting lines to keep the blaze in check. Paul Greever, delivering the address at the dedication of the fire memorial located near where you parked for this walk, described the scene: "These boys for hours fought the raging blaze. They cut timber, and fought the fire in every way known; cut, bruised and injured by fierce scorching blasts as the walls of fire closed in upon them. Some were suffocated, some were burned."

By the end of that fateful summer day, 15 young men were dead and 39 were injured. A shocked crew of survivors fought on for three more days, finally bringing the Blackwater Fire to rest after it had consumed more than 1,200 acres of national forest. "To those families," Paul Greever went on to say, "who mourn here today the loss of a son, brother, husband or father, may there come a solace in the promise of immortality which is held in every beautiful thing—in the trees, the mountains, the streams, and the flowers." Today in these woods you still can find a few charred remains from the Blackwater Fire. But the other components of the forest—the flowers and trees, the birds and animals—have returned, carrying with them that solace and special promise of immortality.

DOG CREEK

Distance: 2.4 miles
Location: Located southwest of Hoback Junction, Wyoming, on U.S. Highway 89/26, the walk begins on the dirt road that takes off from the west side of the highway, approximately 0.55 mile south of mile marker 137. There is a small turnoff where you can park, directly across the highway from our walking road.

While it's possible to drive 300 or 400 yards down this dirt road to where the actual trail part of our walk begins, you'd be missing one of the finest slices of habitat for miles around. After paralleling U.S. Highway 89/26 for a short distance, our road heads west across a small bridge. On your right will be a beautiful wetland, absolutely overflowing with a lush weaving of bird and plant life. Red-winged blackbirds chatter from the stalks of cattails, while an osprey traces arcs in the sky high above the conifers. Mallards and cinnamon teals float quietly in a fringe of reeds. A pair of great blue herons, surprised by your approach, explode from the water into a glorious dance of sweeping wings, soon to take refuge among the tall spruce on the other side of the pond. These herons make routine feeding trips of 25 miles or more, often to fishing sites along the Snake River Plains to the north.

We shouldn't leave this marsh without paying our respects to the common cattail, easily seen just to the east of the bridge. This is perhaps the most widely used wild plant in the United States. Even today people eat the tender insides of the young shoots (they're rather like cucumbers), boil the spikes to eat the flowers off as one might do with an ear of sweet corn, and bake the starch-laden root stalks in fire pits or grind them into meal. Besides

Osprey

being a good source of tinder, Indians commonly placed cattail "fuzz" in baby wrappings to prevent chaffing, and also wove the leaves of the plant into mats that served as flooring in the family tipi. Geese and even elk will eat young cattail shoots in the spring, while pheasants, marsh wrens, and red-winged blackbirds hide their nests in the tall stalks.

Continue west on this dirt road for about 200 yards, to a point just past a corral on the right. Here the actual trail begins, meandering above a pleasant, open creek bottom peppered with asters, sticky geraniums, harebells, timothy grass, and yarrow. This latter plant, 1 to 2 feet high with clusters of small white flowers and almost fernlike leaves, is often passed off as just another weed. In fact, yarrow is one of the most widespread healing herbs in the world, having been used by everyone from Native Americans to old world herbalists, and for amazingly similar purposes.

Perhaps the most common use of this overlooked little plant was to crush the leaves and apply them to bad cuts and lacerations in order to control bleeding. Laboratory experiments have identified the presence of a chemical called achellein, which reduces the clotting time of blood. (The name of this substance, as well as the genus name of yarrow, *Achillea*, comes from the belief that the ancient Greek Achilles used yarrow, or a related plant, to help control bleeding in his soldiers during the battle of Troy.) Several North American Indians used a tea made from the leaves to break fevers, and at least one Rocky Mountain tribe boiled the plant in water to create a solution that helped aching muscles and joints.

As you walk along the north side of Dog Creek, you'll be afforded a glimpse to the west of the forested flanks of the Snake River Range, a surprisingly rugged collection of limestone and shale peaks, fresh, tumbling creek water, and yawning meadows bursting with wildflowers. These rugged mountain folds were trapped extensively during the 1830s, in the brief heyday of such legendary frontiersmen as Davy Jackson, Jedediah Strong Smith, and William Sublette, heroes whose free trapper lives ended abruptly when silk hats suddenly replaced beaver as the nouveau look on the streets of Boston and Paris. The majority of those notoriously uninhibited rendezvous you may have read about, where trappers drank, lied, drank, purchased wives, drank, and in their spare time, traded beaver pelts for food and staples for the coming year, took place south of here, along the wide sage plains that line the Green River Valley.

A short distance into the walk, about 50 yards past the point where the trail becomes a single footpath, is a tiny spring guarded by a remarkably big grandfather Engelmann spruce. This grand old patriarch is perhaps 300 to 400 years old. Imagine what pageants of adventure have passed beneath its great arms, what range of humanity took rest against its strong trunk. Past this old tree 40 yards, to the left of the trail, are the remains of a beaver dam, courtesy of the furry fellow who brought to the United States the entire romantic, boisterous era of the free trapper. Once an area is sufficiently flooded, beavers build fine lodges complete with protected underwater entrances. Nearby, below the level of freezing ice, a cache of aspen or willow branches is kept on hand to feed mom, dad, and the kids through the long, cold Wyoming winter.

Our turnaround is located 1.2 miles into the walk at a point where Beaver Dam Canyon and Creek spill into Dog Creek from the southwest. Those so inclined may want to explore this side canyon for the chance of seeing its namesake, the beaver. Whether you set eyes on this furry engineer or not, you can hardly go wrong with a slow, aimless drift through the canyon's quiet collage of nooks and crannies.

GRANITE CREEK

Distance: 2.5 miles
Location: Follow U.S. Highway 189/191 south out of Hoback Junction for approximately 12 miles to Granite Creek Road and head east. You'll reach a parking lot for Granite Creek Hot Springs in 10 miles. Park here and cross Granite Creek to the Hot Springs facility; our northbound trail takes off from between the plunge pool and the creek.

When the Plains Indians tried to tell French trappers that the people of these mountains were known as "always hungry," the French, not being adept at sign language, misread the sign—both hands passing over the stomach—as "big bellies," or Gros Ventres. And so the people and the mountains have been known this way ever since. While these 25 square miles of high country may lack the abrupt drama of the Tetons, they nonetheless form a fantastic tapestry of grassy summits and wind-scoured badlands, soft-shouldered hills and peaks, deep gorges of red, gray, and purple rock. The Gros Ventre Wilderness supports an excellent population of wildlife, such as bighorn sheep, bear, and moose, and was once the main migration corridor for thousands of elk bound for Jackson Hole each year at the first slap of winter.

These mountains are much older than the Tetons. While the eye-catchers here are the sheer granite walls to the northwest, much of the Gros Ventre is composed of layers of colored sedimentary rock, formed over countless millennia at the bottom of ancient seas. These seafloors were later uplifted by violent forces deep within the earth, their outer flanks eventually colliding with an overthrust block slipping slowly to the northwest. Many of the well-defined shapes you see today are the result of more recent geologic activity—creeping rivers of glacial ice, and the incessant pounding of wind and weather.

If all this is not enough to entice you, surely the hot mineral waters near the trailhead will. Although a commercial facility, this pool, built in 1933 by the Civilian Conservation Corps, is still wonderfully close to its humble beginnings. You still walk down a dirt road, pay your money to a couple of kids, and change your clothes inside a plain old cabin with wooden pegs driven into log walls. Then you dash across the grass and slip into clear, hot mineral water, bubbling into the pool beneath a backdrop of towering rock walls and pockets of cool, green forest. Hot springs rely on the fact that fresh water continually percolates through the earth to a layer of searing hot rocks. These rocks, which often overlie a magma chamber, heat the water to great temperatures, a process that increases the pressure enough to allow it to again rise to the surface of the earth.

The view of the sheer granite walls that make Granite Creek Canyon so special is particularly good during the first 0.25 mile of trail. These walls plunge to ground level in a series of short steps, each fall broken by a steep ridge peppered with hardy trees, sinking their roots into rock cracks on the edge of oblivion. Trees are another agent of erosion that is sometimes overlooked. Their powerful root systems split the rock along tiny fault lines, causing it to eventually fall and crumble on the ground below, piles of rubble one step closer to becoming soil.

If you're walking this path in midsummer, at 0.3 mile you'll come to a beautiful meadow of asters, cinquefoil, thistle, scarlet gilia, and balsamroot. This latter plant, easily identified by its large, olive green arrow-shaped leaves, produces tasty seeds not unlike those of the sunflower. Many Indian peoples also ate the tender inner section of the immature flower stems. You'll wind your way in and out of wildflower meadows and pockets of fir, spruce, and an occasional aspen for another 0.35 mile, eventually reaching a small pond on the fringe of a grassy meadow. This is a fine example of pond succession, a neat trick of nature where water is turned into wildflowers. As the plants that surround the pond's perimeter die and drift to the bottom, they are broken down and accumulate as layers of soil. This slow but steady process decreases the depth until finally it reaches a point where plants can live successfully across the entire surface of what was once open water.

From this point the remaining water fills in fairly rapidly. What was once liquid is simply an extension of the surrounding meadow.

If you're here in late July or August, about 50 yards past the pond on the right you'll see what appears to be a collection of sunflowers from which someone has plucked all the yellow petals. It looks as if a desperate, love-struck teen came through here playing "she loves me, she loves me not," each time getting the wrong answer. These are western coneflowers and they bear their flowers not in long rays like most composites but as a collection of tiny blooms on a dull-colored cone.

Our turnaround point is at a long jumbled line of granite talus, approximately 1.25 miles into the walk. Here you'll likely hear the strained, high-pitched "eeek, eeek" of the pika, sometimes referred to as "rock rabbit." It takes a sharp eye to actually see one of these dancing bundles of fur, since whenever possible they travel through passages created by the haphazard jumbles of broken rock. A farmer of sorts, the pika actually harvests various types of vegetation—often 15 or 20 different species at a time—and then lays the food out on flat rocks to dry. Once properly cured, he gathers it up and stores it away for winter, when he will still be active under a deep blanket of snow.

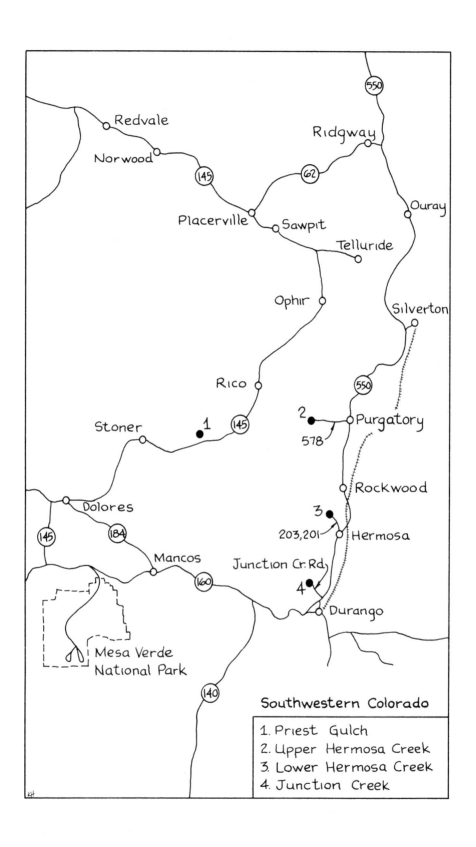

Redvale

Norwood

145

Ridgway

550

62

Ouray

Placerville   Sawpit

Telluride

Ophir

Silverton

Rico

550

Stoner   1   145

2

578   Purgatory

Rockwood

Dolores

145   184

3

203, 201   Hermosa

Mancos

Junction Cr. Rd.

160

4

Durango

Mesa Verde
National Park

140

Southwestern Colorado

1. Priest Gulch
2. Upper Hermosa Creek
3. Lower Hermosa Creek
4. Junction Creek

Southwestern Colorado

PRIEST GULCH

Distance: 2.5 miles
Location: The trail takes off from Priest Gulch Campground, located on the north side of State Highway 145, approximately 25 miles northeast of Dolores, Colorado. The walking trail leaves off from the north side of the campground, adjacent to campsite 7. Leave your vehicle near the campground entrance, as parking at the trailhead is very limited.

Priest Gulch traverses the very best of the Colorado forests. Aspen blanket the hills and hummocks as far as the eye can see, their soft canopies streaked here and there with the dark olives and frosty blues of Engelmann and Colorado blue spruce. Though beautiful any time of year, the shrinking days of autumn trigger a particularly splendid change in the aspen, as the airy green color of chlorophyll drains from the tree, leaving a sea of blazing gold leaves shimmering in the October sun.

Many a mountain man used to scan the high pockets of the Rockies in search of the aspen's fluttering leaves and striking white trunks. For to find them often meant finding the beaver, who has a particular penchant for the sweet bark of the tree, and a wily way of using the twigs and branches to construct dams and lodges that the best of engineers would envy. (The beaver keeps a stash of aspen branches beneath the freezing level of its pond, thereby ensuring a good supply of food throughout the winter.) Beaver continue to munch aspen bark in wet pockets of this forest, while deer and elk browse the leaves and twigs.

The same shift in hat fashion (from beaver to silk) that ultimately saved the aspen-loving beaver from being trapped to extinction sent the mountain man the way of the passenger pigeon.

127

"We are done with this life in the mountains," wrote mountain man Robert Newell, who 150 years ago saw the writing on the wall. "Done with wading in beaver dams, and freezing or starving alternately—done with Indian trading and Indian fighting. The fur trade is dead in the Rocky Mountains, and it is no place for us now, if it ever was."

This is a fairly gentle walk. After two very short climbs in the first 0.2 mile, the path levels off to become an easy streamside meander. At 0.5 mile into the walk you'll come to a small meadow 50 yards long, spackled with the white umbels of yarrow blooms, and the lemon-colored heads of the yellow salsify. Salsify was introduced into this country from Europe, where it has been cultivated for nearly two millennia for its tasty, fleshy root. Depending on who you ask, a cooked salsify root tastes like parsnip, artichoke, or even oyster (hence one of the plant's nicknames, "oyster plant"). Salsify has been extremely successful in its colonization of the new world, in part due to its efficient dispersal method of launching thousands of tiny seeds into the wind on tiny white parachutes.

Just before leaving this small meadow, note the two large dead trees (snags) on your left. While many people would look at these according to the number of cords of firewood they would produce, such trees are actually very important to resident wildlife. Three-toed woodpeckers, for example, would relish either of these snags as a place to rear their young, as might the beautiful, weasellike marten.

Throughout this section of trail, particularly along the stream just after leaving this first meadow, you'll notice the long, slender leaf bunches and, in June and July, the beautiful lavender flag flowers of the Rocky Mountain iris. This is one of the most beautiful of all the mountain wildflowers, and only grows in areas where water lies close to the surface of the ground. The fresh roots are reported to contain strong poisons, although when dried they have been used for decades as a treatment for syphilis, as well as to create a strong diuretic.

Past the first meadow 60 yards the trail wanders through a forest of conifers draped with lace lichen. After reaching a second open area in 1 mile, cross the stream and begin a gradual climb up a narrow ridge. Just after topping this ridge at 1.25 miles, you'll enter one of the most beautiful aspen meadows you could ever hope to find. These lovely trees, some 80 to 100 years old, form a stunning fringe around a grassy parkland peppered with iris, yarrow, and salsify. To the west is a high wall wrapped in spruce and aspen that separates this drainage from Little Taylor Creek, while in the distant north stands the high, lush ridge line of Stoner Mesa. If you make a short descent down a 35-foot hill on your right, you'll come to a very secluded section of Priest Creek—a perfect pocket in which to sit and soak up a Rocky Mountain afternoon.

UPPER HERMOSA CREEK

Distance: 2.8 miles
Location: From U.S. Highway 550, just north of the main entrance to Purgatory Ski Area, turn west onto Forest Road 578, following signs for Sig Creek Campground and Hermosa Park. Continue past the campground for several miles to a road taking off to the left across a meadow to the East Fork of Hermosa Creek. Park here and cross the stream on foot. The walk continues on this road for 100 yards, becoming a trail after crossing through a gate.
Note: This trail has several gates; please be sure to close each one as you pass through.

This is a beautiful walk through a combination of high open meadows and spruce–fir forest environments, ending at a small streamside park. A hundred years ago the road through this park (the one you came in on) was a toll route connecting the mining region around Rico with transportation facilities at Rockwood, 15 miles north of Durango. Since any worthy investor was hesitant to back a mining region unless there was an adequate, reliable means of transporting the ore, road building in the 1870s was pursued at a feverish pitch, often over some of the most incredible topography imaginable. Yet building these roads, often blasting through solid rock, was only the beginning. Gatekeepers were employed to collect fees, and the constant beat of weather meant work crews armed with picks and shovels had to be on hand to fill in ruts, as well as to clear the endless flows of mud, rock, and snow. Toll road fever began to wane in the 1880s with the arrival of the railroads. At that point, mining camp promoters quickly shifted their energies into trying to woo the iron horse into their particular pocket of the San Juan high country.

In 0.3 mile there are fine views off to the right of the mountains that give rise to Hermosa Creek. From here the watercourse tumbles southward for more than 20 miles through stately forests of Engelmann spruce, Douglas-fir, ponderosa, juniper, and white fir, finally unleashing its precious cargo 10 miles north of Durango into the Animas River. This gentle trail follows the course for nearly the entire distance.

As the path turns south, Hermosa Creek begins to enter a shallow ravine cut through the meadow, flanked on the west by fine collections of aspen peppered with spruce and fir. Aspen are especially adept at colonizing disturbed ground, although if no further disturbances occur, they ultimately will be replaced by the more shade-tolerant spruce and fir you see growing here. These conifers then form what is known as the climax forest.

The open ravine continues to drop southward, becoming narrower and narrower until the grassy creek banks are eventually replaced by forest. In 1.5 miles you'll reach the East Fork of Cross

Steller's Jay

Creek, just after passing through a wooden gate. Cross this stream and continue on for about 50 more yards, where you'll find a small grassy area beside Hermosa Creek, with a sheer rock wall exposed on the far side. This is our turnaround point.

This is a very good place to meet some of the common feathered residents of this forest—the black crested head and bright blue body of the Steller's jay, the blunt gray body and piercing scream of the goshawk, and that ever-busy fluffy gray insect eater, the mountain chickadee. This latter bird sports nearly the same familiar tune (chick-a-dee dee dee) as does its lower-altitude cousin the black-capped chickadee. Always found near coniferous forests, in severe winters these hardy little birds may work their way down to the lower stretches of Hermosa Creek, where the sting of winter is a bit less severe. Also keep an eye out here for red crossbills (the name refers to the specially evolved crossed bill, perfect for opening pine cones) as well as golden-crowned kinglets and pine siskins.

Pine Grosbeak

LOWER HERMOSA CREEK

Distance: 3 miles
Location: From U.S. Highway 550, 0.25 mile north of mile marker 32, turn west onto Hermosa Creek Road. Immediately after making this turn, take a right onto La Plata County Road 201. Follow this for 4 miles; it reaches a dead end at the trailhead.

For much of its 30-mile tumble from the high, rugged peaks of the central San Juans to the northwest, Hermosa Creek is paralleled by a wonderful footpath, the two of them meandering through a vast, endless quilt of rich forest communities. As you'll see on this walk, simple turns of the trail can have surprising consequences. For instance, a small drainage nook hidden from the warm, drying fingers of the sun will support a flush of life far different from that which surrounds it. You'll find an entirely different array of flowers peppering the ground, and the dull, blunt complexion of ponderosa and fir will yield to the summer-bright greens of aspen and alder. With such changes, of course, comes a different array of animal life—the buzz of honeybees where there were none before, glimpses of mule deer looking for leaves to browse, and the light chirp of bushtits instead of the raucous calls of Steller's jays.

The trail begins in a semiopen coniferous forest, with fine, broad views of Hermosa Valley stretching to the northwest. In 0.25 mile you'll see another trail taking off at a sharp right angle to join Jones Creek, but other than this, there should be no intersections confusing enough to divert your attention from the pleasures underfoot. It was on just such forested mountain trails that the proud Ute Indians once roamed summer through fall, gathering herbs and berries, hunting elk, deer, and rabbit—then preparing the meat and tanning the hides that would often be traded with other tribes in the uplands of northern New Mexico. Every component of this forest had a name, and more often than not, a use to these people. Roots and bulbs, pine nuts, seeds from various grasses, acorns from the Gambel oak that grows so profusely here—even the Abert's squirrels that dance and chatter in these ponderosas—were considered important food sources. Branches from willows and alders were used to make water baskets, which were then sealed with the

132

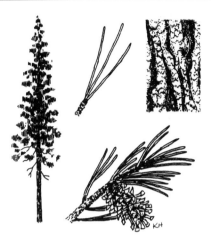

Ponderosa Pine

pitch from the conifers that surround you. Sweet sap was collected from aspen in the spring. Here then, was firewood, housing material, clothing, trade items, dinner, and dessert.

According to a Ute legend, long before any people roamed the earth, the creator Sunawavi began to collect and cut sticks that he then placed in a large bag. Day after day this went on, much to the curiosity of Coyote, who had stood nearby watching the entire process. One day, while Sunawavi was away, Coyote could no longer contain himself and opened the bag. When he did, thousands of people ran out and scattered in every direction, each speaking a different language. When Sunawavi returned he was extremely angry. He had planned to distribute the people evenly across the land so that they could live in peace, but now there would be much war, each tribe trying to get better and better land. Considering the small collection of people who remained in the bag, Sunawavi decided to name one group the Ute. They would remain few in number, but be endowed with great courage, able to stand against all others.

And so the story seemed to unfold, at least until the arrival of hungry miners to the San Juans in the latter half of the nineteenth century. The Utes were not aggressive fighters; they sold a major portion of the high country to the north to the U.S. government simply to avoid a war. Yet still the newcomers wanted more, until Sunawavi's special people were removed from all but a minuscule section of Colorado territory. Today in this part of the state, only words hint at this nearly forgotten people—Ouray, Ignacio, Uncompahgre, Weminuche—words and the sprawl of the vast green forests that nurtured them for countless centuries.

Notice as you walk along an exposed, south-facing bench that in about 0.3 mile the vegetation changes dramatically. Instead of ponderosa and white fir there is a profusion of Gambel oak interspersed with juniper. This latter tree, readily identifiable by its beautiful blue "berries" (they're actually the tree's cones), is sometimes mistakenly referred to as cedar. Once consumed by the Utes, today the "berries" are an important food source for many birds. Roughly 1 mile into the walk, the trail cuts across the sheltered drainage of Swampy Creek, an environment rich with wildflowers, shrubs, and even deciduous trees.

Although ponderosa pines have been present throughout much of this walk, adding a stately, truly western feel to the landscape, nowhere are they more beautiful than at our turnaround point, approximately 1.5 miles from the trailhead. Here these trees are exceptionally large, at least two hugs wide, growing in a beautiful, open parkland perched on a rim high above Hermosa Creek to the southwest. In fact, if you leave the trail and walk to your left for 30 or 40 yards, you'll find an abundance of perches beneath these great trees. These are just perfect for mentally drifting away with the summer breezes that routinely roll out of the La Plata Mountains several miles to the west. Though the ponderosa is often cited as the most common pine on the North American continent, here it seems anything but common. In this slice of mountainscape these cinnamon-colored giants are real magic, most uncommon in the amount of beauty they offer to those who linger beneath their outstretched arms.

JUNCTION CREEK

Distance: 2.6 miles

Location: From Durango town center, head north on Main Street until you reach 25th Street, and turn left. This street first becomes Junction Creek Road, and then, at the point where it enters the San Juan National Forest, it turns into Forest Road 543. You'll reach our trail after a short drive through the forest, on the left side of a horseshoe turn to the right.

This walk will take you through a mixed conifer forest that blankets the bottom and sides of a lovely, meandering mountain valley. The artist responsible for much of this scenery is Junction Creek. This fine little stream on your left has sliced its way through these thick slabs of sedimentary rock for thousands of years on a headlong dash from the high reaches of the La Plata Mountains. A century ago this waterway ran dark with sediments from mining operations near its headwaters; today only spring snowmelt and summer showers cloud its otherwise crystal complexion.

The early portion of the trail winds through a narrow open area, complete with a mat of tall grass cradling the cinnamon trunks of the ponderosa. This tree, also known as yellow pine or, when young, as blackjack pine, tends to grow in relatively open parklands like this one. Held against a distant range of mountains or a flush of Colorado sky, it seems to sing the essence of the American West. Many Indian peoples of the area collected the seeds of the ponderosa, which they ate raw or made into bread.

Also common along this section of the trail is Gambel oak, a member of the beech family whose thickets of lobed leaves often can be found woven into the ponderosa understory. While the nuts of nearly all of the oaks served as major sources of food for Native Americans, Gambel oak was especially prized since its acorns tended to be less bitter than those of other varieties. Preparing acorns meant first grinding them into a fine meal, often in a stone mortar or metate. The ground nuts were then placed in a basket lined with leaves and water was poured through them to remove the tannic acid. Acorn meal could be stored for long periods in pottery containers and its flavor (as well as that of acorn mush) could be altered by adding other nuts or berries or even meat. Like

135

Downy Woodpecker

the nuts of the pinyon, so important a food source was Gambel oak that it actually influenced the ebb and flow of large bands of people. Today common consumers of Gambel oak are mule deer, which have a fondness not for the nuts but for the plant's thick leaves.

The trail continues above the creek through collections of purple asters, scarlet gilia, and yarrow. Besides depending on adequate moisture from summer showers, the particular blossoms that you see splashed onto this landscape depend a great deal on what time of year you happen to be here. Were you to drift very, very slowly through this forest you'd see a soft, carefully orchestrated explosion of yellows, scarlets, and creams, each bloom marking the steady drift of summer toward autumn. Beyond blooms, a beautiful fusion of greens can be seen here, created by the outstretched arms of blue spruce, alder, ponderosa, and cottonwood.

Down the path 1 mile keep your eyes and ears open for the raucous call and deep blue flash of Steller's jays, the soft toot of nuthatches, and the sporadic drum of sapsuckers.

While most people realize the influence of fire and disease on this landscape, few of us stop to consider that the dry, loamy soil underlying this forest also adds a great deal to the pace of change. At 1 mile into the walk you can look high across the creek and see evidence of a large slide of land, now patiently being stabilized once again by the long root fingers of young conifers. Just to your right at this point, on the bank alongside the trail, is a collection of exposed root systems—more evidence of how much of this land is routinely carted off by wind and water. The hold that these trees and plants have on the mountainsides forms a tenacious net—one which a careless fire or misplaced clear-cut can destroy easily.

At 1.2 miles, near the Quinn Creek drainage, the pathway enters one of those pockets that add such surprise and fascination to walks in the southwest mountains. Protected from overexposure to the sun and fed by fine lines of water, the land here shifts dramatically from a coniferous forest that is fairly bereft of under-story life, to a land exploding with aspen, yellow cut-leaf coneflow-ers, box elders, chokecherries, mountain maples, and thimble-berries. Something very different is happening here. The dry, fine-edged odor that laced the ponderosa parks has melted into air that runs thick with damp earth and herbs. The lilt of bird song is heavier; a cool moisture rubs your face and arms. It is a profound lesson in the power that both water and exposure have to alter the face of the land.

In 0.1 more mile is our turnaround, at a point where the trail joins another pathway coming in from the left. This is the south-ernmost portion of the newly constructed Colorado Trail, a remark-able 470-mile dance across the high country from Durango to Denver.

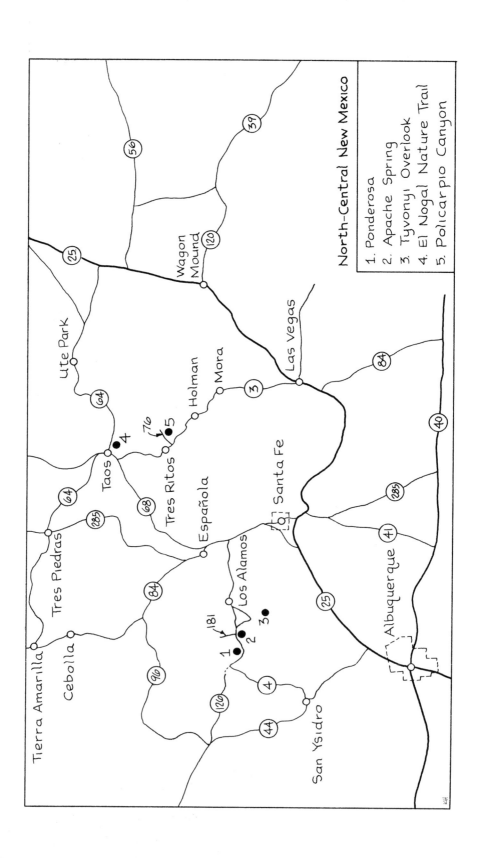

North-Central New Mexico

1. Ponderosa
2. Apache Spring
3. Tyuonyi Overlook
4. El Nogal Nature Trail
5. Policarpio Canyon

North–Central New Mexico

PONDEROSA

Distance: 1.8 miles
Location: This trail is located on the north side of New Mexico Route 4, west of Las Conchas Campground, and 0.35 mile east of mile marker 35. This small, grass-covered pathway, actually a cross-country ski trail, is visible from the highway behind a Forest Service gate. A small pull-off area is located immediately adjacent to the trail.

I must admit that I have a strong love affair going with the ponderosa pine, certainly one of the most stately trees of the entire Rocky Mountain chain. Unlike California, where it shares the stage with Jeffrey pine, here it is the only cinnamon-and-sugar colored giant standing guard over the drier, grass- and oak-covered mountain slopes found between 4,000 to 8,000 feet. I can still see the movie cowboys of my boyhood shuffling their horses through the ponderosas, and usually around sunset, I swear I've spotted Hoss Cartwright's big white hat disappearing just over the next ridge.

Almost as soon as you pass through the gate adjacent to the highway you'll be in magic timber. The leaves of aspen and tall, slender meadow grasses wave in the wind, while a fine mat of scarlet gilia, harebells, asters, lupine, and yarrow lend splashes of color to the soft green conifer blanket. The yarrow you'll see growing along this pathway—the plant with clusters of tiny white flowers and fernlike leaves—is one of the most heavily used medicinal plants in the world. Even it's genus name, *Achillea,* is a reference to the Greek warrior Achilles having supposedly used a relative of yarrow to stop bleeding in the wounds of his soldiers at the famous battle of Troy. In old Europe the plant was known as "soldier's wound wort." (Science long ago verified that the alkaloid

139

present in yarrow does in fact reduce the clotting time of blood.) Native Americans also used yarrow in this way, as well as to help break fevers and treat aching muscles.

After walking 0.25 mile you'll reach another gate. The ski trail, which in national forests is marked by blue diamonds, takes off to the left. We'll continue straight, however, climbing gently through an area that was burned by a forest fire more than a quarter century ago, and was then replanted with ponderosas in 1962. While these trees have done well, they are nonetheless a long, long way from reaching the giant proportions of the timber you saw along the first stretch of trail. When it comes to forest growth, 25 years is a drop in the bucket, a ponderosa grove taking more than ten times that amount of time to reach full maturity. In this sense the growth of a forest can provide some sobering thoughts about time, making us at least halfway conscious of things such as centuries and millenniums.

In less than 0.1 mile from this second gate you'll reach a T intersection. Take a left here, but before you do make sure you take notice of where you've come from; this is an easy path to miss on the way back. Not all of the large ponderosas on the land were killed by the Las Conchas fire. Many were removed because they were badly infested with a parasite known as dwarf mistletoe, which, if not eradicated, could have easily been spread to the young planted trees. You can recognize dwarf mistletoe by its yellow or orange blooms lining the branches of a ponderosa, or, more commonly, by the disfigurement it brings to the tree. Mistletoe sinks a vast network of roots beneath the bark to collect the nutrients it needs, in the process severely interrupting normal growth patterns. Large swelled areas, and clusters of stunted branches known as "witches brooms," are common indicators that the parasite has gained a firm hold. It may take 15 or 20 years for the ponderosa to die; its death is often the result of attacks by insects or other infections that gain access to the weakened tree.

A short distance from the last left turn, past some beautiful New Mexico locust trees, you'll reach another fork in the road; stay to the right, on the fainter of the two paths. At this junction you'll have a fine view of the high peaks and ridge lines to the north that make up a small part of the Jemez Mountains, a name derived from a Tanoan Indian word for "the people." This beautiful quilt of high country also happens to embrace the Valles Caldera, the sunken remnants of a crater that spewed enormous quantities of magma and ash across the landscape 1.2 million years ago, some of it reaching as far as present-day Kansas. This almost perfectly circular crater, more than 13 miles across, is located immediately to the north of where you now stand. You can get a fine view of a small portion of it by driving east a short distance on New Mexico Route 4 (the road you parked on).

Continue walking west through huddles of young aspen and ponderosa, the former straining to claim their place in the sun before one day being edged out by conifers. The road soon begins a gentle descent, and again enters the mature forest at 0.9 mile. This is our turnaround point. You can, however, keep going. This pretty little road ambles through the ponderosas a bit longer before it rejoins the fast lanes of the highway.

APACHE SPRING

Distance: 3 miles
Location: The trailhead for this walk is located on the south side of New Mexico Route 4, 1.7 miles west of the point where the route splits, one going to Los Alamos, the other going to Bandelier National Monument. (Also located at this road split is Ponderosa Group Campground.) The trail is along a fire road, closed off by a gate a short distance from the highway. Because thick timber makes the trailhead and small parking area very difficult to see, I recommend pulling off the highway 35 yards east of the trail, where Forest Road 181 takes off to the north.

Just a few miles to the south of this beautiful forest quilt the land dances to a much drier song. Standing down there in the landscape of sheer rock, surrounded by pastel layers of volcanic ash and pumice that have been carved into abrupt desert canyons, it is almost impossible to imagine that such richness could be so close at hand. For so many creatures, life in the West flows with the rise and fall of mountains. Plant communities change quite rapidly as

141

you climb, a thousand vertical feet of mountain being equivalent, as far as the vegetation is concerned, to a northward trek of several hundred miles. The ancient Indian peoples in the Bandelier region knew this well. They chose to live in the lowlands for the warmth and longer growing season, but came regularly to these mountains to hunt large game, to gather the nuts of the pines and oaks, and to harvest the sturdy logs of the ponderosa for use in construction.

This walk begins in a fine collection of white fir, aspen, ponderosa, and a few Gambel oaks. These last two trees were important to early peoples of this region, the former providing seeds that could be ground into bread, while the latter produced acorns that were less bitter tasting than those of other oaks. (All acorns, however, were leached in water to remove tannic acids before using them in mush, breads, and so forth.) Since the ponderosa dominates the show here, this is a perfect chance for you to get to know this stately giant a little better. It's rough, cinnamon-colored bark is assembled in layers of a thousand shapes, like the pieces of an impossibly complicated jigsaw puzzle. All sorts of imaginary creatures can be found clinging to one of these trunks. Some of the larger ponderosas in this forest may be more than 350 years old, having begun their stretch toward the sky about the time that the Pilgrims had settled into life at Plymouth Rock and Rembrandt was busy creating masterpieces.

At 0.25 mile the road makes a smooth right turn. Before you is one of the finest little mixed conifer meadows you're ever likely to see. At the east end, an old logworm fence snakes through the tall grass, with a pair of absolutely remarkable white firs serving as sentinels on either side of the road—two blue-green skyscrapers forming a striking portal to the meadow beyond. More than likely you'll see red squirrels, or at least hear their incessant chattering, as they go about the serious business of collecting nuts (or even birds' eggs) along the branches of these great conifers.

At 0.5 mile you'll reach a junction of roads. Our route—which may or may not be signed—is the more well-worn path that takes off to the right. While on the outbound walk this junction shouldn't cause any particular problems, be careful on your return that you don't let a pleasant forest stupor cause you to miss your turn. With this turn you'll have entered a drier, more exposed ridge

Abert's Squirrel

line sporting a more homogenous growth of ponderosa as well as a couple of beautiful stretches of New Mexico locust. In early summer this latter plant produces soft, satiny clusters of light pink flowers that can halt the most hurried traveler. These blooms, as well as the seeds that come on during autumn, were common sources of foods for Indian peoples of the region.

By the time you've walked a mile, you will have entered some of the less severe signs of the 1977 La Mesa fire, a violent, human-caused inferno that took 2,000 firefighters 8 days to control, but not before it burned more than 15,000 acres of forest. Throughout the twentieth century firefighters suppressed nearly every forest fire they could get their hands on. This aggressive policy actually resulted in a tremendous build-up of dead wood. If a forest then did catch fire under dry conditions, like this one did, there was simply no stopping it. (Firefighters reported flames on the La Mesa fire of 150 feet!) To avoid such disasters happening again, today's foresters carefully burn accumulated downfall. This also tends to return valuable nutrients to the soil and promotes the growth of ground plants that produce good graze for wildlife.

This does not, of course, excuse careless handling of fire by humans. Controlled fires and haphazard burns with no supervision are two very different things. Being careful with fire is especially appropriate in New Mexico. South of here in the Lincoln National Forest, a small bear was rescued in 1950 when a 17,000-acre forest fire obliterated his home in the Capitan Mountains. After being treated in Santa Fe for severe burns, the little bruin went on to some rather great things, most notably being christened with the name Smokey the Bear. The scars from Smokey's fire are still visible today and will be for several more generations.

Past a roadside strewn with asters, gilia, and harebells, you'll begin a descent in 1.3 miles that leads to the boundary of the Bandelier Wilderness. From this point make a gentle fall on a forest trail for 0.1 mile, keeping your eyes out at the bottom of the ravine for a very faint pathway taking off to the left. This leads in 40 yards to Apache Springs, surely one of the finest, most relaxing little pockets of greenery to be found anywhere in the state. Surrounding the old stone catch basin, built by the Civilian Conservation Corps in the mid-1930s, is an absolute wonderland of sights, sounds, and smells. There are currants and raspberries, fir and oaks, alders, elders, and aspen. Lavender sticky geraniums line the ever-so-gentle flow of spring water; soft green Rocky Mountain maple leaves shimmer in the afternoon sun. This entire setting, the result of just the right amount of water in a fold of land that has the proper soil and exposure, is a real work of art—a miracle, in fact—that will sustain you for many daydreams to come.

TYUONYI OVERLOOK

Distance: 2.4 miles

Location: Go to Bandelier National Monument. Turn right into Juniper Campground, just past the monument entrance station. Continue to the campground amphitheater parking lot located on your left. Our trail takes off from the far side of this parking lot. (The Frey Trail also takes off from here; watch the signs to make sure you're on the right path.) As soon as the walkway leaves the parking area, it forks; stay left, and make a horseshoe turn to the left onto the Tyuonyi Overlook Trail.

This enchanting national monument wears the name of Adolph Bandelier, an ethnologist who spent much of the late 1800s here exploring possible connections between Pueblo Indian cultures and the great Meso-American civilizations that existed far to the south. This region of New Mexico contains a plethora of ancient ruin sites, from the faint cave remnants west of the Rio Grande River that date back nearly 4,000 years, to the more common stone structures you'll see along this walk, most built between A.D. 1100 and A.D. 1500. In fact, no one knows how many archeological sites Bandelier does contain. Conservative estimates put the number at about 5,000.

This is a fine, relaxing walk across a finger of the Pajarito Plateau, a small part of the 10-million-year-old, 2,000-square-mile volcanic field that forms the fabric from which much of this part of the New Mexico landscape is fashioned. It is thanks to such violent, massive, steaming flows of pumice and volcanic ash (tuff) pouring over the land that this beautiful collection of canyons and cliffs exist today—cliffs that yielded easily to the stone scrapers of early residents, who turned their small, natural pockets and caves into rooms for living and storage.

Your trip across this thick block of volcanic tuff will be through a lovely forest of pinyon and juniper, sprinkled here and there with handsome ponderosa pine. Depending on the time of the year you walk the trail, the open areas are likely to be peppered with the blooms of ground plants, including aster, paintbrush, groundsel, and broom snakeweed. The latter two plants, when seen in appreciable quantities, are indicators of disturbed soil. Look for their yellow cluster blooms along roadways, trail edges, and especially where the land has been overgrazed. Unfortunately, overgrazed land is never hard to find in the West. One can only daydream about how the land must have looked 200 years ago, so much of it having been praised by early explorers for its fine grasses.

Another plant hard to miss here during midsummer to late summer is mullein, the thick, 2- to 4-foot-tall hairy stems that dot so much of the open areas near the trailhead. This biennial was introduced from Europe, and now blankets much of the North American continent. Though not particularly beautiful, mullein has an impressive record of use by humans. Leaves were sometimes smoked as a tobacco substitute. Unlike tobacco, however, the leaves of mullein contain elements that Native Americans

145

found to be quite effective in soothing irritated tissues. Some of these chemicals are found in modern skin-softening lotions. Mullein is at its best in sandy or rocky areas where few other plants can survive.

Soon the open spaces become fewer, and the path begins meandering through a classic pinyon–juniper forest, sporting an occasional ponderosa and mountain mahogany. Pinyon, which, like juniper, produces delicious nuts, form an extensive forest belt between 4,000 feet and 6,500 feet. Stretching for nearly 40,000 square miles, the "p–j" forest can be found from New Mexico into Colorado, south into Texas and Mexico, west into Arizona and Nevada, and east into Oklahoma. These two trees have an uncanny way of growing on you. You never know what beautiful surprises may lie waiting around the next juniper—a prickly pear wearing a coat of beautiful, delicate yellow flowers, or a yucca flying a stout staff of rich creamy white blooms. Birds and small mammals consume the "fruits" (actually cones) of the juniper, while mule deer can often be seen grazing in their protective cover.

At 1 mile you'll pass the point where the return loop takes off to the left. Keep going straight, past a partially excavated habitation site, and about 0.1 mile later, past a circular shrine thought to have been a place of worship for the early residents of the Pajarito Plateau. Just past this shrine site the trail ends on a promontory, with wonderful views of Frijoles Canyon below, dominated by the long green fingers of cottonwoods lining El Rito de los Frijoles, and the remarkable ruins of Tyuonyi. This beautiful structure, containing 250 ground-floor rooms and 3 kivas, or ceremonial chambers, was constructed in the early 1300s. Adolph Bandelier reported that "Tyuonyi" was a Keres Indian phrase for "place of treaty," which alludes to a territorial pact made between the Keres and their neighbors, the Tewa.

Here at this overlook are one-seed juniper, datil yucca, and splashes of lichen staining the rocks with beautiful colors. Lichen is actually a mix of two plants—a coat of fungus forming a protective coating over an inner layer of algal cells. This is truly a symbiotic relationship where the whole is more durable than the sum of its parts. Lichen can produce food and grow at any temperature above 32 degrees Fahrenheit—15 to 20 degrees above what most plants can manage. It can store more than its own weight in water and needs nothing more than an occasional splash of dew to keep growing. There is no more hearty form of life to be found anywhere in the American West.

EL NOGAL NATURE TRAIL

Distance: 1 mile

Location: Heading southeast out of Taos on U.S. Highway 64, El Nogal is the first picnic ground you'll come to in the Carson National Forest, and is located on the right side of the road. The trail takes off just to the left (east) of the entrance way, crossing a wooden bridge over Rio Fernandez de Taos. Once over the bridge, turn left onto the nature trail.

For those who are unfamiliar with the classic braid of riparian and pinyon–juniper life zones that paint so much of the New Mexico landscape, this small Forest Service nature trail is a fine place to make acquaintances. A handout has been prepared by the Forest Service that is keyed to numbered posts along the 1-mile path. These brochures are not always available at the trailhead. You may want to stop in at the Taos Ranger Station (112 Cruz Alta Road) to pick up one before coming out to walk.

The first few feet of this walk are along a beautiful streamside collection of mountain alder and lanceleaf and narrowleaf cottonwood. This latter tree was actually discovered far to the north by Lewis and Clark during their famous trek to the Pacific in 1804 to 1805. All cottonwoods, as well as poplars, willow, and aspen, contain varying degrees of chemicals that are closely related to today's aspirin. Indeed, Native Americans have for centuries used teas made from the bark of cottonwoods to reduce fever and inflammation.

As the Forest Service brochure notes, the change as you step even a few feet away from Rio Fernandez de Taos (also known as Taos Creek) is a remarkably abrupt one. Whereas a few feet back the land was thick with trees and grasses, now there is sage and rabbitbrush, along with a few clumps of rice and blue grama grass clinging to the sandy soil. These plants were, and to some degree still are, important to the Indian people for whom this was home. Rabbitbrush (its name alludes to the fact that rabbits find it quite tasty) has been used for centuries to produce a beautiful yellow dye and baskets were woven with its branches. The sagebrush you see here has been widely used as both a stomach tonic and as a treatment for worms. Despite what you might have heard, however (or what the Forest Service brochure alludes to), this is definitely not the kind of sage that has been used traditionally as a cooking herb. Try a few healthy pinches on your next baked chicken and I guarantee you'll end up ordering out for pizza.

Just past stop 6 you'll enter the fringes of a pinyon and juniper woodland. These two beautiful trees are truly signature species of the southwest uplands. Often found growing in tandem like this, they cover millions of acres in Utah, Arizona, and New Mexico. Juniper has been used in sacred ceremonies of regional Indian peoples for centuries. Pinyon is most recognized for its sweet edible nuts, easy to find in local food markets in the fall. Because humans were hardly the only ones that relished the nuts of the pinyon—deer, jays, squirrels, bears, and packrats go out of their way for them—Indians often collected the cones in late summer before the cones were ripe, heating them in fire pits to melt the binding resin and release the nuts. The gathering of pinyons

Utah Juniper

148

was a major family event. There is some evidence suggesting that entire village sites were located according to their proximity to healthy pinyon groves.

On the back side of this loop is a small rest area that affords wonderful views toward Taos and the Rio Grande Valley to the west. From this fine little perch the stage of what has been a rather staggering amount of history and intrigue is visible. The Rio Grande, or "great river," has been just that, from the time that Juan de Onate led a sizable group of Mexican colonists to take possession of its "meadow grounds, pastures, and passes" for the glory of the King of Spain in 1598. This is a lonely, often hauntingly beautiful river, born in the rugged high country of the San Juan Mountains of southern Colorado. From there it tumbles over 1,800 miles—though the length of New Mexico (the only river to do so), along the western edge of Texas, and finally into the Gulf of Mexico.

The village of Taos, in contrast, located just a few miles from where you now stand, is just as filled with fascination. Perhaps a corruption of a Tewa Indian word meaning "red willow place," Taos was settled nearly 400 years ago, years before the Pilgrims set foot on Plymouth Rock. For two centuries the Taos trade fairs were frequented by a variety of Indian, French, and eventually American traders. In the later 1800s and early 1900s this village, like its neighbor Santa Fe, mysteriously blossomed into a unique haven for well-known artists and writers.

As you make your way westward along this high bench, take a minute to notice the vegetation on the other side of the highway. While of the same pinyon—juniper mix, there is obviously a wider spacing among the trees across from you. This is due to the fact that they are growing on a south-facing slope, which offers much more exposure to the drying effects of the sun. While the same amount of rain and snow falls on both sides of the highway, the side you are walking on is simply able to hold onto the moisture longer, which means it can support a greater density of plant life. It is in large measure these nuances of exposure, along with the dramatic rise and fall of plain and mountain, that allow the intricate threads of life to weave their magic into this singularly beautiful landscape.

POLICARPIO CANYON

Distance: 1.5 miles
Location: Heading east on New Mexico Highway 3, turn left (east) onto Forest Road 76, 0.4 mile east of mile marker 50. Proceed for 3.6 miles to a small road taking off to the right. Follow this road across a bridge to another road taking off to the left. Turn left and park; begin walking east on this road.

I hesitate to even suggest a trail that is also open to motorized vehicles. (Woods walking with motorcycles is about as satisfying as waltzing to Muzak.) Yet those who can get on this trail early in the morning, or on an off-season weekday, will find that it traces a most enchanting line through the best of the forested Sangre de Cristo high country.

The walk beings in a fine spruce–fir forest, with nooks and crannies peppered with beautiful adult aspen, now in the glory years that come before they eventually yield the stage to the more shade-tolerant conifers already rubbing branches with them. By 0.2 mile into the walk, Rocky Mountain maple, dwarf juniper, and an occasional blue spruce and alder have joined the scene, along with a lovely quilt of streamside wildflowers, including sticky geranium, false Solomon's seal, violets, groundsels, harebells, and pentstemons.

Such rich forests also give rise to a fine collection of birds and mammals. One of the easiest creatures to spot, or at least hear in this forest, is the chickaree or red squirrel. (Red squirrels are found from here to Alaska, and east to the Carolinas. In the intermountain West, however, they are not red at all, but rather gray with a slight tinge of rust.) It is most often this industrious little nut lover that you'll hear scolding you as you pass beneath the branches of Engelmann spruce. While you'll have no trouble hearing the chickaree, it is not always so easy to spot. Look for piles of pine cones and scales—called middens—that are its signature. Because many generations of chickarees live in the same place, some of these midden piles may grow to 1 foot or more deep and be 20 to 25 feet across! Chickarees often store unopened cones in the loose, moist soils of middens; the coolness of the pile keeps the cones

Red Squirrel

unopened for future meals. Abandoned middens are excellent places to find the small, ground-hugging plant known as kinniki-nick, which Indians mixed with red-osier dogwood bark to make a popular smoking mixture. Chickarees nest in the forks of conifers, or, if possible, in hollow logs and tree holes abandoned by wood-peckers. Young are born in May or early June and nurse through midsummer.

Of course, where there are chickarees there are animals who prey on them. In this forest that typically comes down to one of three predators: martens, coyotes, and gray foxes. Of these, the marten is the most troublesome to the chickaree, since this beau-tiful weasel-shaped mammal is as perfectly adept at maneuvering through trees as is the red squirrel. This, combined with the fact that martens will often eat 30 percent of their total body weight each day, hardly makes them a welcome sight for the chattering chickaree. Other mammals in the immediate area include bobcat, striped skunk, raccoons, and mule deer. The muddy ground next to Policarpio Creek makes an excellent place to look for the tracks of these mammals.

Continue climbing gently through gardens of wildflowers and conifers laced with stringy fronds of goat's beard. You'll find the still pools and shallow rapids of your streamside companion to be perfect places to find dippers, or, as they are known in Great Britain, water ouzels. These are perhaps the most enjoyable of all the mountain birds. What they lack in color, they more than make up for in charm. I saw a particularly fine dipper dance in a pool about 0.7 mile into the walk just before the trail leaves the stream drainage. The dipper feeds on insects found at the bottom of such streams and to that end spares no effort to obtain them. In deeper rapids and pools you often can see them nimbly swimming with half-outstretched wings, a graceful display that should serve as an inspiration to competitive aqua dancers everywhere. Occasionally the dipper will stop on a rock and—what else?—dip! This unexplainable behavior consists of a delightful series of bobs, making the bird appear to be dancing to some catchy music, unavailable to human ears.

At 0.75 mile the trail climbs up and away from the stream into a fine meadow fringed by mountain ridges clad with dark green blankets of conifer. This is our turnaround point. Notice the dramatic difference in vegetation in this more exposed pocket of high country. Here the streamside plants have been traded for those that are satisfied to sink their feet into somewhat drier soil. Besides a

Dipper

wonderful array of grasses, look for yarrow and the beautiful yellow flowers of shrubby cinquefoil, which is an excellent plant to stabilize easily eroded soil. The name *cinquefoil* is a French term meaning "five leaves." If you look closely, you'll find they extend in five segments, somewhat like the spread fingers of a human hand.

Coyote

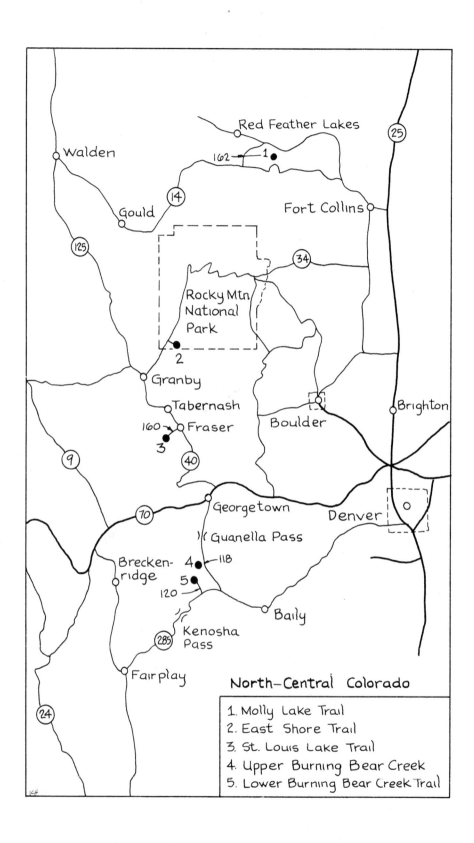

Red Feather Lakes

25

Walden

162→ ● 1

14

Gould

Fort Collins

125

34

Rocky Mtn.
National
Park

● 2

Granby

Tabernash

Brighton

160→ ● Fraser
● 3

Boulder

9

40

70

Georgetown

Denver

)|(Guanella Pass

Brecken-
ridge

4 ● →118

5 ●

120→

Baily

285

Kenosha
Pass

Fairplay

24

North-Central Colorado

1. Molly Lake Trail
2. East Shore Trail
3. St. Louis Lake Trail
4. Upper Burning Bear Creek
5. Lower Burning Bear Creek Trail

North–Central Colorado

MOLLY LAKE TRAIL

Distance: 2 miles

Location: Heading north on U.S. Highway 287, northwest of Fort Collins, turn left on Red Feather Lakes Road. Proceed west for 24.6 miles, turning left (south) onto Country Road 162. Continue for 2 miles. Our walking road is Forest Road 267, located on the east side of county Road 162. Park at the junction of these two roads and begin your walk through a gate to the east.

The walk to Molly Lake is along an ever-so-gentle roadway that the Forest Service has closed to motorized vehicles. A series of numbered posts have been placed along the route that correspond to information on a sheet available at the trailhead, making the walk a perfect one for learning a few of the more common plants that pepper this western-looking landscape.

Occasionally on this walk you'll see piles of slash in the forest. These are the result of efforts to control infestations of the mountain pine beetle, which attacks both lodgepole and ponderosa forests. The eggs of these insects are laid beneath the bark during August and September, the nutrients in the trees providing food for the larva throughout the winter. By the following summer the surviving larvae have turned into flying beetles that take off to attack other conifers nearby. A fungus carried by these small beetles attacks cells in the tree used to transport nutrients up the trunks and out to the branches. Unlike the slow death caused to both ponderosa and lodgepole by the parasite dwarf mistletoe (visible at stop 3), conifers hit by mountain pine beetles are typically dead within 18 months following the initial infection. Trees weakened by other forces are particularly susceptible to pine beetles.

Healthy stands are usually safe, especially with a little help from hungry resident woodpeckers, who find the beetles quite tasty.

There is a very pleasant mix to this forest—shiny greens of ponderosa and lodgepole, dark mats and spires of dwarf juniper and Douglas-fir, and shimmering stands of aspen that are particularly beautiful when their leaves melt to gold in the crisp air of autumn. Also growing in dark, shiny mats (complete with light pink bell flowers in the spring or red berries in the fall) is the beautiful creeper known as kinnikinick. The name *kinnikinick* is an Algonkian Indian word applicable to any of several plants used in traditional Native American smoking mixtures. Kinnikinick was just one part of homemade tobacco, frequently being added to red willow or red-osier dogwood leaves. This mixture became a favorite of the trappers who roamed this high country during the first half of the nineteenth century.

Because the name kinnikinick is occasionally given to other plants, it's sometimes safer to refer to this lovely little creeper by its other common name, bearberry—a title that refers to the fact that most bears find the fall fruits much to their liking (the Latin species name means "bear's grape"). Most humans find them more palatable if they are boiled first. Kinnikinick leaves are a source of the tannins used to cure fur pelts, and in Russia they remain important for this use. In addition, some Native American people made tonics and diuretics from the plants; the Cheyenne used the berries for treating colds and flu.

Stop 10 will allow you a close inspection of a tree killed by a porcupine's insatiable appetite for tender tree-top bark. Porcupines are the largest land rodent in this area (beavers are larger), and, when spotted lumbering across the floor of an open forest, can look remarkably cumbersome. In trees, however, these slow-moving pincushions are really quite graceful. Their love for the inner bark of conifers can wreak havoc in a forest, often by completely girdling the trunk of the tree, thereby stopping its nutrient flow, or by destroying the entire upper section of the tree by removing its bark. Porcupines are also famous for chewing on sweat-soaked tool handles and canoe paddles. Despite a popular belief, porcupines cannot "shoot" the quills that line their backsides.

Just before reaching the turnoff to Molly Lake there is a rough path leading to an overlook of the Lone Pine Valley. Standing above this long, lonely roll of timber and grass, this seems like a particularly appropriate name—the kind a cowboy might dream up some moonlit autumn night while out checking the doggies. In fact, if ever there was a place where the sunsets should be accompanied by harmonica music, this part of Colorado is it.

Just under 1 mile is a small road taking off to the left. This is the route to Molly Lake, a pretty little watering place for deer and cattle. It is framed on the north by rolling hummocks of grass, and on the south by fine clumps of aspen, their leaves fluttering with every sigh of summer breeze.

EAST SHORE TRAIL

Distance: 2.5 miles
Location: Head north out of Granby on U.S. Highway 40, and turn right onto U.S. Route 34. Proceed for approximately 11 miles, and make a right turn 0.9 mile past mile marker 11, at a sign reading "Arapaho National Recreation Area." Then immediately make another right turn, following signs toward Shadow Mountain Dam. Park at the dam and walk across it to the east side. Our walk begins here, taking off to the south (downstream) along the Colorado River.

This stroll along the western fringe of Rocky Mountain National Park is a true delight. The land, a soft mix of lodgepole forest and riparian meadows, forms a quiet, mellow quilt of high country. Though gentle, there's also a wonderful sense of wildness here— a thick, exciting feeling that pervades so much of this national preserve, perhaps the most beautiful of all the high-mountain parks. Besides sporting a stunning collage of rocky peaks, more than a hundred of which soar to over 12,000 feet, Rocky Mountain National Park has an almost overwhelming collection of hanging glacial valleys, plunging waterfalls, and cold, crystal streams. One of these watercourses, visible on your right, flows through a gentle glacial valley and forms the quiet, clear beginnings of the greatest river in the West—the mighty Colorado.

A short distance from the Shadow Mountain Dam you'll find yourself in a beautiful meadow stitched with sedge, marsh marigolds, elephantella, shooting stars, and calypso orchids. Here you may spot the hanging wings of a red-tailed hawk, running sky surveillance on the upper fringes of this grassy area for a tasty deer mouse or ground squirrel. Hawks and eagles in general play an extremely important role in this ecosystem by controlling the population of such small mammals. If left totally unchecked, these prolific little rodents can quickly overpopulate, eating themselves out of house and home in very short order.

Also eyeing the rodent population here with an anxious stomach is the coyote, which late-evening walkers often can hear engaging in a rousing chorus of yips and yowls from the inner pockets of the lodgepole forest. There are few animals that seem to have as tenacious a survival instinct as the coyote, especially in the face of vigorous human attempts to eliminate them. (The name *coyote* comes from the Aztec word *coyotl*, or "barking wolf.") Indeed, this beautiful little canine seems more abundant than ever, conducting business from Costa Rica to Alaska, from the thick of the wilderness to the backyards of suburban areas that have encroached upon its territory.

Golden-mantled Ground Squirrel

One of the reasons coyotes have been so successful in hanging on to a shrinking environment is that when it comes to dinner, they are very open to suggestions. The ground squirrels, voles, rabbits, mice, and pocket gophers living in this area provide a significant portion of their diet. Coyotes also will eat birds, snakes, weasels, and even skunks! They will consume carrion or garbage if either is readily available.

Coyotes may spend several years with the same mate. The male becomes extremely busy in the spring as he scours the countryside looking for enough food to feed both himself and the nursing female. Five to seven pups are born without hair, unable to open their eyes for nearly two weeks. The home den is left behind when the youngsters are about ten weeks old, at which time they join the family in wide-ranging hunting forays. The kids will strike out on their own in the fall, just about the time that aspen leaves begin raining down on the forest floor.

At 0.25 mile you'll cross a marshy grassland environment on a wooden walkway. At the far end is a fork; stay to the right. A short distance later you'll enter private land, so be sure to stay on the trail as you make your way through this stretch of classic lodgepole pine forest. (The lodgepole is an easy tree to identify in this area, since it is the only one with its needles growing in bundles of two.) Lodgepole can form dense blankets of timber in the Rockies, and is found in scattered stands from Mexico to Alaska, making it one of the most widely distributed pines in North America.

While most of this long, quiet stretch of forest is a homogeneous blanket of lodgepole, there are a few mats of dwarf juniper and kinnikinick lending splashes of green against the dull carpet of lodgepole needles. One of the reasons that these needles accumulate in such thick layers before breaking down is that they, like most pine needles, are covered with a waxy coating that is especially impervious to bacteria. This trait, combined with an arid climate that really doesn't promote decay, has resulted in deep layers of needles on the floor of many conifer forests of the West.

Into the walk 0.75 mile a trail from Grand Lake comes in from the left. Grand Lake is a beautiful, deep, natural lake to the north of here, formed by the lateral and terminal moraines of two distinct glaciers that ground their way across this landscape during the last glacial epoch, which ended roughly 25,000 years ago. Continue straight, past an area of timber that has been shredded by a ferocious windstorm, finally joining the Colorado River again in another 0.5 mile. This lovely fringe of river shore is a perfect place to soak up the very best of the Rocky Mountains. It's an unforgettable experience to sit here and ponder the fact that this tranquil, whispering ribbon of water is the mighty architect of Colorado's Glenwood, Utah's Glen and Arizona's Grand canyons, patiently peeling away grain after grain of rock for countless millenniums to create some of the most splendorous rock labyrinths the world has ever known. The waters you see here are embarking on a remarkable 1,400 mile journey to their ultimate destination at the Gulf of California.

SAINT LOUIS LAKE TRAIL

Distance: 2.4 miles

Location: Head south out of Granby on U.S. Highway 40 for approximately 15 miles. At 0.9 mile south of mile marker 226, in the center of the town of Fraser, turn right (west) onto Eisenhower Drive. Take a left on Norgren Street and then a right on Mill. This leads to our trailhead, 12.6 miles from where you first turned off the highway.

While this walk requires steady climbing, it offers a fine soak in a classic central Rocky Mountain spruce–fir forest—a place with layer after layer of dark, wild beauty. After crossing a wooden footbridge over Saint Louis Creek, the path meanders along this cold, frothing mountain stream, most of the summer lined with sticky geraniums, gentian, columbine, pipsissewa, and monkeyflowers, and beautiful purple shooting stars in the more open areas. Pipsissewa and monkeyflower often were used by Indians of the region, the former to break down kidney stones (its common name is derived from a Cree Indian phrase for "breaking into pieces"), and the young leaves of the latter as raw greens. Pioneers in the West who picked up on this use of monkeyflower often referred to the plant as wild lettuce.

There is a special color and moist coolness to a high country spruce–fir forest. The great blankets of snow that fall here—sometimes several feet in a single day—linger long into the summer, tight huddles of green aprons shielding the snow from the warm fingers of the sun. In 0.25 mile you'll break out of the forest briefly to skirt a meadow brimming with grass and willow. After climbing a short rise away from the stream, however, it's back into the thick of the woods, this time into a more mature slice. Old, stately Engelmann spruce tower above the footpath, forming a hushed cathedral. Some of these trees have stood long enough to see the entire exploration and settlement of Colorado and the Rocky Mountain West.

Spruce and fir represent what is known as a climax forest, meaning that they form the last in several stages of plant succession, commonly beginning with grasses and proceeding to shrubs and aspen, and finally to spruce and fir. Like several other species of trees, both spruce and fir are able to to sprout from low branches coming into contact with the ground, a phenomenon that increases as the growing environment becomes more severe. Although mammals and birds are not usually as numerous in a spruce–fir forest as in other, lower-timbered areas, this walk seems to have a peculiar abundance. Deer and elk are joined by martens and snowshoe hares, while three-toed woodpeckers, pine grosbeaks, nuthatches, pine siskins, and creepers add to the feathered population. Especially common along the upper reaches of the trail are Clark's nutcrackers. At first glance, it may appear that this bird consumes pine nuts without bothering to even swallow them. Actually, they have a special storage pouch in their cheeks that allows them to collect several goodies and then pack them away to distant dining areas.

In 0.8 mile is a creek crossing, and 0.2 mile later, you'll have the rather unusual treat of stereo streams on your right and left as you make your way up the back of a narrow finger of land. Look off to your right in this area for young Engelmann spruce. The year I was here several were showing the effect of black snow mold—a dark, molasses-looking glob that hangs off of lower branches. Snowpack often holds these branches against the ground through the spring, which is actually a necessary step for the branch to sprout as a new tree. But if the snow lingers too long, snow mold fungus is able to establish a hold on the tree.

At just over 1.1 miles the trail tops a small plateau, overlooking a beautiful stream. Our turnaround point is the bank of this stream, reached by making a short, sharp descent to the right. Besides being a great place for wildflowers, take a look at some of the delicate groundcovers lying at the cool, moist feet of the spruce and fir. Twinflower is here, with a few wood nymph and wintergreen plants adding to the lot. In the lower reaches of this forest you can see the delicate lavender fairy slipper, also known as calypso orchid. This latter name is taken from the beautiful sea nymph in Homer's *Odyssey*.

UPPER BURNING BEAR CREEK

Distance: 3.5 miles
Location: Go along Forest Road 118 (Guanella Pass Road), just south of Burning Bear Campground. You'll find a large parking area on the east side of the road for access into the Abyss Lake Scenic Area and Mount Evans. Park here and walk south along the highway for 0.15 mile. Our trail takes off to the right, heading northwest, adjacent to a horse corral.

This walk along upper Burning Bear Creek—a corruption of "burned bare"—is a stroll through an absolutely delightful high country collage of clear, tumbling waters, yawning meadows, and thick, green forests. The trail begins in a meadow of shrubby cinquefoil, with excellent views to the north of the soaring spine of the Continental Divide, just west of Guanella Pass. In about 50 yards the path makes a sharp left turn onto a footbridge crossing Burning Bear Creek. Suddenly a hushed veil of forest drops around you. There is a pungent smell of conifers and the springy feel that comes with walking a path thick with years of fallen needles. Burning Bear Creek now flows in a whisper off to your right, a twisted course of oxbows and meanders, visible only occasionally between clumps of willow.

While nearly everyone is drawn to the carpet of growth that sprouts from the banks of a mountain stream, few of us stop to ponder the myriad life that exists in the water. Living in a stream like this one is not an easy proposition. The strength of these currents can be a formidable force to deal with, especially in early to midsummer when they are fed by snowmelt. Some insect larvae have developed disc-shaped suction cups at the rear of their bodies with which they anchor themselves to the surface of rocks. Also, it's important to note that most stream insects set up housekeeping in locations well away, or at least protected from, the main pull of the currents—most often in the nooks, crannies, and crevices provided by the jumble of the streambed rocks. Since going out for food is so dangerous, most of these creatures depend on delivery service for their meals. Some have funnel-shaped appendages that are used to collect passing plankton. The caddis fly actually weaves a small net that it floats into the stream to trap bits of food.

This assemblage of tenacious stream creatures makes up a great deal of the trout's daily diet. Trout, of course, also have to contend with the relentless force of currents. Over millions of years they have developed a long, lean shape that offers little resistance to flowing water. They also spend the majority of their time in quiet pools formed by large rocks or sharp bends in the stream.

Just over 0.25 mile into the stream you'll reach a section of trail marked by signs reading "Snowpack Studies—Please Stay on Trail." This is a joint project between the Forest Service and the Soil Conservation Service used to predict the amount of spring runoff likely to occur from these mountains.

Watch out along this stretch of trail for mountain chickadees, Steller's jays, Clark's nutcrackers, and the beautiful yellow body and heavy beak of the evening grosbeak. These birds tend to congregate when food is hard to find, and late autumn or early spring walkers may see dense bands around a good supply of seeds or buds. Also in these woods are red crossbills, the male of which is a rust-colored bird about 6 inches long, with a bill that is actually crossed at the ends. It's no accident that this peculiar design happens to be perfect for inserting into pine cones and splitting the scales open, making it easy for the bird to remove the nuts with its tongue.

The path bends slowly around toward the left, offering in 0.75 mile fine views of the red, iron-rich peaks to the west that

163

Evening Grosbeak

form the lower ramparts of the Continental Divide. A long, lovely meadow will accompany you westward for nearly half a mile, coming to an end as you enter a thick cloak of lodgepole pine forest. This tree, one of the most widespread on the North American continent, got its name from the fact that thin lodgepoles were once commonly used by various Native American peoples to construct their tipís, or lodges. Lodgepole is one of a group of trees sometimes referred to as "fire pines," a name derived from the fact that the majority of the tree's cones will not open until licked by the flames of a forest fire. This ensures that the tree, which does best in open sunlight, will be among the first to grow again after a fire has destroyed the existing forest.

Speaking of fire, notice here the fairly large amount of dead timber lying on the forest floor. The dry conditions in the West mean far less bacterial activity occurs on the forest floor than, say, in the woods of the East. It requires a long, long time for these dead trees to be broken down into soil again. Before the arrival of modern man, periodic fires, usually the result of summer lightning strikes, would race through the forest. The ground would be cleared of such debris, while harmful parasites would be killed off and nutrients returned to the soil. By adopting a policy of stopping all forest fires, we inadvertently caused a buildup of combustible materials on the forest floor. When a big fire does strike in such a forest, it can be much more devastating than it would have ordinarily been, since the increased amount of fuel allows it to rage hotter and higher than it would have normally. Such lessons did not go unheeded; today you'll often see controlled burning projects in the national forests specifically designed to reduce the fire load on the forest floor.

In 1.7 miles the trail makes a gentle descent from a low bench, dropping to the same level as a small stream that has been gurgling off to your right for the last 0.25 mile. This is our turn-around point. Before heading back, though, leave the path and walk north a short distance to this watercourse. Here you'll find several quiet pockets of willow and aspen, washed in the cool whisper of water as it dances down the bed rock. This is a particularly delightful place to bird-watch, picnic, or for long afternoon snoozes in the mountain sunshine.

LOWER BURNING BEAR CREEK

Distance: 1.3 miles
Location: From U.S. Highway 285, 0.6 mile east of mile marker 207, turn north onto Forest Road 120. The trailhead and a small parking area are on the right, 2.7 miles north of U.S. Highway 285.

Whereas the upper reaches of the Burning Bear Creek Trail meander along the forested feet of a soaring mountainscape (see page 162), the stroll along this lower end of the pathway is a bit more subdued—a short, sweet amble along a tiny mountain stream singing through a hushed huddle of aspen. In autumn this trail is particularly appealing, the aspen leaves glimmering like gold dust in the late September sun, the smell of dry grasses wafting through the cool Colorado air. Although the path (actually an old roadway) climbs throughout its 0.65 mile, all but a very short stretch 0.2 mile into the walk is fairly gentle. Do keep in mind that the first section of trail passes through private lands; please respect the privacy of these landowners by staying on the roadway.

Just 100 yards into the walk you'll be met by your gurgling stream companion. This delightful little watercourse, known as Lamping Creek, gathers its waters to the northwest of here, just a few miles this side of the Continental Divide. True to the definition of the Continental Divide, its waters are bound for the Gulf of Mexico, first via the South Platte River across the windswept prairies of northeast Colorado, then along the Platte, drifting through the long reaches of Nebraska grain fields until it reaches the Missouri River south of Omaha. It finally reaches the mighty Mississippi at St. Louis, which will carry it 700 miles further southward, melting into Gulf waters through a sprawl of marshy fingers just outside of Venice, Louisiana.

For the moment, though, the stream is just a friendly trickle through the aspen forest, slowly nursing life onto its banks in the form of beautiful wildflowers and stout mountain alders. The bark of this latter tree seen near the beginning of the trail was often boiled by Indian people of the region to produce a beautiful red to orange dye. Moccasins and feathers were dyed routinely, and tended to hold this color quite well without any additional preparation. The women of tribes to the north reportedly made a tea from alder bark that helped them regulate their menstrual periods.

You'll come to a faint road taking off to the left 0.2 mile into the walk; this is a private driveway, so continue straight up a short but relatively steep section of trail. At the top you will have left behind many of the aspen in favor of a mixed conifer forest of lodgepole, juniper and an occasional bristlecone pine. Bristlecones are the oldest living things on earth. Core samples taken from trees in the White Mountains of California revealed several bristlecones to be more than 5,000 years old! It's incredible to think that such trees were beginning to grow before construction of the Great Sphinx—a full thousand years before the mysteries of Stonehenge came to Salisbury Plain.

Bristlecones are the hardiest of trees, achieving their greatest splendor under conditions of poor soil and frightful cold that other tree species find totally intolerable. Growing slowly in such places, their wood becomes extremely dense, a collection of small, tightly clustered cells that are impervious to either insects or decay. They are unflinching survivors, the old trees often carrying nutrients to a single living branch via a thin line of bark, the rest having been soured away by a thousand seasons of wind and ice.

The trail continues to climb steadily along a bench perched above Lamping Creek, lined with fine collections of yarrow, cow parsnip, and sticky geraniums, as well as an occasional columbine or monkeyflower. This is a lovely stretch to leave the roadway and spend some time streamside, listening to the lilt of chickadees and the buzz of nutcrackers. Also in here you'll notice a sizable collection of aspen stumps whose trees were long ago chewed down by beaver. (Look at these closely; you still can see the rodent's narrow teeth marks in the weathered wood). Beavers, with their incredible efficiency at cutting trees and flooding large areas of ground, have perhaps more impact on the land than any other mammal besides humans. The size of these tree stumps should convince you that their timber-harvesting operations are hardly limited to saplings.

A beaver's pond provides a protective area around its lodge, while the deep water allows for food storage beneath the winter ice. This environment also favors the growth of alder, willow, and cottonwood, which happen to be among this furry engineer's favorite foods. The fate of the beaver in this area is not known. Quite possibly, though, the pond slowly filled with sediment until it could no longer support the beaver's preferred life-style.

At just over 1.6 miles is our turnaround point, where the stream crosses the road. More ambitious walkers can continue up the trail for quite a distance before encountering any severe climbs.

DESERTS

Though not particularly expansive, the fingers of the desert that reach into the Rocky Mountain states are perfect places to wander on foot. Bypassed by the moisture-laden air systems that lose their cool, liquid cargo on the nearby mountains, life and landscape here have a striking clarity—a clean, crisp look that stays with you long after you have left these lonely, windswept soils. The fact that most of these desert pockets are fringed by high plateaus or even expansive mountain ranges makes them all the more irresistible. The contrast of high and low, hot and cold, makes for a truly enchanted landscape, where you can trace a long line of life tumbling across highlands thick with timber, down through cottonwood-lined canyons, finally arriving at the shimmering desert floor. In parts of New Mexico, the dance of mountains and desert is so extreme that you can be skiing in the morning, and drop down for a rich, warm sun bath among the yucca and greasewood by midafternoon.

The four great desert systems of the United States lie between two massive lines of mountain peaks, the Rockies in the east, and the Sierra Nevada in the west. Only two of these systems, however—the Chihuahuan to the south and the Great Basin to the north—actually lay claim to portions of the Rocky Mountain states.

The Chihuahuan is the desert of southern New Mexico and perhaps the most classic of any you will tramp through in the pages of this book. Here are 175,000 square miles (more than a third of the continent's total desert land), stretching almost from the center of the enchantment state to the Sierra Madres of Mexico. In New Mexico it occurs as a series of tongues lying between north–south mountain ranges and high plateaus. The common vegetative fabric on this pastel landscape is one of greasewood, tarbush, lechuguilla, yucca, prickly pear, and cholla cactus. Yet this hardly completes the picture, as any nook, cranny, or mountain slope will have its own particular signature of shrubs, grasses, and forbs, depending on altitude and exposure to the sun. The sight of spindly ocotillo branches sprouting brilliant scarlet flowers, the fluttering cottonwood canopies that line the major washes here, and the rich mats of sunflowers, marigolds, groundsel, and primrose, are visual delicacies not soon forgotten.

The elevation, and therefore moisture content, in many regions of the Chihuahuan Desert is high when compared to other dry-land areas, a trait that tends to produce more plant material. This, in turn, results in high concentrations of small mammals such as antelope squirrels, pocket mice, and black-tailed jack rabbits. And still further down the chain, this then leads to healthy populations of predators, including foxes, coyotes, mountain lions, and birds of prey. While the actual number of species, especially bird populations, comes nowhere near to equaling those of the forests and mountains, the spaciousness of desert fauna can make many of them easier to see. Because many of these creatures tend to be nocturnal, serious wildlife watchers would do well to spend a moonlit night beside a Chihuahuan Desert water hole.

The other desert arm, this one reaching into western Colorado and Wyoming, is that of the Great Basin. Besides being the second largest of the American deserts, this is by far the highest and coldest of the lot. It was given its name by the frontier explorer John C. Fremont, who, during an exploration of the region in the 1840s, became convinced that the entire region was completely without drainage to the ocean; hence it was called the Great Basin of the West. There are actually scores of different basins in the region, spiked with more than 150 separate mountain ranges. It is the almost endless rise and fall of this landscape that led geographers to dub the region as the Basin and Range province.

You will find that the Great Basin Desert lacks the variety of large plants visible in the Chihuahuan provinces far to the south. This high tapestry is woven primarily with big sagebrush, along with healthy collections of saltbush, Mormon tea, ricegrass, galleta, and wheatgrass. Despite the lack of variety here, the increased elevation of this particular section of the Great Basin creates larger plants, which occur in somewhat greater concentrations than can be found in the lower reaches of the same desert in Nevada and western Utah.

As you may have guessed, fewer plant species, which means fewer seeds and opportunities for browse, tends to result in fewer birds and mammals. But special treats are waiting here. Many of our walks provide excellent opportunities to see the fleetest of all the North American mammals—the pronghorn. Also here are coyotes, badgers, and foxes. A wide variety of raptors soar above the Wyoming basins and the Colorado Plateau, including kestrels, golden eagles, Swainson's hawks, and ferruginous- and red-tailed hawks.

Whether in the high, cold fingers of the northeastern Great Basin, or the low, hot sands of the northern Chihuahuan, the problem of surviving in these climates is one that has been met with some remarkable evolutionary solutions. Ord's kangaroo rats, for instance, receive all the moisture they need from the plants they eat. Daylight hours are spent in a network of burrows in which holes can be plugged to regulate both temperature and humidity. Likewise, pronghorn are able to exist quite well without water. Some researchers suggest that certain herds may never take a single drink. Also in the pronghorn's favor is its wide-ranging appetite; it is able to gain sustenance from cacti and sagebrush, both of which many animals will not touch.

Plants, rooted to their environment, are even more remarkable in their abilities to survive the extremes of desert life. Ocotillo will drop its leaves under conditions of drought and then sprout an entirely new crop after the next good rain. The lechuguilla will wait patiently through the roll of seasons—often for decades—storing up nutrients from the scant amount present in the desert soil. Then, in one remarkable spurt of growth, a towering stalk perhaps 6 feet high and laden with creamy yellow flowers will appear. It offers its seeds to the ground, and then withers and dies. In order to increase its chances for propagation, globemallow will flower once in the spring, and if there are sufficient rains, again during the summer.

When walking the desert, allow your attention to focus more

on the nooks and crannies lying at your feet than on the lilt of distant peaks and valleys. The bottom of a small wash, a hillside shaded from the blast of the summer sun, a thin draw split by a seep of fresh water—these are the magic places of the desert. It is here that you'll discover some of the most startling of life's miracles, unforgettable when held against the desert's vast, shimmering stillness and the long, soft swell of rock and sky.

Colorado Plateau

WHIRLPOOL CANYON OVERLOOK

Distance: 3.2 miles

Location: Head north from Dinosaur National Monument Headquarters on the Harpers Corners Road. Just north of mile marker 22, on the right side of the road, is the Echo Park Overlook. Park here and walk back south along the Harpers Corners Road for 0.1 mile until you come to a dirt road taking off to the west. This is our walking path.

If you've ever had a desire to amble across the middle of nowhere, this is the walk for you. You'll be following a small dirt ranch road that seems to almost float through a vast blanket of pungent sage, the distant line of eroded cliffs and mountains shimmering like mirages in the summer sun. Turkey vultures with enormous 6-foot wing spans hang on the desert thermals, carving circles in a parched blue sky. If you stand completely still for a moment, you'll notice a remarkable lack of sound here. To look across this tremendous yawn of open space, unable to cock an ear to even the slightest whisper or lilt of bird song, is a strange, almost overpowering experience. It can be a real relief to again strike up the comfortable rhythm of feet tapping time against the dirt.

If you haven't noticed them already as you drove on the roadway up to the trailhead, this walk may introduce you to large, reddish brown to black insects known as Mormon crickets. These 2-inch-long creatures are actually a form of wingless grasshopper, their nickname deriving from the extensive damage they did to the crops of Mormon pioneers in 1848, until they were finally gobbled up by California gulls. In some years their populations absolutely explode, and millions of them—both dead and alive—can be found lining the pavement of the Harpers Corners Road. Strangely, when

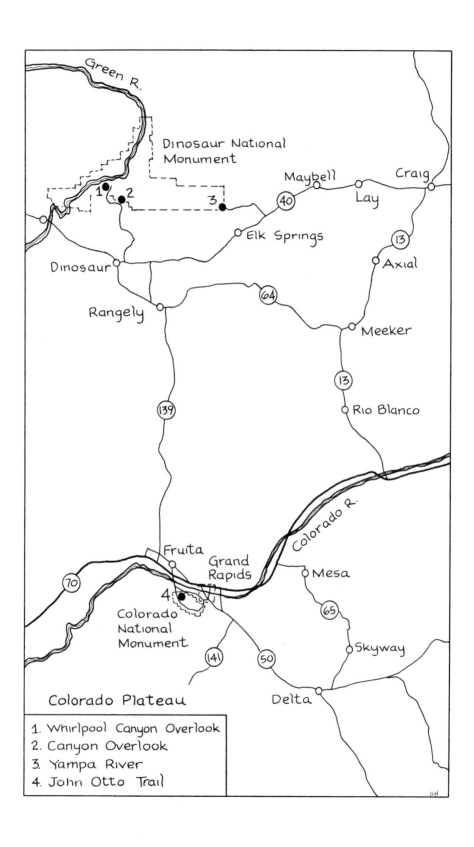

Green R.

Dinosaur National
Monument

Maybell   Craig

Lay

40

13

Elk Springs

Axial

Dinosaur

64

Rangely   Meeker

13

139   Rio Blanco

Colorado R.

Fruita

Grand
Rapids   Mesa

70

4   65

Colorado
National
Monument   Skyway

141   50

Colorado Plateau   Delta

1. Whirlpool Canyon Overlook
2. Canyon Overlook
3. Yampa River
4. John Otto Trail

such large numbers occur, the insects will often begin a mysterious migration in an apparently random direction, never stopping or detouring around any obstacle in their path, be it a river, fence, or even a sheer cliff.

You can tell the female of this species by the long pointed structure (ovipositor) that extends from the abdomen. Eggs are laid in the soil during the summer and will hatch the following spring. While these insects may hardly seem like a palatable paté to us, for some regional Indian people they were a very important source of food.

In 0.8 mile you'll pass through a fine collection of junipers, and then begin descending gently, soon reaching a place where the land drops away into a magnificent canyon. Here in these layers of rock is a story stretching back toward the early pulses of life on earth. The upper gray shales and limestones before you rest atop 500-million-year-old reddish brown rocks that once formed head-lands on a vast, silent sea known as the Ladore Ocean. Beneath even this is the billion-year-old red quartzite that forms the roots of the Uinta Mountains. The narrator of this incredible tale is the Green River, 2,500 feet below you and just out of sight, cutting downward deeper and deeper into the foundations of the earth.

It was in 1869 that the intrepid one-armed explorer John Wesley Powell became the first man to descend the mighty Green and Colorado rivers on the back of a boat. Having already lost one of his craft at Disaster Falls and very nearly losing another one at Hell's Half Mile (both in Ladore Canyon), Powell was hardly a stranger to the incredible force that the Green could muster. Thus it was probably not with complete calm that Powell and his men approached the mouth of the canyon that lies before you, now choked with even more fury since the addition of the Yampa's liquid cargo.

"All this volume of water," he writes, "confined, as it is, in a narrow channel and rushing with great velocity, is set eddying and spinning in whirlpools by protecting rocks and short curves, and the waters waltz their way through the canyon, making their own rippling, rushing, roaring music." Through difficult lining and por-taging maneuvers, Powell's party made it past the point where you now stand, to find a wider but even faster river further down.

"What a headlong ride it is!" he later wrote, "shooting past rocks and islands. I am soon filled with exhilaration only experienced before in riding a fleet horse over the outstretched prairie." Floating later in the calm waters of Island Park just to the west, Powell decided to christen this Whirlpool Canyon, the narrowest of all the gorges they had seen thus far.

The road continues along this edge, becoming fainter and fainter, finally fading out completely a couple of hundred yards from where it first joined the edge of the canyon. Continue along the ridge past the end of the road for another 200 yards through a pinyon–juniper forest to a narrow open area strewn with rocks. This is our turnaround. From here you can look north into a deep canyon that lies along the Island Park geologic fault. This beautiful gorge, its floor carpeted with tall grass and cottonwoods, was carved by Jones Hole Creek, which runs as clear as crystal into the murky waters of the Green. The word *hole* was a term typically given to the valleys of the West by early trappers and explorers.

CANYON OVERLOOK

Distance: 0.3 mile
Location: Head north from Dinosaur National Monument Headquarters on the Harpers Corner Road. Turn right at the signed road to the Canyon Overlook and Picnic Area, just north of mile marker 15. A short distance after making this turn the road will fork; the left branch goes to the picnic area and the right goes to the overlook. Park at the overlook.

The view from the Canyon Overlook is one to remember, with mile after mile of folded stone, licked by wind and sculpted by patient fingers of water into a fantastic tapestry of domes, cliffs, and twisted canyons. Standing on this high perch looking into the rugged landscape below, there is a strong feeling that the park brochure is correct: this place is, and seems likely to remain, "a secret of the present, known to few travelers."

This walk is much shorter than most of our other treks. I've included it because it offers a wonderful opportunity to see how

Evening-primrose

what may seem like subtle environmental differences can completely alter the vegetative complexion of the earth. Leaving your car parked at the Canyon Overlook, begin the walk by descending the paved road to the picnic area lying just to the north. While this stretch can of course be driven, the warm smell of sage and sand on the wind, the clean summer skies overhead, and the rush of rabbits and squawk of jays make a slow saunter on foot the only truly appropriate way to travel.

Depending on the time of your visit, you'll likely find the roadway fringe leading to the picnic area dappled with color—the deep blues of lupines, the fiery reds of scarlet gilia, and the soft white petals of the primroses. As is common in other parts of the monument, junipers and pinyon pines add a smattering of blunt green to the scene. These trees seem especially beautiful when viewed from a distance, as you can see in the great sweep of forests visible far below in Pearl Park, tossed like a tattered quilt at the bare feet of a sandstone gulf.

While you may have noticed a couple of changes in the look of the plant life as you made your way down, things really begin to get interesting about the time you reach the turnaround circle adjacent to the picnic area. Here in this small island surrounded by concrete is a small huddle of aspen, a tree usually no more at home in a high slice of desert than would be the beavers that relish its sweet white bark. From here things become even stranger. Walk

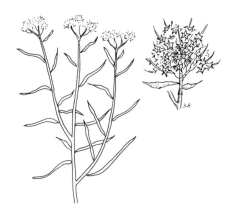

Rabbitbrush

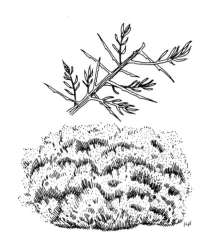

Greasewood

out along the small finger of land that extends beyond the picnic area in a clockwise direction. Joining the occasional pinyon pine and juniper is a beautiful assemblage of curl-leaf mountain-mahogany, as well as several fine old Douglas-firs. Almost nowhere else along this drive, most of which is through a land washed with sage, rabbitbrush, and greasewood, will you see this kind of plant community. So why here?

The first thing that may come to mind is elevation. Remember that the higher you go, the cooler the air becomes. Since cool air cannot hold as much moisture as warm air, moisture-laden clouds rising over an uplifted landscape tend to drop their water at high elevations. In many places near here you can be standing in shorts in a warm, dry desert, looking at 3 feet of snow on the high line of the surrounding mountains. But your elevation here is only about 5,800 feet—substantial, but less than many other sections of the Harpers Corner Road.

If elevation doesn't adequately explain these beautiful aspen and Douglas-fir, the next thing to consider is exposure—how the land is oriented to the sun. And so we find that this is a great part of the secret to this arboreal oasis. The face of this land finger slopes gently downward almost due north, the one direction that offers the least amount of exposure to the sun. Rain that falls here stays a little longer, because the warm, dry fingers of the sun do not sink in and pull it from the earth. The snow that falls here when the sun is lying far to the south lasts a little longer, melting drop by drop into the soil instead of evaporating quickly back into the atmosphere. These extra drips of water, each one bringing the promise of life, are what enable the trees you see here to survive when all around there is the strong song of the desert.

Looking north and just slightly east from the overlook at the end of this promontory, hidden in the folds of Weber sandstone, lie the grassy glades of Echo Park. Here the Green River exits beautiful Ladore Canyon to join the Yampa, which has been on its own stunning journey through the grand twists of rocks known as the goosenecks. Together they will twist like a great snake, past the rugged roil of Whirlpool Canyon and the silence of Island Park, through the sunlit gorge of Split Mountain, and out into the sage-covered flats beyond.

More than a hundred years ago, Echo Park was the home of a quasi hermit named Pat Lynch. The life of this feisty Irishman was never dull. He was once stranded and held prisoner on the coast of Africa, and was also a naval veteran of the Civil War, reportedly with the crew that sunk the Merrimac. He came to settle in this rugged land in the vicinity of Echo Park, laying "claim on this bottom for my home and support." Often living in caves once used by Indians, Lynch grew to love this place as few Europeans had before him, or have since. It is wonderful that today you can still lose yourself in his footsteps, meandering along the Green, up Moonshine Draw and down Iron Springs Wash, finding the land still filled with that piercing, silent beauty that haunted Pat Lynch until the day he died.

YAMPA RIVER

Distance: 2 miles
Location: From U.S. Highway 40, approximately 40 miles west of Craig, Colorado, turn north on a signed highway toward Deerlodge Park Campground. The walk begins from this camping area, approximately 11 miles from U.S. Highway 40.

By the time the Yampa River reaches this beautiful parkland, it already has traversed an amazing variety of environments. Rising 100 miles to the east, in the high spruce–fir forests that flank the Continental Divide, the Yampa tumbles through meadows splashed with wildflowers and across floodplains heavy with sage, eventually punching its way westward through the hard heart of the Juniper Mountains. Here at Deerlodge Park it makes a slow, lazy amble through these grandfather cottonwoods before disappearing into a silent, mysterious world of 300-million-year-old limestones and ancient quartz sand dunes, now hardened into a maze of shimmering white canyons.

This walk begins beneath the arms of the great Deerlodge Park cottonwoods, along a path following the south bank of the Yampa through a blanket of tall grass. Besides forming an extremely beautiful environment in which to walk, the vegetation that grows along the Yampa was once part of a great garden of useful plants that Indians relied on heavily throughout their daily lives. Various parts of the cottonwood, for example, contain populin and salicin, both related to the active ingredient in common aspirin. Native Americans of the region were using cottonwood (and, to a lesser extent, aspen) to break fevers and reduce inflammation long before the first Excedrin headache. Some Indians ate the sweet sap of the cottonwood, and the buds and fruits were used to produce colorful dyes.

As you continue along the river, look for the stiff, segmented hollow stems of horsetails, also known as scouring rush. This latter name hints at the fact that early peoples used the abrasive stems of the plant to polish stone pipes and arrowheads. Pioneer women would routinely dry and bundle the stems to clean pots, pans, and even wooden floors. Before such things as sandpaper and fine grades of steel wool, British woodworkers used horsetails as their primary means to finish cabinets and fine pieces of furniture.

The braid of trails running through the grassy areas that fringe the Yampa sandbars can become faint in places. You may wish to do a little walking in the upper reaches of the sandbars themselves, noting the surprising amount of life that can spring from these sandy soils, including an abundance of cottonwood seedlings and tamarisk. Once out of the cottonwoods, in about 0.25 mile, you'll enter a much more open area covered with sagebrush, cactuses, rabbitbrush, and saltbush. The leaves and seeds of the rabbitbrush—the tall bush with slender leaves and great clusters of tiny golden flowers—are a favorite of the cottontails you may see dashing across your path.

If you're walking through this area during mid- to late summer, you'll undoubtedly spot the black and white plumage and long tail of the magpies, or at the very least hear their harsh cries coming from along the river corridor. Magpies typically do not congregate during the nesting season, but suddenly become much more sociable after the rigors of parenthood are completed. Their harsh yak! yak! can be rather startling after the gentle croak of the ash-throated flycatchers, or the somber coo of mourning doves.

Just under 0.5 mile into the walk you'll come to a parking lot. This marks the western terminus of the road system into Deerlodge Park. (If you happen to be walking out along the sandbars, this parking area will be on your left at the point where a large block of sandstone protrudes to the edge of the river.) We'll follow a footpath leaving from the southwest corner of the parking area, climbing up through the rocks onto a small bench above the river.

From the parking area to our turnaround point, the look of the land is quite different from what came before. Across the river are large blocks of severely tilted sedimentary rock, evidence that these lopsided peaks were squeezed up on either side by enormous pressures inside the earth. Later erosion by wind and water, a process that occurs rather quickly in soft sandstones, gave these rocks the dramatic face they wear today. Grain by grain, the relentless forces of erosion are delivering these mountains to the Yampa, which carries them away to the Green, and finally to the slack waters behind Flaming Gorge Reservoir.

At 0.65 mile the trail heads away from the river to cross a rocky sandstone wash. Notice how different the vegetation is beneath these narrow walls. Here water is regularly channeled from the face of the surrounding plateaus, allowing a fine garden of wildflowers, cottonwoods, and squawbush to exist. At 0.9 mile our path will turn south, bound for the rocky corridors of Disappointment Draw and Indian Water Canyon. You may wish to exit the trail here and walk along the sandbar to the point where the river disappears into a massive rock cathedral. From here it will continue west as it has done for countless millenniums, cutting first through the soft tertiary sediments and finally the harder limestone and sandstone blocks laid down by a series of ancient oceans.

JOHN OTTO TRAIL

Distance: 0.5 mile
Location: From Interstate 70, take the Colorado National
Monument exit at Fruita. Continue south on the Rim Rock
Drive for 7 miles to the Monument Headquarters and Visitor
Center. The signed John Otto Trail is about 1 mile past the
Visitor Center, on the left (northeast) side of the Rim Rock
Drive.

Any road-weary traveler on Interstate 70 would do well to make a
quick detour into Colorado National Monument. In this tapestry of
quiet sandstone chambers is a world far different from that of
on-ramps and off-ramps, where the monotonous whine of tires
gives way to the whisper of cottontail feet and the coo of rock
doves.

This 20,000 acre pocket of solitude owes its existence to the
fervent efforts of John Otto, for which this trail has been named.
Otto came to the region in 1906 and wasted no time in assuming
the role of chief promoter of the region. Of the Grand Valley below
he would claim that rich soil and abundant sunshine grew "peaches
as big as the moon," and pumpkins "as big as railroad oil tanks."
But he held an even greater admiration for this soaring canyon
country, spending an enormous amount of effort writing letters and
raising money in order to have it declared a federal park. His
perseverance paid off in 1911 when President Taft signed legislation making the area a national monument, with Otto himself as
the first custodian. For this position Otto was paid $1.00 per month.

Otto's antics were the talk of the local grapevine: the way he
would disappear into these canyons for weeks with only his beloved
burros for company; his suggestion to name the preserve Smith
National Monument Park, thinking that such a name would cause
the millions of Americans named Smith to visit the area; the time
he suddenly married Beatrice Farnham from New England (her
wedding present being a burro) to have his bride discover to her
dismay that a tent and pack stove were about as much of a domicile
as John was able to handle.

This walk begins in an open forest of pinyon and juniper,
two trees that occur together throughout much of the southwestern

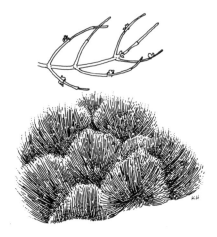

Mormon Tea

United States. On the ground here you'll also see the stiff, multi-jointed green stems of Mormon tea. Its nickname refers to Mormon pioneers who commonly used the plant to make a tasty tea, although Native Americans and Mexicans were using the plant for medicinal purposes long before Brigham Young set foot in Utah. This particular species of Mormon tea has trace amounts of ephedrine, which is recognized around the world for its value as a decongestant. (Asian varieties have much higher concentrations of this chemical.) Many people of the Southwest still drink tea made from this plant to relieve allergy and cold-related congestion.

While this canyon country may look frightfully devoid of any plants that could sustain human life, those who know it well consider it a garden of plenty. Besides Mormon tea, the leaves and "berries" of the juniper provide a treatment for urinary tract disorders, while the pinyon (a good example is 50 yards down the trail on the right) offers delicious, high-energy nuts that contain nearly 60 percent fat. Also, the pinyon produces a quick, hot fire. Early settlers discovered that the wood of the single-leaf ash, also found here, made extremely durable tool handles. And finally, the buds, flowers, and fruits of the yuccas along this trail are fine sources of food, the leaves of the plant once providing material for making rope, sandals, and mats.

The trail descends gently, offering fine views of the Fruita

Valley, 2,000 feet below, framed in the distance by the beautifully layered Book Cliffs. In just over 0.2 mile the path ends at a wonderful sandstone perch. Here you can stand wrapped in warm sun, with a dry desert wind tumbling upon the canyon walls. Listen for the raucous call of the pinyon jay, and the fast rush of wings as swifts dance along the precipices looking for insects. To your right is beautiful Monument Canyon and the 550-foot-high spire of Wingate Sandstone known as Independence Monument. This monolith, as well as the Pipe Organ formation directly in front of you, are remnants of much larger ridge systems, long since beaten back into grains of sand by eons of ice, wind, and water. The one thing that has kept these spires from suffering the same fate is a protective layer of light-colored capstone (Kayenta formation) that consists of rock sediments glued together by silica and calcite. True to his love for this land, John Otto scaled Independence Monument on the Fourth of July in 1910, planting an American flag on the summit.

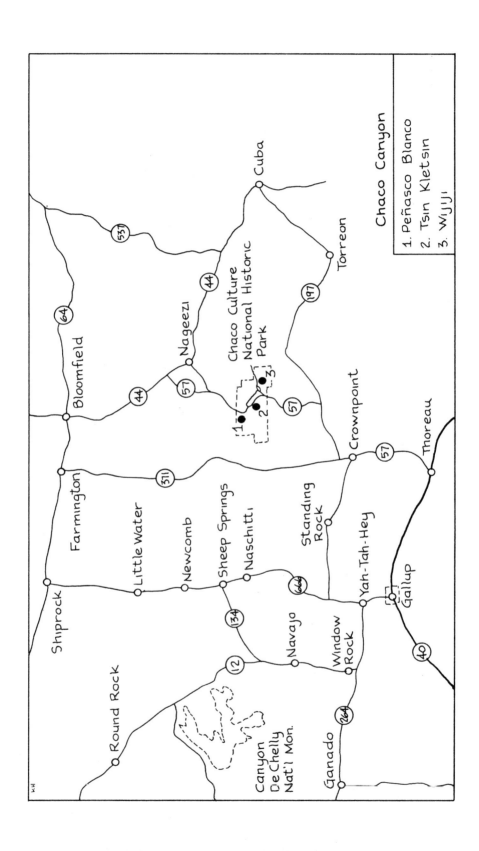

Chaco Canyon

1. Peñasco Blanco
2. Tsin Kletsin
3. Wijiji

Chaco Canyon

PEÑASCO BLANCO

Distance: 4.5 miles
Location: Chaco Canyon can be reached either from the north
or south along dirt roads, which can be dangerously slippery
when wet. For this reason it's advisable to contact the monument for current road conditions before making the trip. If
you're coming from the north along New Mexico Route 44,
head south on New Mexico Route 45 at the small village of
Nageezi. In 13 miles take a left onto New Mexico Route 57
and continue south. You'll enter the park after descending a
steep grade. At the bottom is Casa Chiquita Ruin on the right,
where this walk begins.

Coming from the south, exit Interstate 40 onto New Mexico
Route 197 at the town of Thoreau. Continue for approximately
40 miles and turn north on New Mexico Route 57, reaching the
park visitor center in 21 miles. From the visitor center, head
northwest through Chaco Canyon, following signs for Chetro
Ketl and Pueblo Bonito. Continue a short way past the parking
area for these two ruins to an intersection with a road coming in
from the northwest. Turn right here and proceed for about 1
mile to the parking area for Casa Chiquita on the left.

This walk takes off to the northwest along a service road adjacent
to Casa Chiquita, or "little house." Compared to "great houses"
like Pueblo Bonito and Peñasco Blanco, this ruin is aptly named.
Archeologists think that this almost square structure, still unexcavated, was built sometime between A.D. 1100 and A.D. 1130.
Some of the room rows were two and even three stories tall, built
around an elevated round room. Even on a small scale, the amount
of work involved in building this type of structure was considerable. The walls consist of an inner core of small stones, covered
inside and out with thick veneers of quarried sandstone, carefully

189

shaped into easy-to-fit blocks. One architect has speculated that the construction of Pueblo Bonito, the magnificent "great house" located about 1 mile southeast of here, may have required as much as 100 million pounds of stone veneer! When you also consider that thousands of ponderosa pines had to be harvested for roof beams, and perhaps carried here from the distant mountains, the achievement becomes downright incredible.

Leaving Casa Chiquita, the service road continues to the northwest along Chaco Wash, through a vegetative mat of black greasewood, four-wing saltbush, amaranthus, ricegrass, and broom snakeweed. Each of these plants played a significant role in the lives of people who once made their homes in these canyons. The leaves and spring shoots of four-wing saltbush, a member of the goosefoot family, were eaten regularly, and the seeds ground into meal. Some Navajo people still make a beautiful yellow dye from the leaves and twigs of this plant, as well as mix ground seeds with water and sugar for a drink called pinole. Likewise, the seeds and leaves of the black greasewood were edible, and the wood was commonly used as fuel. Broom snakeweek, the tall, spindly green plant with thin leaves and clustered yellow flowers, derives the second half of its name from the fact that Navajo people use it to treat sheep that have been bitten by rattlesnakes. The plant's leaves are ground and boiled into a poultice, which is then applied to the bite.

About 0.2 mile into the walk the trail comes close to Chaco Wash, where you'll see several beautiful Fremont cottonwoods, named for the famous explorer John Fremont. Pioneers crossing the parched terrain of the southwest always rejoiced at seeing this tree, since it meant that permanent groundwater was not far from reach. Hopi Indians still use the roots of this tree for carving their beautiful kachina dolls.

Into the walk 0.75 mile, just before a side wash comes in from the right, is a large petroglyph panel on a northwest-facing cliff. Researchers have documented Indian rock art in Chaco Canyon that may stretch back 2,000 years. Beginning with simple hand prints and birds and plants made by the early basket makers, these warm stone walls stand as record to a long wave of history. Besides Anasazi images and symbols from 200 years of Navajo occupation,

Four-wing Saltbush

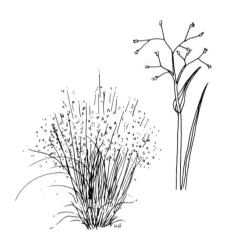

Indian Ricegrass

also in this stone have been recorded visits from the U.S. cavalry, cowboys, and sheep herders who passed through here in the first half of the twentieth century. Though they might not seem so, these petroglyph etchings (as opposed to pictographs, which are painted with dyes) are quite fragile; touching them dislodges the sand grains and hastens their demise.

In another 0.3 mile you'll cross Chaco Wash, profuse with tamarisk, a tall feathery tree with juniperlike leaves. Tamarisk was introduced from the Mediterranean (its name may derive from the Tamaris River in Spain) in an effort to control severe soil erosion caused by years of overgrazing. To that end it has proven to be very effective. Unfortunately, tamarisk is remarkably adept at taking over entire landscapes, using great amounts of groundwater, which is then unavailable for other native plants. Once entrenched, the plant is almost impossible to eradicate. Willows are the other common plant in this wash. They were used by the Anasazi to make sleeping mats; archeologists have found several burials placed on top of mats woven from this species.

Once out of the wash you'll come to a trail junction at the foot of a mesa. The fork heading west leads in 0.25 mile to a rather famous pictograph known as "Supernova." Though no one knows for sure, many archeologists believe that the art panel is a record of a great supernova that occurred during the summer of 1054. (We know the date of this celestial event from having read about it in ancient Chinese records.) The trail to Peñasco Blanco climbs the mesa, and is marked well by a series of rock cairns, which are small piles of stones placed as guideposts along the trail.

Peñasco Blanco, which means "white rock point," is located on a rocky spur atop West Mesa, and offers sweeping views down Chaco Wash. This unusual oval structure, still unexcavated, consisted of more than 160 rooms and 4 great kivas (round rooms perhaps used for social and religious rituals)—2 in the structure's plaza and 2 more just outside the building. It is thought that construction began on Peñasco Blanco around A.D. 900 and continued in five stages through about A.D. 1120. To the northeast is a rather unusual terrace, upon which lies the ruins of a small L-shaped building, which may have been a storage unit of some type as well as a slab that one early archeologist thought might be some type of calendar device.

Could this great house, which lies along one of Chaco's famous prehistoric roads, have served as the controlling governmental unit for the communities that lay beyond? What a fantastic thought to spend a lifetime wandering these lonely canyons and mesa tops, walking these prehistoric roads, probing these remarkable buildings. What a challenge to try to piece together the fantastic social system that existed here—a system so wonderfully complex that some nineteenth-century writers suggested it could only be the work of the ancient Greeks.

TSIN KLETSIN

Distance: 3 miles
Location: Chaco Canyon can be reached either from the north or south along dirt roads, which can be dangerously slippery when wet. For this reason it's advisable to contact the monument for current road conditions before making the trip. If you're coming from the north along New Mexico Route 44, head south on New Mexico Route 45 at the small village of Nageezi. In 13 miles take a left onto New Mexico Route 57 and continue south for 15 miles into the park. A short distance after taking a right turn on a one-way loop road (just past Pueblo del Arroyo), you'll come to a parking lot for Casa Rinconada on the right side of the road. Our walk begins from here.

Coming from the south, exit Interstate 40 onto New Mexico Route 197 at the town of Thoreau. Continue for approximately 40 miles and turn north on New Mexico Route 57, reaching an intersection just west of the visitor center in 21 miles. Take a left at this intersection (onto a one-way loop road), and continue around the loop past the parking area for Chetro Ketl and Pueblo Bonito. Soon after the road makes a horseshoe turn to the left, heading back toward the southeast, you'll come to the Casa Rinconada parking area on the right. Park here.

The walk to Tsin Kletsin, which means either "black wood" or "charcoal place," is a journey through a collection of archeological wonders leading to one of the most expansive, haunting desert views to be found on any trail in the park. Keep in mind that this walk can be a bit of a scorcher in the summer. During these months plan to leave early in the morning, when the coo of mourning doves and the whistle of canyon wrens runs thick off the rock walls, or late in the evening, as the last light of day seeps off the stony fingers of West Mesa.

Before ascending the northern flank of South Mesa, the trail meanders past the ruins of Casa Rinconada, which means "the house in the corner." A short distance from the parking area it makes a quick climb to the edge of a large circular chamber. This is a superb example of a great kiva—the largest in the park and one of the finest to be found anywhere in the Southwest. Though the functional extent of great kivas is not known, they are generally thought to have housed special social gatherings, and were places where important religious ceremonies were performed.

The room against the north side of the kiva may have served as both an entry and storage area for religious items. Some researchers feel that the covered subfloor passage from this room to the chamber allowed for entry into the kiva as if from within the earth. Such a ceremonial maneuver has a link to modern pueblo cultures, who are more than likely the descendants of these Anasazi, or "ancient ones." To them, kivas represent the underworld out of which their ancestors first emerged onto the face of the earth. Their kivas, just like this one, have a symbolic hole known as the *sipapu* (see-pah-pooh), which represents this sacred place of emergence. It's been suggested that tower kivas were simply kivas built on top of one another, each level perhaps representing a former stage of the underworld that the ancient ancestors once passed through.

Leaving the complex of Casa Rinconada, the path soon begins the moderately steep but fairly short climb up to the top of South Mesa. Part way up you'll pass through a very narrow slit in the sandstone, riddled with small pockets and passageways carved from the rock by the relentless beat of wind and water. Soon after this section you'll leave the well-worn path behind. Much of the rest of the journey is accomplished by following a series of rock cairns, which are small towers of piled stones used to mark the way.

The vegetation is fairly sparse on this parched, windswept mesa, consisting predominantly of grasses, broom snakeweed, cliff-

Roadrunner

rose, four-wing saltbush and, in about 0.75 mile, a smattering of juniper. The bark of cliffrose was used by the Anasazi to make baskets and sandals. Juniper is still used by modern pueblo Indians for an array of religious and medicinal purposes.

In 1.5 miles you'll reach the ruins of Tsin Kletsin, an unexcavated structure probably built during the early 1100s. It consists of a central block of rooms, an L-shaped wing to the west, and an arc of rooms to the south enclosing a large plaza. Of particular interest to archeologists is Tsin Kletsin's unique line of sight to other ruins in the Chaco complex. From atop the highest tower here could be seen the great houses of Kin Kletso, Peñasco Blanco, and the Pueblo Alto complex, as well as several "outlier" structures. Moving this site a short distance in any direction would eliminate these sight lines. Could it be, as many researchers have suggested, that the Anasazi constructed an ingenious system whereby the entire complex could be alerted to a stranger's approach?

The view from atop this mesa is absolutely haunting in the depth of its solitude, the long, lonely roll of high desert stretching almost beyond what the mind can comprehend. Only far, far to the north is there any relief—a thin crest of Rocky Mountains painted lightly on the distant horizon. All else, it seems, has been reduced to sun, stone, and silence. Yet strangely, when one stands at Chaco on the crumbling threshold of one of the greatest civilizations North America has ever known, it seems as if the Anasazi never perished at all. Perhaps they are out there still, dancing, singing, riding like turkey vultures on the warm desert winds.

Turkey Vulture

WIJIJI

Distance: 4 miles
Location: Chaco Canyon can be reached either from the north
or south along dirt roads, which can be dangerously slippery
when wet. For this reason it's advisable to contact the monument for current road conditions before making the trip. If
you're coming from the north along New Mexico Route 44,
head south on New Mexico Route 45 at the small village of
Nageezi. In 13 miles take a left onto New Mexico Route 57
and continue south for 15 miles into the park.

Coming from the south, exit Interstate 40 onto New Mexico
Route 197 at the town of Thoreau. Continue for approximately
40 miles and turn north on New Mexico Route 57, reaching the
visitor center in 21 miles. From the visitor center, head east
toward Gallo Campground, continuing past the campground
turnoff to the Wijiji parking area on the right.

It is a major stretch of the imagination to consider that this haunting
collage of quiet, windswept desert washes was once the scene of
one of the most extraordinary leaps of cultural development on the
North American continent. In barely 30 square miles, more than
2,400 archeological sites have been identified, ranging from 2,000-
year-old baskets and sandals found in Atlatl Cave, to the imposing
great houses or towns. One of these (Pueblo Bonito) was a four-
story architectural masterpiece of more than 800 rooms spanning
nearly two acres. Such architectural scope was virtually unknown in
the United States until after the advent of structural steel.

But beyond the actual sites, what really is most appealing
about this entire 25,000-square-mile region is the sense of mystery
that still pervades the entire concept of the "Chaco Phenomenon,"
a term used often to emphasize the remarkable complex develop-
ments that mark the area's peak habitation period during the tenth,
eleventh, and twelfth centuries. How could such a dry, fragile
environment support the kind of numbers that the great houses
seem to suggest once lived here? And, if this was such a populated
area, why have so few human burials been found? In a culture that
had no wheeled carts, what was the purpose of having half a dozen
major road systems, many nearly 40 feet wide and stretching
straight as arrows across the landscape for more than 50 miles? After
having spent 300 years establishing such a fantastic place, why did

Canyon Wren

Loggerhead Shrike

people suddenly begin drifting away during the mid- to late twelfth century? Walking to Wijiji (a Navajo word for the greasewood that grows in the area), it's exciting to ponder these questions.

This walk runs along an old ranch road, and is especially beautiful early in the morning, when the first shafts of sunlight flood the rocky tongues of land lying between Wijiji and Chacra mesas. Canyon wrens flit among the boulders, their crystal-clear, down-the-scale whistles dripping off the warm brown canyon walls. Also here are mockingbirds and loggerhead shrikes, the latter storing their excess catches of insects, small birds, and mice by impaling them on thorns, yucca leaf tips, and barbed wire.

There's an interesting mat of vegetation in this area, one that has changed considerably in the past 40 years. In 1920, an archeologist excavating Pueblo Bonito made the rather extraordinary claim that Edward Sargent, the bad-boy kingpin of early twentieth-century ranching, was running close to 60,000 sheep in this fragile desert ecosystem. Besides the sometimes violent techniques he used to run off the Navajo people who had been here for two centuries before him, Sargent's operation proved to be an absolute disaster for the resources. Where fine grasses once grew, suddenly there was only black sage and Russian thistle. It was not until the mid 1940s, when Sargent lost his grazing lease and the entire monument was finally fenced off, that the land began to recover. (It must be remembered that, after more than a century of heavy grazing, very little of the American Southwest looks the way it did to early explorers.) The abundance of ricegrass in Chaco Canyon is testimony to the fact that the land does begin to heal itself if given the chance.

Wijiji ruins lie 2 miles into the walk on the left side of the road. This structure contained 103 rooms at floor level. Built around A.D. 1110 to A.D. 1115, it may have been one of the last great houses to be constructed in Chaco Canyon. Speaking about the symmetry of the structure, archeologist Stephen Leksen has called Wijiji "the most perfect of any Chacoan ruin." This, he goes on to say, suggests that the building of Wijiji did not occur in several stages over many years, but was instead most likely a single construction event. The masonry here is strikingly uniform, the thin sandstone slabs having been quarried from the top of the cliff located behind the ruin. The opposite rows of holes you see in some of the rooms were anchoring sockets for roof beams. If you look carefully, you'll also see a row of these anchor holes high up along a cliff wall behind Wijiji. A series of portals on the north exterior wall of the ruin, of which two remain today, have never been explained. Oddly, Wijiji shows no signs of having had an enclosed plaza. Since this was the architectural fashion of the day, some archeologists suspect that Wijiji may never have been finished.

Two fine rock-art panels lie behind Wijiji to the north. The closest one, slightly west of the ruins, has a fascinating array of petroglyphs. (Petroglyphs are etchings in rock faces, whereas painted images are known as pictographs. Do not touch these rock panels since this hastens their decay.) Spirals, horned animals, and figures resembling humans—some etched in this stone a thousand years ago—are common themes throughout the park. The finer, more deeply incised images, particularly those depicting plants, are thought to have been done by Navajo people in more recent times.

Southern New Mexico

WHITE SANDS

Distance: 0.7 mile
Location: White Sands National Monument headquarters is located on U.S. Highway 70/82, 13 miles south of Alamogordo. From headquarters, head west into the park on the Heart of the Dunes Scenic Drive. (At headquarters you can pick up a free interpretive guide to this road.) There are numbered posts along this drive that correspond to the interpretive guide. Our walk is to the Back Country Camp, leaving from the south side of the road opposite marker 7.

There is no place in the United States more startling in its sheer degree of shimmering white vastness than the White Sands of southern New Mexico. This is the largest gypsum dune field in the world. Driving to the westernmost point of the loop road, which you may want to do before you begin this walk, will tug at your senses in ways that they have never been pulled before. Part way in, a fine layer of gypsum grains begin to scatter across the roadway, lightly at first, but building slowly until they completely obliterate the pavement. When well packed, the grains look remarkably like a frozen surface. You drive slow, your foot poised on the brake, thinking that at any minute you might slide off the road on this icy surface. Massive, bright white shoulders of sand rise around you, consuming the view in every direction. It is as if you had slipped through space to another planet, one whose surface is covered by a strange, shifting quilt of warm desert snow. So striking is this dune field that it is one of the last earth forms identifiable by astronauts, visible from fully halfway to the moon.

This 300-square-mile field of sand owes its existence to a complex set of geologic events. The 150-mile-long Tularosa Basin,

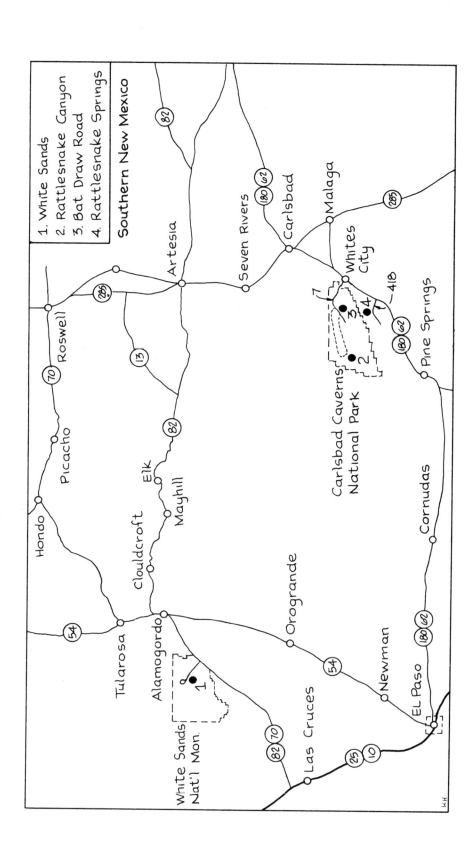

Southern New Mexico

1. White Sands
2. Rattlesnake Canyon
3. Bat Draw Road
4. Rattlesnake Springs

of which the white sands are only a small part, began forming hundreds of millions of years ago when a series of ancient seas invaded and retreated from the area, laying down beds of sediment thousands of feet thick. Some 200 million years later, the same series of uplifts that created the Rocky Mountains also thrust this land skyward. This particular region happened to be bordered by large north–south fault lines, allowing it to sink slowly back into the earth much later, to form a giant, enclosed basin. Because there is no outlet, all the bits and pieces of rock carried by rainwater from the surrounding high country end up trapped in this basin. So far, the rubble has accumulated to a depth of almost 2,000 feet.

To form the sands themselves required first that rain and snowmelt carry down gypsum from the surrounding mountains. Since gypsum is dissolved in water so easily, it poured out of the high country into this basin in great quantities, much of it flowing into the waters of Lake Otero to the southwest. When changes in climate caused Lake Otero to disappear, a massive field of minerals was left, including the selenite from which much of this sand is derived. (Broken flakes of selenite crystal are actually brown, but the wind stirs them violently, scratching their surfaces white in the process.)

All that was required from this point was the arrival of wind—at least 17 miles per hour—to launch these grains into the air. When sand is stopped by a ground object, the grains begin to

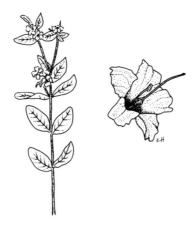

Desert Four O'Clock

build higher and higher on the windward side of the obstacle until they have covered it completely. A crest eventually forms on the mound, leaving it looking like a great white ocean wave frozen in the desert. These crests in turn form launching ramps for new sand grains, which blow out over them and fall down the other side. In this way dunes actually move, or "migrate" along their lee side, which is to the northeast in this case.

Since paths, rock cairns, and every other conventional system of trail marking soon would be obliterated by the blowing sand, you'll make your way along this walk by following a series of numbered posts southward. Once away from the road you'll find this to be a stunning, beautiful world. Rubber rabbitbrush and soaptree yucca race the wind to keep their heads above the migrating dunes. Sometimes blowing sand becomes packed firmly into a plant's fine web of roots. When the dune moves on, beautiful gypsum pedestals remain, like those visible to the left a short distance into the walk. Despite the fantastic adaptability of these plants, as well as about 60 other species found here, vegetation living on the dunes owes much of its existence to a strange, little-understood mix of bacteria and algae that thrive in this shifting world. Without them, there would not be enough nutrients for these plants to survive.

As you continue south along a high ridge of sand, you'll have good views of the San Andres Mountains to the west and the

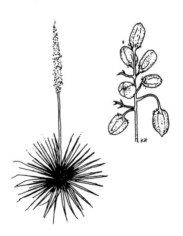

Soaptree Yucca

Sacramento Peaks to the east. The names of both of these ranges attest to the deep Spanish–Catholic roots of New Mexico. The former range was named for Saint Andrew and the latter for the Holy Eucharist. (Since certain saints are hallowed during different times of year, the name that a place ended up with often depended on the month it was discovered.)

Near marker post 5 you'll be able to spot several cottonwoods growing in the nearby dunes—rather a surprise, since cottonwoods never grow in places where there is not permanent groundwater fairly near the surface. In fact, in some of the lower areas of this dune field water may be less than 3 feet beneath the ground.

As you climb the hummocks behind the designated back country camping area, take a minute to sit down and notice how rich and satisfying this environment is. There are the brown heads of ricegrass and the sweet scent of rosemary mint hanging on the desert wind. A short line of whiptail lizard tracks arc across the sand, stopping abruptly at the point where a Swainson's hawk suddenly carried him off for dinner. Every so often the air runs thick with bird song—the loud whistles of a Bullock's oriole or the flutey melodies of a western meadowlark. Though the white sands

Chihuahuan Spotted Whiptail

are indeed a harsh place to live, they are hardly devoid of wonders. Here the world has struck a special balance, a carefully evolved, Spartan harmony between an unforgiving climate and the indomitable flow of life.

RATTLESNAKE CANYON

Distance: 1 mile

Location: To reach Carlsbad Caverns, head south out of Carlsbad on U.S. Highway 62/180 for 20 miles to Whites City. Turn west on New Mexico Route 7 and proceed for 7 miles. A signed, 9.5-mile scenic loop drive takes off to the west just before reaching the park visitor center. The signed Rattlesnake Canyon Trail is located on the south side of this road, approximately 4 miles from the starting point of the loop.

The vast majority of visitors to this national park head 750 feet straight down, bound for the spectacular medley of limestone chambers that make up Carlsbad Caverns. What most don't realize, however, is that there's also a very engaging world up on top, found in the endless folds of rock and sky, in the yawning plateaus and quiet, hidden nooks of the Chihuahuan Desert.

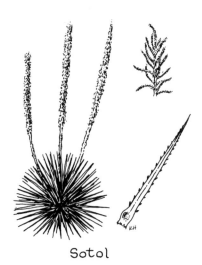

Sotol

The Rattlesnake Canyon walk offers a good taste of the rugged drainage systems that have been sliced into this ancient ocean reef, as well as the thin green cover of plant life that has woven itself across these rocky shoulders. The trail begins with a quick westward descent into a small wash. Following this for a short distance, it then crosses over to hug the north face of a large thumb of rock, the wash falling away in a mad tumble toward the bottom of Rattlesnake Canyon. Along this stretch you'll see a fine collection of desert plants, including one-seed juniper, sotol, lechuguilla, and New Mexico's state flower, the soaptree yucca.

Every one of these plants as well as dozens of others found in these canyons were used by the people who once lived here. One-seed juniper provided good firewood, and the shreddy bark of the tree was used in making mats, sandals, and even cloth. You might at first confuse sotol (a member of the lily family) with the yucca, but its sawtooth-shaped leaves and tall stalk with tight clusters of tiny white flowers are unique. The Apaches roasted the "heart" of the sotol plant in stone-lined pits, made a fermented drink from the sap, and wove the tough, flexible leaves into baskets and mats. Lechuguilla, with its collection of foot-long swordlike leaves (and, in some years, a 6- to 10-foot-tall flower stalk), provided fiber, food, and drink, while the tall, palm-shaped soaptree yucca gave rope, food, and a soapy cleanser that could be squeezed

Cholla

from the plant's roots. Though some people confuse the yucca with the agave, the yucca has white fibers curling back from the edges of its leaves.

The trail continues around this protrusion, the land opening up with each step. By 0.3 mile you'll have gained a sweeping view of the sharply eroded rockscape to the southwest. This area has a rugged, untamed look to it, as if desperados might still be holed up in the stony side pockets of Rattlesnake Canyon, plotting a bust of the Butterfield stage.

John Butterfield's mail stage ran just to the south of here, twisting along the soaring Guadalupe Ridge. Butterfield was a mail stage operator from the East, and in 1857 he was awarded a post office plum worth more than half a million dollars a year to construct a stage system that could deliver mail between St. Louis and San Francisco. The 2,800-mile run was to be made twice a week and each trip was to take no longer than 5 days to complete. Remarkably, Butterfield was able to get the entire system running within the single year the government had allotted him. While for the most part the mail rode east and west no worse for the wear, the same could not be said for Butterfield's passengers. Most found the ride through these vast spaces to be a bone-shaking horror of dust and heat; more than a few decided to abandon the trip long before their stage ever rolled onto California soil. Unfortunately, the Overland mail line had hardly settled into a comfortable routine when Texas seceded from the Union, and no longer allowed passage of the U.S. mail. The operation was moved north and sold in 1862.

Our turnaround point is reached in 0.5 mile, just before the trail begins a zigzag plunge into the drainage below. Those who wish to make this descent will find themselves wrapped in a thick blanket of wash vegetation, reaching in another 0.5 mile a fine amphitheater formed by the intersection of two canyon systems. This is a particularly good place to see a variety of desert bird and animal life. As you head back from our turnaround point, keep your eyes open along this stretch for ocotillo and Engelmann prickly pear. Ocotillo is a strange-looking collection of spiny, spindly branches, typically growing 5 to 10 feet high. If you see tiny green leaves running up and down the ocotillo's branches, it has rained here in the not too distant past. As the soil dries these will wither and fall off, helping the plant to avoid a loss of moisture from water escaping through the leaf pores.

BAT DRAW ROAD

Distance: 2.5 miles
Location: The walk is located in Carlsbad Caverns National Park behind the visitor center. It heads east along the old entrance road to the park, right beside the main entrance to Carlsbad Caverns. Alternatively, you can take the nature trail behind the visitors center and come out on our walking road just a short distance from the main cavern entrance; you would then turn right onto this road. Those beginning near the main cave entrance may have to tell the ranger where they are headed, since this is a holding area for cave tours.

You may be surprised on this walk at how you can meander a couple of hundred yards from the spot where most of Carlsbad Cavern's 800,000 yearly visitors gather, and suddenly find yourself wrapped in the peace and quiet of the Chihuahuan Desert. The ravine you'll be following (Bat Draw) derives its name from the fantastic explosion of Mexican free-tailed bats that pour out of the cavern entrance most evenings from May to October. Hundreds of thousands of these nimble fliers spin out of the cave like a small cyclone, always flying out counterclockwise, then pouring down this dry land for the insect-laden banks of the Black and Pecos rivers. The amphitheater on your left at the beginning of our walk is devoted to this spectacle. Each evening, other than during inclement weather, a short interpretive talk is given before the free-tails pour out of the cavern to begin their all-night forays. Mexican free-tails live at the highest population density of any mammal in the world. Adults will typically form cozy roost packs of 1,800 animals to the square yard!

It was these bats, or more correctly the feces or *guano* they produce, that brought the first Europeans into this largest of North American caves. Guano is a valuable, nitrate-rich fertilizer and

Mexican Free-tailed Bat

collections here during the first two decades of this century ended up on farm crops throughout the country. It was not until almost 1920 that tourists began coming here in earnest; the earliest were lowered two at a time into the cavern in large metal buckets. Though this cavern system has been explored thoroughly since it became a park in 1930, there are still stories yet untold. Another passageway was just discovered in 1987; as of this writing, its full course is still unknown.

The old entrance road you're following is through a fine mat of Chihuahuan Desert vegetation. You'll see plenty of soaptree yucca, recognizable from the curled white fibers on the edges of its leaves. Also here is a small evergreen tree known as one-seed juniper, as well as snakeweed, algerita, catclaw acacia (watch out for the thorns!), and Engelmann prickly pear. The large purple fruits visible on the prickly pear during late summer are known as *tunas;* hence the common name of tuna cactus. They are quite tasty, though over the last hundred years they have shifted from a mainstay of desert Indian people into a novelty candy and jelly business. An abundance of prickly pear, along with snakeweed and Russian thistle, can be an indication that the land has been over-grazed. Since in many areas outside these park lands overgrazing is the rule rather than the exception, prickly pear continues to claim new territory each year. At about 0.5 mile the path branches left, marked by a sign and a series of rock cairns (small rock piles used as trail markers). From here you'll follow a shallow ravine with a ridge of land on your right that will drop away as you reach the 1-mile point.

From the flat ridge top at 1 mile, high on a 400-mile-long ancient ocean reef, you'll be afforded an expansive view of a vast dry tableland, with only the mighty Guadalupe Mountains check-ing the long drift of desert far to the southwest. Not far from here the Overland mail stage bounced its way west from St. Louis to California, the desert dust and wind licking at its wooden wheels. Here also were outlaws, some lurking in the caves that dot this reef, and some, like Blackjack Ketchum, riding fast on lathered, thirsty horses in mad dashes for the Mexican border.

To the north and east of where you now stand was the domain of Henry McCarty, or, as his gravestone in the old Fort Sumner cemetery declares, "alias Billy the Kid." By the time

Black-tailed Jack Rabbit

Sheriff Pat Garrett gunned Billy down in a dark room at the age of 22, he had amassed an amazing reputation. At least one eastern newspaper painted him as a dashing outlaw dressed in black buckskin and silver bells, sporting $300 jewel-bedecked hats. But, as a the special correspondent to the St. Louis *Globe Democrat* wrote from Lamy, New Mexico, after the Kid's death in 1881, "He needs no bogus silver spurs stuck on his heels by a Philadelphia scribbler to send him galloping down to a bloody and dare-devilish immortality in the annals of this strange, wild territory. The simple story of his hideous career would fill a volume written in letters of fire and blood, and give a better idea than all the inventions of pen-and-ink extravaganzas of a thousand correspondents, of the desperadoism that has for years cursed New Mexico and retarded the development of the richest region on the continent."

RATTLESNAKE SPRINGS

Distance: 0.3 mile
Location: Head south out of Carlsbad, New Mexico, on U.S. Highway 62/180, for approximately 24 miles to County Road 418. Turn right and follow signs to Rattlesnake Springs Picnic Area. Park in space provided adjacent to the restrooms.

Whether you've never seen a true desert oasis before or have spent half your life rambling from one water hole to the next, you'll find Rattlesnake Springs to be one of the finest, most enchanting places that a trickle of water has ever given birth to. The distance to be covered barely qualifies this as a walk at all. But there is so much to be seen here, such a rich, tightly woven tapestry of life, that even a hundred yards can take the better part of an hour.

In particular, this is a place for birds of all feathers. The small unit of land surrounding the spring, as well as the picnic area where you parked, form a small sub-unit of Carlsbad Caverns National Park. This is co-managed with a 14-acre parcel immediately to the south owned by the Nature Conservancy; together they provide critical habitat for several of the more than 250 species that have been sighted in the immediate area. This is the only breeding area in the entire state for eastern bluebirds and orchard orioles; the latter can sometimes be seen in the branches of the plains cottonwoods so common to the area. Perhaps new to your New Mexico bird list will be the Bell's vireo, often quite willing to entertain your curiosity, and the varied bunting; either may be seen in the mesquite thickets surrounding the oasis.

From the parking area, walk west on the dirt road and pass through a National Park Service gate at the far end of the picnic ground. The land to your left contains a lush mix of plains cottonwoods, black willow, and a virtual jungle of sunflowers in late summer. To the right is a beautiful grove of Russian olives. This was a tree frequently planted throughout the Southwest as a windbreak, which ultimately escaped the civilized life and has since done quite well on its own. Just beyond this grove to the north, as if an invisible climate line had been drawn, lie the northern reaches of the Chihuahuan Desert. Here is a much more measured collection of life that includes mesquite, princes plume, little-leaf desert sumac, feather dahlia, western soapberry and catclaw acacia.

Because the Chihuahuan Desert experiences slightly greater precipitation and cooler temperatures than other deserts of the Southwest, you'll find more grasses here than you might expect (at least in areas where they haven't been grazed out of existence).

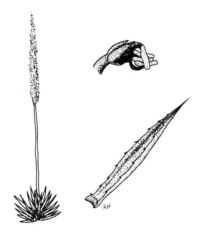

Lechuguilla

213

There are also more agaves, particularly the lechuguilla. This plant, practically the trademark of the Chihuahuan Desert, was used by desert Indians to make sandals, mats, and baskets. Because it may take more than 15 years for a lechuguilla to store enough food to launch its towering 6- to 10-foot flower stalk, you'll never see all the plants in one area flying their beautiful lemon blossoms in the same season. Beautiful as it is during bloom, this is not a plant to tangle with; its pointed leaves can easily puncture an automobile tire.

Visible to the north through the thick line of vegetation is towering Capitan Reef. This is a massive, 400-mile-long precipice made up of billions of marine plant and animal skeletons deposited here by ancient oceans more than 200 million years ago, then cemented together by a thick crust of lime. Soaring on the desert thermals that routinely rise along this wall are turkey vultures, those unsufferably homely but tremendously graceful birds that make a most sensible living off of dead flesh. Rattlesnake Springs is an important stopover for turkey vultures migrating south in the fall.

Soon you'll come to a Park Service residence on the right, just past Rattlesnake Springs itself—a beautiful rock-lined pool built by Civilian Conservation Corps workers in the 1930s, fringed on the south and east by thick curtains of Johnson grass. These springs provide the 28,000 gallons of water used each day in Carlsbad Caverns National Park.

Globemallow

214

Return to the picnic area the way you came. If you're interested in getting to know more of the feathered residents of Rattlesnake Springs, take a right past the Park Service gate at the west end of the picnic ground, and then another right on a small trail leaving from a set of corrals. You can stroll for about 60 yards along the Nature Conservancy wetlands—a wonderful spot to see long-billed marsh wrens, vireos, vermilion flycatchers, and perhaps even a green heron. If you do cross the fence into this area, do not in any way disturb the marsh. Sitting along this path in the cool shade of a plains cottonwood, the air thick with bird song and the flash of colored feathers, is a rare, delicious treat—one more of the Chihuahuan Desert's many surprises.

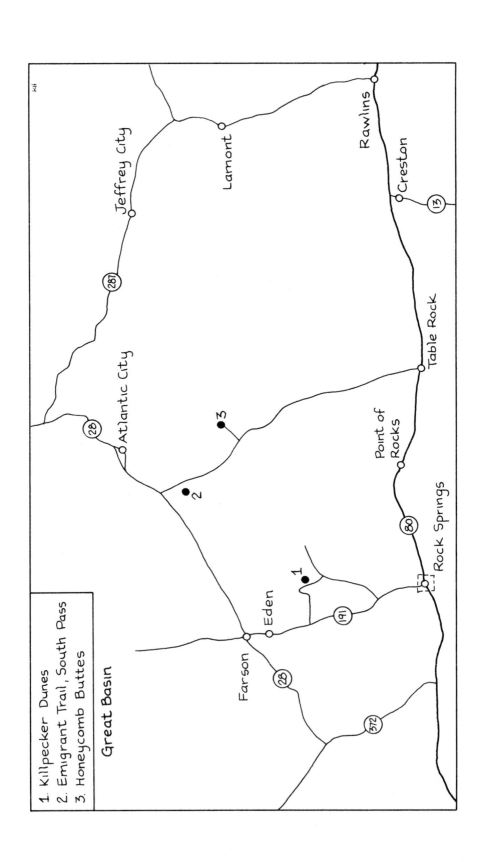

1. Killpecker Dunes
2. Emigrant Trail, South Pass
3. Honeycomb Buttes

Great Basin

Great Basin

KILLPECKER DUNES

Distance: 3.2 miles
Location: Head north out of Rock Springs on U.S. Highway 191. Go 0.3 mile past mile marker 10 and turn east onto Sweetwater County Road 17. (There is a sign marking this turnoff as "Tri-Territory Site.") Continue on Sweetwater County 17 for 15.4 miles and make a left turn. Continue on this road for 6.3 miles, to a small two-track road taking off to the right. Drive to the end of this road and park beside an old railroad bed, approximately 0.65 mile from your last turn. Begin the walk by heading north (left) on the railroad bed.

This walk, through a long, lonely reach of Wyoming desert, follows the bed of an old railroad built 30 years ago to haul iron ore from the Atlantic City Mine. Although much of the area you will be traversing is currently under study for wilderness designation, very few people ever come to this windswept quilt of sage and sand. The dunes you'll see here, the majority of which lie to the east and north of this walk, are just a small slice of a sandy field that stretches from Idaho all the way into the Sand Hills of Nebraska—making them second in size only to the dune fields of the Sahara.

The further you immerse yourself into this environment, the more incredible it becomes. There are secret draws running into great hummocks of bare blond sand, where one can easily imagine being adrift in the wilds of Arabia. During the winter, larger fields of ice and snow accumulate along the lee side of the dunes. The blowing wind eventually covers these fields with an insulating blanket of sand, forming what is known as an eolian ice cell. These cells, located throughout the Killpecker Dunes, release their cool cargo through the summer into small ponds that dot the area. Because of this unique phenomenon, you'll find a surprising variety of waterfowl here, as well as mule deer, and the only desert elk herd in Wyoming.

Bobcats, mountain lions, coyotes, red foxes, and kangaroo rats also live in this wild maze of stone and sand, and patient explorers will find many of their tracks in the moist soils that surround the ponds. (As for the Ord's kangaroo rat, on a hot day you should look for small burrow entrances that have been plugged with earth; such coverings are used by the animal to regulate temperature and humidity inside the burrow.) A special thrill here is to glimpse a band of wild horses running through the sage, flying their manes in the desert wind. There are approximately 1,500 wild horses in this region, which represent roughly 60 percent of Wyoming's total number of these animals.

As you climb from the parking area up to the old railroad bed, notice the towering, pointed butte off to the east. This is a volcanic plug known as the Boar's Tusk, uncovered over countless millennia as the relentless forces of wind and water peeled the softer rock from around it, leaving broad, sage-covered valleys at its rocky feet.

Turning to the north, you'll begin your walk through a

Mountain Lion

218

broken carpet of big sagebrush, greasewood, and rabbitbrush. The sagebrush and greasewood are special favorites of the pronghorn, which you may see grazing in scattered bands across the flat lands. These beautiful animals, with their brilliant white rump hairs that can be raised to alert other members of the herd to danger, are the best runners on the continent. They are remarkably fast, able to achieve speeds of 70 miles per hour. But sometimes even more important to their survival is their endurance. Most pronghorn are able to lope along at 30 miles per hour for more than 15 miles, a pace that will leave even the most determined predator with its tongue hanging in the dust. Add a pair of eyes that can spot movement miles away, a need for very little sleep, and the ability

Pronghorn

to eat almost anything that grows (including cactus), and you've got one of the truly great survivors of the American West.

Several ponds can be found along this walk. One of the first ones of substantial size is located on your right about 0.5 mile into the walk. Notice the carpets of saltgrass lining the fringes of these water pockets, which for part of the year sport a beautiful cloak of gold. In another 0.5 mile on the left is a fine water pocket lined with reed grasses and Baltic rush. Those who approach quietly may see a small flock of mallards floating here in the summer sun. The ponds that pepper the Killpecker Dune vary greatly in size and range in depth from several inches to 8 feet. Some are quite sterile, whereas others support a wide range of life, including tiger salamanders, tadpoles, and freshwater shrimp in the deeper pools. The best time to see tiger salamanders, which are the largest land-dwelling salamanders in the world, is late in the evening after a good rain.

After 1 mile you'll actually enter the wilderness study area, marked on both sides of the road by small brown signposts. In 0.3 more mile is an excellent covey of pools on the right side of the railroad bed, framed to the east by a tapestry of sand dunes and grassy bluffs. This is an excellent place to leave the railroad bed and do some serious rambling in this amazing environment. Work your way back 0.2 mile or so to the fringes of the dune fields. Walk up the quiet draws. Notice how the drooping heads of the bunch-grasses trace lazy circles in the warm sand. Look for the tracks of harvest mice and short-horned lizards, and for shore birds, who often come here to feed along the edges of these cool, clear pools of water. Slowly make your way cross-country toward the south, rejoining the railroad bed near where you parked your car.

EMIGRANT TRAIL, SOUTH PASS

Distance: 1.5 miles

Location: Head east on Wyoming Highway 28 to the Continental Divide, which is marked by a sign along the road. Shortly after this sign, 0.25 mile east of mile marker 33, turn right (south) onto Sweetwater Country Road 74. In 2.9 miles you'll cross a small, two-track road. Park here and begin your walk along this road to the west.

If there is one walk in all the American West that feeds a fantastic array of historical fantasies, one route thick with daydreams of the dramas that were staged there would have to be the Oregon Trail. For more than two decades, families, farmers, gold seekers, politicians, preachers, and prostitutes rolled across these 2,000 miles of trail on their way to new beginnings. They came by horse, by mule, by trail wagon, and by foot. Some would recount it as the greatest adventure of their lives, while others were destined to return to the East by the same route, convinced that the tales of milk and honey that drove them to the West were lies. Still others would never make it, ending up in crude, shallow graves along the trail—victims of disease, exhaustion, or the wrath of Indians.

In the long, arduous journey from Independence, Missouri, to Oregon City, in Oregon's Willamette River Valley, South Pass was a breath of fresh air. No route offered an easier crossing of that high spine of the Rocky Mountains known as the Continental Divide. In fact, many emigrants didn't realize they had crossed the divide at all until someone gave a joyous shout at setting eyes on Pacific Creek several miles west of here, realizing that its waters were flowing west instead of east.

The actual discovery of this important pass came along before the first of 350,000 westbound emigrants began cutting wagon ruts through these fields of sage. In the early 1880s, the great financier John Jacob Astor had attempted to dip his fingers into the money pots of the fur trade by buying the Canadian North West Company, which the owners flatly refused to sell. Undaunted, Astor launched an all-out effort to capture the fur trade of the entire western sector of the continent. He kicked things off with a rather ill-fated exploration of the West led by Wilson Price

Hunt. Another one of Astor's men, Robert Stuart, returning from the west coast with important dispatches, inadvertently stumbled across the route that would eventually become South Pass. It would be 14 years before the first wheeled vehicle rolled across this route, and 30 years before wagons full of emigrants began crossing it in earnest.

So exceptional was this route that it was shared by several westbound trails. In 1847, Mormons began streaming across the pass bound for Utah, fleeing persecution in the East. A year later, when gold was discovered at Sutter's Mill in California, thousands of eager miners headed over South Pass for the Golden State. Still a dozen years further down the road, the Pony Express mail route began using South Pass on the courageous, galloping horseback rides to carry mail between California and Missouri. A station for the Pony Express lies just a few miles west of here at Pacific Springs.

As you begin your walk west along this short stretch of the Emigrant Trail, on your left will be the Oregon Buttes, a set of rugged, dome-shaped towers rising from this high, flat tableland. This area is a favorite nesting site for raptors, so keep your eyes to the sky for soaring golden eagles and red-tailed hawks. Also common along this road are several large, round dens that serve as homes for coyotes and foxes. Like the raptors, they too are here to dine on the plethora of mice and ground squirrels that frequent these lonely reaches of the high desert.

About 0.25 mile into the walk, you can look off to your right (north) and see the ramparts of the Wind River Range, one of the most beautiful of all the western mountains. In the middle 1800s, the famed explorer John Charles Fremont climbed one of the higher peaks, which now bears his name. Like most of the mountains of the Rockies, this one saw an influx of miners pouring into the area with hopes of finding riches in its granite folds. It was in part the stampede to this area, along with an amazing influx of workers who came to build the Union Pacific Railroad line, that led the residents of the region to press for a territory to be called Wyoming, which was granted in 1869. Unfortunately, neither hopes for gold at South Pass nor the railroad construction jobs lasted very long. Just a year later, most of the newcomers had moved on, leaving the entire territory with a scant 9,000 people.

At 0.75 mile you'll enter a fenced area with two markers in the center—one for the Oregon Trail, and the other commemorating the first European women to cross the pass in 1836. You can continue walking this stretch for several miles, but we'll make this our turnaround point. It's the perfect place to grab a seat next to a clump of sagebrush and cast your thoughts out onto the Wyoming winds. How amazing all this must have looked from the seat of a buckboard 140 years ago. What a strange mixture of feelings were surely brewing in the families that had come so far—feelings of fear, of hope, of sheer exhilaration for the lands that lay ahead to the west.

HONEYCOMB BUTTES

Distance: 4.8 miles
Location: Exit Interstate 80 to Bar X Road, located approximately 46 miles east of Rock Springs, Wyoming. Proceed north on Sweetwater County Road 21 for 41.9 miles, where you'll turn right (north) onto Sweetwater County Road 74, following the sign toward Oregon Buttes. From this intersection 4.3 miles, take a faint road heading off to the right (northeast). Drive 2.5 miles (stay left at the fork 0.6 mile in) to a large wash at Bear Creek. Park here and continue walking to the northeast on the same road. Do not attempt this drive after a rain!
Note: Continue north along County Road 74 past Oregon Buttes to reach the Oregon Trail walk described on page 221.

If you're up for a trek through country so wide and lonely that it can leave you feeling like the only person on earth, then Honeycomb Buttes is definitely the place for you. Here wild horses still thunder across the bunchgrass plains and large herd of pronghorn huddle in the sagebrush. Golden eagles and red-tailed hawks hang on the desert winds, attentions fiercely tuned to the ground below for the tiny flash of a grasshopper mouse or kangaroo rat. The Buttes, visible to your left as you begin the walk, are a complex maze of sharply eroded shale canyons where, at least in modern times, very few human feet have trod.

This little-known tract of land is a part of the Red Desert, in turn cradled by the warm windswept arms of the Great Divide Basin. This basin is the unique product of a split in the Continental Divide that occurs to the southeast, one branch of its rocky spine running past Rawlins, and the other heading toward Pacific Springs to the west. Although most of us were taught in geography class that raindrops falling on the slopes of the Continental Divide either go to the Gulf of Mexico or the Pacific Ocean, such is not the case here. No raindrop, no snowflake, no stream leaves this basin. Were the climate to change even slightly toward the wet side, this would once again be an inland sea.

To your left along the first section of this walk are fine views of Continental Peak on the left and the Oregon Buttes to the north, the latter once a prominent landmark to pioneers on the Oregon Trail. On the far horizon, 40 miles to the north, lies the mighty, snow-capped massif of the Wind River Range. The

Burrowing Owl

plant life along the first 0.5 mile of this road is a loosely woven mat of rabbitbrush, sage, and greasewood, as well as a mix of wheatgrasses and prairie cordgrass. It was this latter tall, stout plant that fueled many of the overly optimistic mid-nineteenth century reports that this region was a paradise, with grass growing "high as a horse's belly."

At 0.6 mile the road begins to deteriorate into a layer of cracked bentonite, a no-nonsense sign that this is the last place on earth you should be with a car after a good thunder shower. Around this area you'll pass through a small depression where water routinely accumulates, partly due to a clay lining beneath the topsoil that keeps it from percolating into the earth. These playas, as they're called, are easy to spot because of the conspicuous lack of sagebrush, which is quite intolerant of saturated soil. When they occur as large tracts lined with carpets of bunch and wheatgrasses, dry playas can look remarkably like slices of the Serengeti Plain, shimmering in the summer sun.

Continue along this road until you reach the North Fork drainage, approximately 1.4 miles into the hike. From here we'll leave the road, working our way along the streambed for about 1 mile, to a quiet, windswept amphitheater of red and gray shale. There are countless nooks and crannies in this soft-shouldered maze, each one serving up solitude in portions that few of us are used to receiving. There is growing support for making portions of the Red Desert into wilderness, a proposition that seems more likely to happen now than a few years ago, when energy prospectors combed these flats and draws.

There are those who continue to think of this area as a veritable wasteland; one government official, in fact, suggested that it was "the perfect place for a nuclear waste dump." But as we continue to fill the long reaches of the West with progress, we will need more and more of these spare, lonely places, these subtle flows of rock and sky. In some ways it is here, and not at the shores of blue alpine lakes, that we find the real essence of wildness—a polished mirror of sorts, reflecting a face quite different from the one we have grown accustomed to seeing.

PRAIRIES

The eternal illimitable sweep of the undulating prairie im-
pressed on me a sense of vastness quite overwhelming. . . . I
know not when I have felt so forcibly conscious of my own
insignificance, as when struggling through this immense
waste, and feeling as though I were suddenly carried back-
ward into some remote and long past age, and as though I
were encroaching on the territories of the Mammoth and the
Mastodon.

—JOHN PALLISER
Solitary Rambles and Adventures
of a Hunter in the Prairies, 1853

While many people have learned to enjoy the subtle beauty of the deserts—their quiet vastness, their shimmering, secret pockets of colored blossoms and textured sandstones—the lands that make up our prairies have, for the most part, gone unnoticed. Indeed, a hundred years ago these great expanses of grass were themselves known as deserts. They were areas that would never be settled—places to get across, to endure on the way to somewhere else, like the rich valleys of Oregon and California or the gold fields of Colorado and western Montana. The elk, pronghorn, and bison, the teams of migrating bird life that were supported by these rich mats of grasses and forbs—numbers rivaling those of any plains region on earth—were no more than curiosities. Hundreds of thousands were shot for sport from passing trains or by dudes on horseback looking for nothing more than the thrill of killing.

In the mid-nineteenth century, cattle were driven to the northern prairies from Texas to get fat on the lush grasses. Fifty years later, eager to fill the last empty spaces of the West, people swarmed to the prairies to homestead. Unfortunately, homestead laws required that a certain number of acres of each parcel be put into crops, and so for the first time, many of America's most fragile grasslands felt the sting of the steel plow. A particular problem was the size of the homestead grants. Settlers were at first given 160 acres, which was later increased to 320. Still, this was hardly enough in a land that required 40 acres to manage a single cow. Overgrazing was soon the norm.

Meanwhile, the Native Americans, who had lived along these braids of cool, quiet water in these rich, hauntingly beautiful grasslands for thousands of years, watched civilization roll west. Helpless to stop it, they were angry at those who would engineer such a conquest of Mother Earth. Above all the land's bounties, the Plains Indians especially revered the grasses, since they regularly brought bison, elk, pronghorn, deer, and birds. Despite relentless efforts to turn reservation Plains Indians into farmers, many would have none of it, believing it total madness to tear into the living skin of a land that had sustained them for so many generations.

The retribution that many tribes believed would happen to those who took the land for granted did occur. In the 1930s, a fatal mixture of overgrazing, plowing, and drought turned living carpets of prairie grasses into millions of acres of blowing dust and hummocks of sand. Street lights burned all day long in the darkened streets. Layer after layer of Colorado dust settled onto the Capitol in Washington, D.C., and onto decks of ships 300 miles out in the Atlantic Ocean.

In themselves, the fantastic storms of the dust-bowl days were not unprecedented. The prairie was, in fact, built by wind-borne soil, which over countless millennia accumulated in the central plains to depths of several hundred feet. What had changed at the hand of humans were the conditions under which such events would occur. Removing the plants that covered the prairie was like "turning up the volume" of the already mighty wind. Instead of conquering the West, we suddenly found ourselves more vulnerable than ever to one of its greatest forces.

When Resettlement Association agents arrived to buy up the worst of the homesteader's lands, they found that many had already left, totally abandoning their homes and goods. Some were seen driving cars or trucks piled high with possessions west to California; others, either without cars or money to fuel them, walked by the sides of the roads, hoping for a ride to anywhere. The government appropriated moneys to acquire these lands, either by outright purchase—typically $2 per acre—or by simple payment of delinquent taxes. (By 1930, almost 70 percent of the plains homesteaders were delinquent on their taxes.) The lands were slowly restored by the Soil Conservation Service through the seeding of crested wheatgrass, along with windbreak and erosion control projects. These "land utilization projects," or, as they were later known, "national grasslands," remained in the hands of the government, which today manages them primarily for grazing and energy development.

Belts of grassland, or former grasslands, actually cover a good portion of the United States. One stretches from Illinois to the eastern sections of the Rocky Mountain states. Another is found between the Rockies and the Sierras and Cascades, and yet another occupies the central and certain coastal sections of California. For the purposes of this book, however, we'll confine ourselves to discussions of the shortgrass and, to a lesser extent, the mixed-grass prairies of the Rocky Mountain states.

As a plant type, grasses began to evolve more than 75 million years ago. They developed in intriguing ways, bringing into the world new methods of dealing with the problems that plague all plants growing in this type of environment. For one thing, the root systems of grasses, especially perennials, tend to make up a very large portion of their total biomass—more, in fact, than a comparable area of forest. These roots allow the plant to tap into water resources lying far below the ground. In addition, since these roots store large amounts of energy, they can easily send up new growth once they had been clipped by grazing animals. Having relatively small leaves reduces the amount of moisture lost through transpiration, and their long, narrow shape allows the strong winds here to flow through without damaging them.

The types of grasses that make up the prairie lands are surprisingly complex. Some are perennials (lasting several years with deep root systems), while others are shallow-rooted annuals.

Annuals, which conduct their business and set seed all in one season, have been able to increase their numbers as the land continues to suffer from erosion and overgrazing. Some grasses, such as blue grama, put out runners that form sod, a trait tending to keep other species from invading their territory. Others, especially those in drier areas, grow in well-spaced bunches. Some prairie grasses conduct photosynthesis in the spring and fall, whereas their neighbors do most of their work through the heat of summer.

Shortly after grasses arrived in the world, animals evolved to take advantage of the bounty they offered. A quick look around the prairie will give you good clues to the attributes that are most appropriate for survival here. Hard to miss is the fact that grasslands offer few places to hide. Thus, if you are a ground bird, an appropriate amount of camouflage will come in handy, as the prairie chicken or savannah sparrow so aptly demonstrate. If you can't blend in, then head underground, like prairie dogs, moles, and ground squirrels. If even that is not an option, then be prepared to run, as the pronghorn that range these vast expanses are most definitely able to do. What's more, pronghorn are armed with extremely good eyesight. In fact, if you can get a close look at one through a pair of binoculars, you'll notice that the eye sockets form the highest part of their skeletal frames—traits that allow them to see the farthest distance possible.

Although prairies have been ravaged as completely as any environment in the West, those who take the time to tramp the last of them will find them to be a rich, fascinating environment. Like the great herds of bison that pushed their way across these lonely lands, life here still seems to ebb and flow in great, unfettered waves. Light washes over the land in blankets of blue and rose, fading at last to darkness; birds rise and fall in clatters of beating wings, and are gone.

Northeast New Mexico–
Southeast Colorado

MILLS CANYON OVERLOOK

Distance: 3.6 miles
Location: From U.S. Highway 56, head south on New Mexico
Route 39 for approximately 14 miles. South of mile marker
125, 0.8 mile, a signed road will take off to the west toward the
Mills Canyon Campground. From this turn in 5.4 miles you'll
see a windmill on the right (north) side of the road. Continue
past this for 0.6 more mile (a total, then, of 6 miles from New
Mexico Route 39) and park. If you look off to the south you'll
see a small two-track road heading up the side of a hill on the
other side of a wash, perhaps 50 yards from where you're
parked. This is our walking road.

Mills Canyon is a beautiful interruption in the otherwise smooth,
gently undulating prairie. The old stock roadway leading to the
rim, the first 50 yards now reclaimed by shortgrass, is a classic
middle-of-nowhere walk, where the sheer enormity of land and sky
tends to shepherd you into an unhurried, contemplative cadence.

This mental drifting is made all the more delightful by
knowing that you are walking very close to the Cimarron Cut-off
branch of the old Santa Fe Trail. Though drier than the original
mountain passage to the north, the Cimarron Cut-off was substan-
tially shorter and flatter, two attributes that quickly turned it into a
principal route of passage. Once you've gained the first ridge on
this walk, turn around and look across the vast prairie to the southeast. What an incredible sight those long lines of blue-painted
Conestoga freight wagons must have made, their iron-tired wooden
wheels creaking along beneath the weight of brightly colored mack-
inaw blankets, metal tools and bolts of calico and silk, the sound of

233

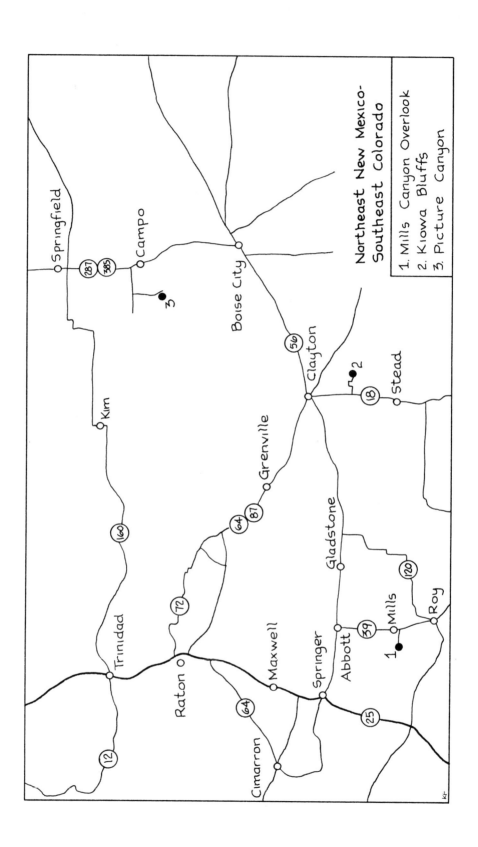

Northeast New Mexico-
Southeast Colorado

1. Mills Canyon Overlook
2. Kiowa Bluffs
3. Picture Canyon

the bullwhacker's whip snapping in the hot, dry air.

Two plants you'll see in fair abundance during the short descent to the wash are gumweed and snakeweed, the latter with clusters of small yellow flowers growing on shrubby, narrow-leafed stems, and the former with one-inch-wide disk flowers surrounded by sticky, curled green bracts. Both plants thrive on disturbed or overgrazed land. The thousands of acres of snakeweed growing on some of the ranges in this area in late summer are testimony to the general decline in the quality of this land over the past century, since years of overgrazing have destroyed the mat of buffalo and grama grasses that once made up the shortgrass prairie.

Working your way up the hill on the other side of the wash, perhaps 100 yards into the walk, you'll find a couple of places where the road is very faint. Once on top of the ridge, however, the track becomes easy to follow again, and remains so for the rest of the walk. As you move west, the land is dotted with cream-colored blackfoot daisies and the soft lavenders of rough blazing stars. Also noticeable is an increase in the number of pinyon and both one-seed and Rocky Mountain juniper, huddling in greater and greater concentrations. At just under a mile into the walk, you'll find yourself in a virtual forest of "p–j," as it's known throughout the Southwest. Also growing in this area is an abundance of wavy-leaf oak, with its shiny blue–green leaves, scattered bunches of blue grama and buffalo grass, and several narrowleaf yuccas. Yuccas have evolved by an amazing dependency on a certain genus of moth as their sole source of pollination. The moth begins the process by collecting pollen from several yucca plants. She then proceeds to a plant, inserts her ovipositor, and deposits her eggs next into the plant's ovary. The moth actually places the pollen she collected earlier on the stigma of the flower, thus ensuring that the plant's seeds will grow, which will in turn provide food for the larvae of her offspring. This is surely one of the most fascinating cases of mutual cooperation in all the natural world.

Also growing in the more open areas along this stretch of the walk will be a few milkweed plants. These are especially easy to recognize once they acquire their pods, which eventually split open on one side to release thousands of silky winged seeds. Milkweed contains toxic chemicals that are actually related to several of the

235

Gumweed

Rough Blazing Star

drugs used in treating heart disease. When monarch butterflies, which eat nothing but milkweed leaves, consume these chemicals, they become toxic to any bird that eats them. What a novel way to avoid ending up as an in-flight dinner for some feathered predator!

In 1.8 miles the road reaches the lip of Mills Creek Canyon. You can see the beautiful Canadian River (thought to be a corruption of *kanohatino*, a Caddo Indian word for "red river") 700 feet below, flowing beneath sheer, crumbling red and buff-colored cliffs. It was after trying to find the source of this river system that Zebulon Pike, for whom Pike's Peak was named, was interned briefly by Spanish soldiers in 1807. He was later swiftly escorted out of Spanish territory and turned loose in the middle of nowhere in southeast Texas. Today Mills Canyon seems far removed from territorial power struggles. Somehow it has kept at least a shred of the tranquility that must have been here long ago when Kiowa Indians led their ponies beneath these warm brown walls, gathering fish, game, and fruits.

KIOWA BLUFFS

Distance: 3.6 miles
Location: Head south on New Mexico Route 18 out of Clay-ton for approximately 11 miles. South of mile marker 362, 0.6 mile, turn left (east) onto a gravel road. In 3 miles this road will make a sharp turn to the north, and in another mile a sharp turn back east. From this second turn proceed east for 2 miles to a smaller dirt track that takes off to the right (south). Follow this road for 0.6 mile to an east–west fence line. A windmill will be on your left. Try to park on the west side of the road without blocking the gate. Our walk takes off on an old roadway run-ning southeast from this spot. To reach it you will have to cross through the gate on the east–west fence, and then cross the north–south fence on your left.

On the whole, managers of the national grasslands tend to meet the couple of hundred inquiries they receive from hikers each year with some skepticism, fairly certain that only a handful of people would really appreciate a day or two ambling across these vast, empty spaces. And, with few or no facilities, difficult-to-navigate road systems, and the general lack of water, perhaps they're right. Yet I found walking the prairie to be wonderful. Lightly rolling oceans of grass and forbs stretch forever in every direction, stroked by the ever-present fingers of the wind. In spring the land is peppered with the reds, lavenders, and yellows of globemallow, daisies, and buttercups, while in late summer and early fall it explodes with miles of smiling sunflowers. And all around there is sky. Sometimes it appears soft and tranquil, other times fierce. But always it floods the senses with its sheer enormity. It is the undisputed master of the scene, the caller of the tune to which, season after season, the prairie must dance.

While there are almost no true native prairie mixes left in this part of the country (or in most other parts, for that matter), this walk does give you a good sense of how diverse grasslands can really be. The sand bluffs we'll be meandering through in the latter part of the walk are particularly significant in that, despite ravages to this country from drought and overgrazing a half century ago, this slice of land is in very good shape. In fact, it supports the only bluestem climax community to be found for many miles, making it as close to the real old West prairie as you're likely to see.

As you make your way to the bluff area, about 0.8 mile from where you parked, you'll be passing through a thick mat of vegetation, indicative of the fact that the 15 or so inches of rain that fall here each year are sufficient to maintain a rich community of

Tahoka Daisy

Common Buttercup

plants. Look for a mixture of side-oats and blue grama grasses, as well as prairie shoestring, snakeweed, groundsel, and narrowleaf yucca. As for the prairie fliers, you should be able to spot kingbirds, rough-winged swallows, brown thrashers, mockingbirds, logger-head shrikes, lark buntings, northern orioles, horned larks, mag-pies, western meadowlarks, and, if you drive along these roads in the summer, wave after wave of lark sparrows. Grasslands can be especially beautiful to the ear, since the birds who live in these open spaces tend to let loose their territorial songs while flying—something that the birds of the forest rarely do.

Besides the above birds, which feed on the bounty of seeds and insects of the prairie, the Forest Service currently has plans to reintroduce the prairie chicken into this area. This beautiful bird once numbered in the millions, ranging from Texas into Canada, and eastward all the way to Ohio. Indeed, they were so numerous that early settlers could often bring down several birds with a single shot. Many are the old reports of the prairie chicken courtship rituals that occurred each year. The birds danced, flashed their tail feathers, inflated orange air sacks on either side of their necks, and of course "boomed," producing a low, dull roar that floated through the crisp February air, often being heard a mile or more away. These mating theatrics took place on special stages, or "booming grounds," which some researchers believe were used over and over, perhaps for several hundred years.

Lark Sparrow

239

One of the most striking creatures of the Western grasslands is the pronghorn, which you may see grazing on the lands surrounding this walk. To say that pronghorns are remarkable is a gross understatement. It is the fastest mammal in the western hemisphere, having been clocked running 70 miles per hour for several minutes. A distance runner as well as a sprinter, it can maintain slower speeds of 30 to 40 miles per hour, for 15 miles at a time, tending to leave many of its predators panting in the dust. (Fawns can run at speeds in excess of 25 miles per hour when they are just 2 weeks old!) Pronghorn can exist comfortably with little or no water, getting what they need from the plants they eat. These plants tend to include all of those that other animals won't touch, even several thorny and poisonous varieties. Both male and female pronghorns have black horns, the sheath of which is shed each year. Those of the female, however, will rarely grow more then 4 inches long, whereas the male's often reach more than 1 foot. During danger the animals can stiffen the glistening white hair on their rump patches, an act serving as a bold warning sign to other animals to shift into high gear. (Pronghorn are often referred to as antelope, which they definitely are not. Unique to North America, they have been given their own family name, Antilocapridae, which translates into "antelope-goat.")

Once into the sandy bluff area, you'll see a fine collection of sand and little bluestem grasses. At 1.7 miles, before our turnaround point at a windmill, an old gnarled tree stands stark against a wash of sky, the only one visible anywhere on this rolling sea of grass, shrubs, and forbs. The tales of heartbreak on this prairie during the 1930s would fill volumes—hopes and dreams of building a solid, independent life on an American homestead shattered by severe drought, overgrazing, and the plowing of thousands of acres that were never meant to sustain intensive farming. In the early 1930s, this county needed 84 schools to serve its ballooning population; today it needs only 3. The scant remains of these sad times— abandoned homes, mineral-poor lands overrun with snakeweed, parched windmill towers creaking in the prairie winds—still can be seen along many of the region's back roads. They are a sober reminder of how fragile our dance with nature really is, how easily this intricate tapestry can come unraveled in careless hands.

Western Box Turtle

PICTURE CANYON

Distance: 3.2 miles

Location: Take U.S. Highway 287/385 south out of Springfield, Colorado. Turn right (west) just past mile marker 13, at a sign marking the turn for a Comanche National Grassland Picnic Area. Proceed west for 8.2 miles, turning left just past a cattle guard onto County Road 18. Go south for another 8.2 miles on this road. A small house will be on your left, with a two-track dirt road on the opposite side, heading west. Take this small road across the cattle guard (0.4 mile) that marks the boundary of the national grassland. Just past this is a fork in the road; park here and begin walking along the left branch.

The secretary at the Springfield National Grassland Office was just a young girl when the first horrendous storm of the dust bowl unleased its dark, gritty fury on this shortgrass prairie. "We called them the black days," she says of the three-day ordeal. "My older brother was out riding broncs at the rodeo arena when it hit. All the people there just sort of huddled together, thinking that it was the end of the world. Some were crying. A lot were praying." Dust was so thick that it was hard to see your hand in front of your face. Men went around with wet kerchiefs held against their noses and mouths, choking and coughing as they called out the names of brothers or fathers or ranch hands lost in the storm. The nostrils of the range cattle clogged and many ended up dead in piles of dust. "For days we had to keep covers on all our food," recalls the secretary. "To eat we'd stick our hands underneath and grab whatever we could."

Buffalo Grass

Here too, in Picture Canyon, the dust sifted down day after day. Despite the overwhelming odds against them, some of the ranchers in the area were able to hang on, a fact that to this day is a source of immense pride for them. But for others it was too much. When the government came in offering to buy this land from willing homesteaders in order to remove it from further agricultural use, they found that a great many of the farms and ranches had been abandoned, more than a few with pictures still hanging on the walls, with cribs and dressers and wooden dolls, all left to the raging prairie winds.

The road begins in typical eastern Colorado grassland fare, with clumps of blue grama, buffalo, and cheat grasses dotting the

Broom Snakeweed

landscape, as well as snakeweed, narrowleaf yucca, and the sticky yellow heads of gumweed. There is a peaceful tranquility to this walk, as you slowly curl southward toward the the mouth of the canyon, carved flat and wide out of the warm, brown sandstones and shales. Later on the right side of the road you'll see erosion-resistant caprock sitting on top of the sandstone, a feature that offers protection from the ravages of the weather. In places these capstones sit atop striking collections of towers and parapets, a medieval fantasy land, complete with clusters of junipers huddling like green-robed monks in the castle wings.

At 1 mile you'll cross a wash, its surface wet during enough of the year to give rise to moisture-loving plants like willow. Also in this area are blue flax, blazing star, and wild prairie rose. At this wash crossing you should begin listening for the sad lilt of the mourning dove, and, to a lesser extent, the cricket trills of the rock wren. This latter bird has the strange habit of constructing a pathway of small stones that lead up to a well-hidden nest.

In 1.6 miles the road will fork. Stay left and work your way to the base of a long cliff line. Here in this pocket is a small supply of permanent water, giving rise to a tremendous collection of plant life not seen before now. On the lower walls of this is an expansive panel of rock art. Incredibly, ongoing research has given some support to the theory that the vertically incised lines making up a part of this rock-art motif are actually Ogam. Ogam is an ancient language, which perhaps originated in the British Isles. If this is true, the "words" you see on these rocks may have been inscribed 1,500 years ago by a Celtic traveler!

While you're studying the astounding possibilities of this rock panel, notice the rings of mud from old cliff-swallow nests, as well as the frequent signs of woodrats in the narrow, protected crevices. Woodrats (or packrats) are incurable collectors, creating gargantuan nest areas filled with everything from barbed wire to pieces of Indian pottery, shotgun shells to bits of handkerchiefs, rope to leather gloves. Woodrats store large quantities of leaves to sustain them during the winter months. The notion that these animals "trade" an item for one that they take is somewhat misleading; in fact, they load themselves up with so many treasures that they usually have to abandon one in order to gain another.

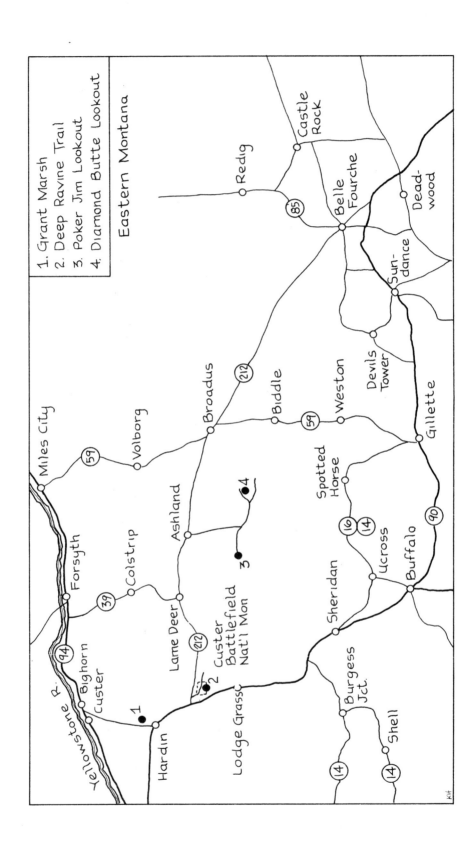

Eastern Montana

1. Grant Marsh
2. Deep Ravine Trail
3. Poker Jim Lookout
4. Diamond Butte Lookout

Eastern Montana

GRANT MARSH

Distance: 1.2 miles
Location: Head north out of Hardin, Montana, on Montana Highway 47 for approximately 7 miles. Go 0.5 mile north of mile marker 7 and turn right (east) at a road signed for Grant Marsh. In 1 mile you'll come to a small, two-track road taking off to the right (south). Turn here, and at the first fork, stay left. In 100 yards you'll come to a T intersection in a large grove of cottonwoods. Park here. The walk begins by heading southwest along the dirt road.
Note: Just after the first fork the road passes through a low spot in the road, which might have water from the marsh lying across it. You may want to get out and check the depth before driving through.

Grant Marsh is one of those little surprises in the middle of nowhere that the road-weary nature buff dreams of finding after a hard day on the asphalt. Framed by the cool, swift, Bighorn River, this is an especially fine place to come during the fall, a pit stop for southbound birds pushed out of Canada by the arrival of winter. The network of shallow pools that exist here, many with thick curtains of reed and cattail spikes drawn across their perimeters, also makes this a good waterfowl breeding area.

Our walk begins in a lovely grove of plains cottonwood trees. The lives of cottonwoods are bound to watercourses and their active floodplains, resulting in the formation not of deep woods but of long, shimmering green lines of woodland painted across the prairie canvas. (Though often extensive, these groves did not seem significant to those who were assessing the land for commercial timber potential. They were, therefore, rarely mentioned by early explorers of the prairie West.) Cottonwoods are famous for their ability to grow rapidly and during the early stage of their lives they may rise several feet each year. Not in the cottonwood's favor, however, is the fact that its seeds have rather stringent requirements in order to take root, and may remain viable only for a couple weeks after being launched from the tree. (Compare this to lodge-pole pine seeds. Locked tightly away in cones that rarely open except during a fire, they may be viable for 40 years!)

Besides providing a great deal of beauty to the prairie rivers they commune with, cottonwoods were very important to the Indians of the northern plains. Among the Cheyenne people, for example, an honored warrior was chosen to select one of these beautiful trees to form the center pole of the lodge used in the sacred Sun Dance Ceremony. Most people familiar with this ritual remember it only for its grueling feats of endurance, in particular, how warriors would hang from poles by strips of rawhide laced into the muscles of their backs and chests. But the "medicine," or visions, that these ceremonies produced were taken very seriously. In fact, it was during the Sun Dance Ceremony of 1876 that Sitting Bull foresaw many dead soldiers "falling right into our camp." Only weeks later, a group of more than 200 U.S. Cavalry men did indeed ride right into a large Indian village where Sitting Bull's people were camped, not far to the south from where you now stand. True to the vision, five companies of 215 men, as well as their leader, General George Armstrong Custer, died that day at the hands of Indian warriors.

Many Indians ate the sweet sap and inner bark of the cottonwood, scraping the latter from the trees with the rib bone of a bison. The buds of the trees produced a beautiful yellow dye that was painted on various articles of clothing, and poultices and teas were made from the leaves, bark, and buds for treating everything from sore muscles to coughs and colds. Warriors of some tribes would rub the sap of the cottonwood on their bodies to mask their scent when stealing horses from enemy camps.

Soon you'll join the Bighorn River, its fast waters running quietly northward to rendezvous with the Yellowstone. (It was at this river junction that General Gibbon crossed the Yellowstone in a rush to aid Custer, only to find Custer and his men already dead for several days on the battlefield.) Lewis and Clark actually named the Bighorn River, as well as the mountains from which it flows, after the regal bighorn sheep, which fascinated them to no end with the graceful way they clambered up and down precipitous cliffs.

The roadway turns to the right and crosses Grant Marsh. Approach this area quietly and you may see green-winged teals floating in the quiet waters, or a red-winged blackbird clutching a cattail spike. Also commonly seen here are migratory American coots, snipes, black terns, and mallard ducks. Just past this marsh is a T intersection. Take a left here and continue along a road lined with kochia. Kochia, sometimes known by locals as fireweed (not the fireweed of the Rocky Mountains), is a tenacious resident of this part of the country. A pest to some, there are ranchers who claim that it offers more nutrition than alfalfa when used as hay.

From this last road junction 0.4 mile you'll reach our turn-around point, on the banks of the Bighorn in a quiet pocket of cottonwoods. This is an especially secluded little nook—a perfect place to cast your troubles out onto the cool, roiling waters of the river, to be lulled into long, summer daydreams by the sound of the wind stroking the leaves high overhead. To make a loop out of this walk, continue straight when you reach the road intersection near the marsh, and then take a right at the junction near the entrance to the wildlife area. Keep in mind that this may require a barefoot fording of any water you might have driven through on your way in. Those who prefer to stay on terra firma should return the same way they came.

DEEP RAVINE TRAIL

Distance: 1.25 miles
Location: Go to Custer Battlefield National Monument. The walk leaves from behind the visitor center, adjacent to the National Cemetery.

For all of the beauty to be found in this lilt of northern prairie hills—their blankets of June wildflowers, their warm, brown shoulders of grass—the area can have a certain haunting, unsettled air to it as well. Perhaps it's just the echoes of all the things that have been lost here. Gone are millions of bison and the great herds of pronghorn, as well as the wide rivers of beating wings that once flowed southward with each turn of autumn. Lost here too were many human beings. As you walk this trail you will see huddles of white marker stones scattered across the prairie, one for each man that fell to angry Sioux and Cheyenne warriors on a warm June afternoon in 1876. Five full companies of the Seventh U.S. Cavalry (in this area, Company E), 215 men total, met their deaths on this windswept field of grass and sage. Perhaps what lends an even greater sense of poignancy to this battlefield is that despite the victory achieved here by the Plains Indians—long considered to be troublemakers because of their refusal to accept the white man's rule—it was really the beginning of the end for these people. Retaliation for Custer's defeat was swift. By 1880, the invisible bars of the reservations were firmly in place. The clothes and fancy tools of the white man had been distributed. Children were taken away from their families to special schools, where signs proclaimed to them that "Tradition is the Enemy of Progress." The Indian spirit seeped quietly back into the prairie soil.

Because of its protection as a national monument, this slice of grassland is significantly closer to what the prairie of 1876 may have looked like (minus the wildlife) than the vast majority of surrounding lands. Bluebunch wheatgrass, thick spike, blue grama, yarrow, and salsify form thick carpets. The sage that grew on this particular slope a few years ago, as well as when Custer was here, was burned off in a fire during 1983.

It's important to realize that for the vast majority of its existence, fire was a fact of life on the prairie. For many creatures the great walls of flame that used to roar across these grasslands, often started by lightning strikes or locomotive sparks, were devastating. Only those animals able to escape to their dens, like prairie dogs, badgers, coyotes, and gophers, or those particularly fleet of foot, like pronghorn, were spared. There were certain plants, however, that actually benefited from these burnings. Blue grama, wheatgrasses, and little bluestem rebounded with new vigor, ultimately providing excellent forage for the animals who lived to benefit from it. It was in large part the turning of soil by

Black-tailed Prairie Dog

pioneer farmers that created earthen breaks, ending the unchecked rage that prairie fires had previously been able to muster.

The most telltale evidence of the 1983 fire can be seen 0.4 mile into the walk at the edge of Deep Ravine. Here the chokecherry and ash trees still wear traces of black on their trunks. By the way, although you will see no marker stones in this ravine, there is substantial evidence that many soldiers of Custer's ill-fated Company E were actually killed here. Such shadowed depressions provided corridors of movement for Sioux and Cheyenne warriors, and for a time likely offered whatever fleeting hopes for deliverance that U.S. Cavalry men may have had.

After marker post 7, walk back a short distance and turn southwest onto a footpath running along the west side of the ravine toward the Little Bighorn River. (The Deep Ravine Trail Guide, available at the visitor center, does not cover this section of the walk.) This is a beautiful 0.25 mile stretch of trail through thick grasses, leading to a bench at the monument boundary overlooking the Little Bighorn. Clusters of tall, stately cottonwoods line the river's meanders, which in autumn frame these quiet waters in flowing robes of gold. There are a thousand secret pockets along this watercourse, peppered with ash, willow, chokecherry, and small congregations of reeds and rushes, all washed by a chorus of bird song. Here too are turtles, herons, trout, frogs, catfish, bass, and even mink; the full extent of their interplay is as little understood as any environment in the United States.

POKER JIM LOOKOUT

Distance: 2.5 miles
Location: From Ashland, Montana, head east on Montana Highway 212 for 4 miles. Turn right onto County Road 484 (Otter Creek Road). Continue south for about 20 miles, turning right (west) onto Forest Road 95, 0.5 mile south of the Fort Howes Ranger Station. After 10 miles, turn right onto Forest Road 801. Continue to follow signs for Poker Jim, which is reached 3 miles from this last intersection.

Even if you never make it past the parking lot, this fire lookout and picnic area, perched atop a high, rolling quilt of ponderosa pine and mixed prairie grasses, will be well worth the trip. According to legend, it was during a fall roundup in the late 1880s that two cowboys—one named Jim—decided to stop chasing dogies long enough to play a game or two of poker. Unfortunately, the boss rode up on the game and decided to fire them both. The place has been known as Poker Jim ever since.

There are a number of things in this forest, such as two-track campground roads, old corrals, and wood-frame fire lookouts like this one, that remind me of that warm, personal-touch feeling of the 1950s and 1960s, when I was getting my first glimpses of such enchanting public lands from the back seat of my father's car. For most of the summer this is a true small-town recreation place, where you'll see a few families scattered here and there riding horses or enjoying a picnic lunch. On one particular summer weekend, however, usually in mid-July, the site becomes much more crowded. It's then that a theatrical touring group arrives on this cool ridge top to perform Shakespeare for the locals. A happy mix of lawn chairs, Budweiser, and *Hamlet* unfolds beneath the wide Montana skies. The production must be a good one; a testimony of sorts is local cowpunchers at the hardware store bedecked in John Deere hats and "Shakespeare in the Park" T-shirts.

On a clear day the view from the Poker Jim fire tower is a fine one. To the northwest is a fascinating maze of badlands, carved by the Tongue River and the surrounding creeks. The running water makes graceful, meandering slices through the soft mudstone and Tongue River sandstone, often leaving strange collections of towers and fluted buttresses. Most of the formations in this area are protected by brittle caps of scoria, or clinker. Scoria is a beautiful brick red rock common throughout much of the region, actually the result of untended fires burning beneath the surface of the earth. Dry underground coal seams sometimes ignite, either through lightning, prairie fire, or spontaneous combustion, and can burn for hundreds of years. The heat generated by these burns rises into the stone layers above, baking them much the same as if they were in a giant kiln. Since scoria is a dead giveaway for those looking for coal seams, it comes as little surprise that this region is on the threshold of major coal development.

Unfortunately, in this case such development means sacrificing one of the best prairie rivers in the entire West. The Tongue, in its sinuous flow to the Yellowstone, is a gentle, unspoiled floating stream that hums through a line of canyons and grasslands overflowing with deer, fox, fish, and birds, including nesting double-breasted cormorants and migrating sandhill cranes. Recently approved coal development plans will shatter the silence of this special river. Mining operations in the area may even jeopardize the actual flow of the Tongue, which could have very sorry consequences for many of the furred and feathered creatures who live along its banks.

In the other direction from this perch, 70 to 80 miles to the southwest, are the beautiful Bighorn Mountains, named by Lewis and Clark for the bighorn sheep in the area. It was this mountain massif that caused so many headaches for prospectors looking for a shorter route from the Oregon trail to the gold fields of Montana. John Bozeman and John Jacobs set out to pioneer such a route in 1863. The pair's first outing took them along the northern and western edge of the Bighorns, during which time they were robbed by Crow Indians and forced to eat grasshop-

251

pers in order to survive long enough to reach their destination on the North Platte. Nonetheless, Bozeman and Jacobs's route was destined to become the major path for northwestbound pioneers; some evidence suggests that as many as 85 percent of all those heading to the Montana gold fields did so on this trail. The Indians, however, remained determined to protect the Bighorns—one of their last unspoiled hunting grounds—from further intrusion. The bitter fighting that resulted led to the wagon road being dubbed the "Bloody Bozeman."

Begin your walk by descending the hill road you were just on, passing through lovely folds of grass and ponderosa spiced with the orange, white, yellow, and lavender of mallow, phlox, coneflowers, and horsemint. These "pine breaks," as they're sometimes called, pepper much of the northern plains. In some ways these plains are a subdued version of the Black Hills, similarly populated with white-tailed deer, porcupines, small mammals, and a variety of magnificent raptors. As you make your way down the hill, notice the shrub growing along the road with the three-part, lobed leaves and, in summer and fall, red, hairy berries. This plant is commonly referred to as squawbush, due to the fact that its supple stems were used frequently by Indian women to weave baskets. Two other common names give clues to additional characteristics of the shrub: "skunkbush," because some find the crushed leaves to smell like skunk, and "lemonadeberry," because

Little Bluestem

the tart berries were often mixed with water for a drink that tastes remarkably like lemonade.

In 0.3 mile you'll reach the intersection you passed on the way up. Take a right this time, heading west. Notice the rather large pocket of dead timber off to your left. This was the result of a 300-acre fire that burned here in the summer of 1980.

The walk continues westward and at 1 mile the road begins a descent toward our turnaround point, in a mixed prairie parkland of wheatgrasses, Idaho fescue, and little bluestem. In places where the soil is somewhat sandy, watch for narrowleaf yuccas, which add a peculiar splash of Southwest desert to these cool green mats of Montana grassland.

DIAMOND BUTTE LOOKOUT

Distance: 1.8 miles
Location: From Ashland, Montana, head east on Montana Highway 212 for 4 miles. Turn right on County Road 484 (Otter Creek Road). Continue south for about 20 miles, turning left (east) onto Forest Road 127, 0.5 mile south of the Fort Howes Ranger Station. Approximately 15.75 miles from County Road 484, a fork takes off to the right of Forest Road 127 toward Powder River. Continue straight. The walking road to Diamond Butte Lookout (the tower is clearly visible from Forest Road 127) is 2.3 miles past this junction. Park along Forest Road 127.

If you ever find yourself looking for a job far removed from the madding crowd, in a place where the empty land rolls away in a vast sea of grassy swells and ponderosa islands, where wind and sky offer the only communion, then being a fire lookout at Diamond Butte might be worth considering.

The lookout itself is visible from the very beginning of this walk, standing as lonely sentinel atop a thumb-shaped headland at the brink of the prairie sea. Look for kochia (locally called fireweed) along the edge of the road as well as a smattering of wild roses and squawbush, the latter sporting clusters of red, hairy berries. These tart berries stimulate the flow of saliva, and were often chewed by pioneers crossing these vast expanses to help alleviate thirst. Beyond the roadside fringe lie vast mats of grasses—wheatgrass, Idaho fescue, little bluestem, and blue grama—rippling under the fingers of the wind. Depending on what time of year you're here, scarlet mallow, phlox, prairie coneflowers, and horsemint in the fall lend delicate splashes of color to the scene.

Though to some this land may look harsh and barren, it is in fact one of the most productive regions on earth, having been a cradle of civilization for Indians for thousands of years. During the ice ages, this particular region did not feel the cold tongues of glacial ice that ground south out of Canada into much of the northern United States. It thus became a protected home for large populations of humans. Hundreds of archeological sites have been found here, some of which date back more than 9,000 years. So too, of course, were there animals. Millions and millions of bison, pronghorn, elk, bear, and coyotes roamed these swells, while flocks of migratory birds were so extensive that their passing actually darkened the prairie sky. In fact, for sheer numbers of life forms, this region actually rivaled, and perhaps surpassed, Africa's great Serengeti Plain.

These grasslands came into being in large part because of the creation of the Rocky Mountains. The high peaks of the Rockies pushed moisture-laden, eastbound air upward, causing it to drop most of its liquid cargo in the cool air of the high country. As a result, those lands lying to the east in what is known as the "rain shadow" became dryer. This dryness, as well as a general cooling of the climate, turned the region from a place of wet forests and ferns into one marked by great expanses of drought-tolerant grasses and forbs capable of supporting enormous populations of grazing animals. (Evidence that a very different type of climate once existed here is found in the region's expansive coal seams, which are really just layers of dead plant material that accumulated from ancient swamps. This plant material first existed as peat, and later under enormous pressure turned into coal. It is estimated that a billion tons of coal may exist in this immediate area along what is known as the Knoblock seam.)

Into the walk 0.5 mile you'll be able to look down to the left and right into a pair of small draws. Notice how deciduous plants such as willow are seen nowhere else but in these small ravines, their lives tied to the thin tether of water that courses down these drainages from the surrounding lands. Watch for meadowlarks, ruby-crowned kinglets, and loggerhead shrikes flitting in and out of the draws.

When you reach the fire lookout itself, take a minute to sit on the edge of this promontory and fly a few fantasies on the face of the wind. The wind itself, ever present here, is worth a thought or two. Each year it propels Russian thistle (tumbleweed) across the land, allowing each plant to scatter hundreds of thousands of seeds across the landscape, thus ensuring that the species will survive. In the winter it scours the ridges and hilltops clean of snow, allowing the pronghorn to reach the sagebrush they need to stay alive until the return of spring. The wind also strokes the blades of the old Aeromotor windmills, filling water tanks, allowing Angus and Hereford cattle to survive.

But for Sioux and Cheyenne warriors that lived here in the late 1870s, the wind was no friend when armed with the cold knives of winter. It was then that the new Americans, enraged by the defeat of Custer and his men on the Little Bighorn, began to strike in earnest. Clothing, tipis and food supplies were burned, allowing the icy winds to drive the people to quick defeat. A great many froze to death. After one such winter attack on a Cheyenne village in the Bighorns, a dozen babies were found frozen at their mothers' breasts. Finally, weary of winter warfare, and indeed, of a lifetime of fighting, the last of the Plains Indians presented themselves to area forts and laid down their weapons for good.

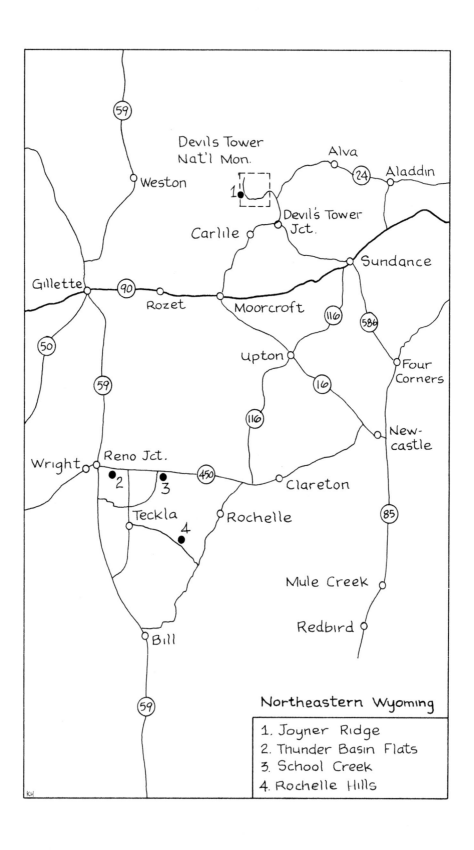

Devils Tower Nat'l Mon.

59

Weston

1

Alva

24

Aladdin

Devil's Tower Jct.

Carlile

Sundance

Gillette

90

Rozet

Moorcroft

116

586

50

59

Upton

16

Four Corners

116

New-castle

Wright

Reno Jct.

2

3

450

Clareton

85

Teckla

Rochelle

4

Mule Creek

Redbird

Bill

59

Northeastern Wyoming

1. Joyner Ridge
2. Thunder Basin Flats
3. School Creek
4. Rochelle Hills

Northeastern Wyoming

JOYNER RIDGE

Distance: 1.7 miles
Location: Go to Devils Tower National Monument. There is one main road in this monument. Approximately 1 mile before reaching the visitor center, a smaller, paved route takes off to the left (north). Follow this a short distance to a signed parking area for the Joyner Ridge Trail. This is a loop trail; begin by taking the left fork.

It is with good reason that Wyoming is occasionally referred to as the "state of firsts," especially when it comes to natural resources. Yellowstone became America's first national park in 1872. The Shoshone National Forest, immediately to the east of Yellowstone, was the first national forest. And, thanks to Theodore Roosevelt, in 1906 this preserve became the nation's first national monument. (Perhaps the most surprising of all in Wyoming's string of "firsts," though, has nothing to do with the natural world. In 1869, the Wyoming territorial legislature became the first known governing body in the world to grant women full rights to vote and hold public office.)

Even from a distance, this great spire that is Devils Tower is certainly an intriguing curiosity. But when you get close enough to stand at its base (a full 1,000 feet across) and see its beautifully fluted sides soaring 867 feet into the Wyoming sky, it becomes a thing of astounding stature. At the beginning of this walk you'll have a fine view of the tower off to your right, across a beautiful quilt of mixed grass prairie peppered with ponderosa pine. (Movie viewers may recognize this amazing landmark from a scene in *Close Encounters of the Third Kind.*)

Devils Tower is really a column of igneous rock. Sixty

million years ago, about the time that the Rocky Mountains were on the way up and dinosaurs were on the way out, this tower was a giant, molten volcanic neck lying more than 1,000 feet below the surface of the earth. As it cooled underground, the volcanic rock fractured into the beautifully fluted four-, five-, and six-sided columns that you see today. While the igneous rock that makes up Devils Tower is quite hard, that which surrounds it—sandstone, shales, limestone, and gypsum—is quite soft. Thus over millions of years the patient forces of wind and water wore away the surrounding landscape, leaving this enormous citadel to stand watch over the surrounding plains.

As you might have guessed, Devils Tower represents an irresistible temptation to climbers. In fact, today over more than 1,000 people make their way to the top each year. The first ascent of the tower was made by a local rancher named William Rogers on the Fourth of July, 1893, to the cheers of more than 1,000 onlookers; two years later, Rogers's wife duplicated the feat. Perhaps the most celebrated trip to the top was made by George Hopkins in 1941. George didn't climb a single foot, but rather dropped to the 1.5-acre rock platform by parachute. Unfortunately, a rope the plane dropped for him to make his descent missed its mark and fell over the side, leaving George stranded for six days until a young mountaineer from Dartmouth was brought in to rescue him from his high, windy perch. The event received an extraordinary amount of public attention.

As you make your way along the Joyner Ridge Trail (named after a former custodian of the monument), notice what appear to be very segmented environmental lines between the ponderosa forest and the grasslands. Actually, there is no such firm line. Prairie and forest are in a constant dance, advancing and retreating according to the climate of preceding years. In the forest to the left keep your eyes open for white-breasted nuthatches, wood pewees, mountain bluebirds, and hairy woodpeckers; on the mixed-grass prairie to the right watch for nighthawks, loggerhead shrikes, meadowlarks, kingbirds, and savannah and lark sparrows, as well as red-tailed and sharp-shinned hawks. This latter bird can put on an extraordinary flying show, darting through open forests and woodlands with phenomenal ease in its pursuit of small birds and mammals.

In 0.75 mile you'll come to a bench running on the edge of a large ravine. Far below in the distance is an open prairie parkland of bluestem, blue grama, and needle and thread grasses, narrowing into a bottleneck below you fringed by deciduous woods. The trail will descend in a series of switchbacks into the ravine 0.1 mile from where you first join this ridge top. From here you can get fine views back up toward the tops of the sculpted sandstone cliffs, each curve of rock throwing back pale, parched colors in the morning sun.

At the upper end of this bottleneck you will enter a wonderful woodland, a soft collage of bur oak, green ash, ponderosa pine, chokecherry, and wild plum. Rouse yourself early enough to walk here just after sunrise and you'll be treated to a marvelous chorus of bird song—chickadees, northern orioles, redstarts, yellow warblers, warbling and solitary vireos, red-breasted nuthatches, and gray catbirds, to name a few. As you make your way up this ravine the forest becomes less dense, and occasional cuts in the canopy let in enough light to allow grasses to rise from the path. (Watch for white-tailed deer in here!) Look for tall clumps of prairie cordgrass lining the roadway. This species typically reaches heights of 3 to 4 feet, and extensive fields growing further to the east made many early settlers think they had arrived in the land of milk and honey.

At the end of the ravine is a large open parkland of mixed prairie—in fact, the very one that you were following along the first section of the walk. A short distance past an interpretive sign at the beginning of the park, take the path leading off to the right, which will take you back to the parking area. But before you get in your car and drive away, take one last look at Devils Tower. Considering its deeply fluted sides, it is not hard to believe the legends of countless Indian tribes of the region about how this structure came to be. In one form or another, they say that a giant bear was attempting to get at a small band of people, most of whom had the good fortune, magic, or physical agility to end up high above the earth on the platform of Devils Tower, just out of reach of the great bruin. The deep furrows you see in the side of the pillar were made by the bear's claws, as he tried in vain to reach the frightened humans. A beautiful painting depicting this legend hangs today in the visitor center.

THUNDER BASIN FLATS

Distance: 1.5 miles
Location: The walk is located at Thunder Basin National Grassland. From Wyoming State Highway 59, 3 miles south of Reno Junction, head east on Wyoming State Highway 450, toward Newcastle. Just over 3 miles from this junction, turn onto a small dirt road taking off to the south. This road forks just south of the highway; park at the fork and begin your walk on the right branch.

Thunder Basin National Grassland, rarely even noticed by travelers blasting past on Wyoming State Highway 59 toward Yellowstone, is actually a rich tapestry of varying environments—broad grassy plains, quiet shimmering creeks, and unexpected pockets of forest and badlands. The paths we'll walk in this region will explore three of these ecosystems, beginning with a walk across the long reaches of a yawning expanse of grass and sagebrush, capped by a wide, blue arc of Wyoming sky.

There are several plants visible at the beginning of this walk that you will see again and again as you walk or drive across this slice of high prairie. Let's begin by taking a look at big sagebrush, the plant sporting a woody stem and blunt, gray-green leaves that exude a pungent odor when crushed. This plant covers literally millions of acres in the American West, and is the most common type of artemesia, or "wormwood" found in the deserts of the Great Basin. Big sagebrush is no relation to the sage used as a cooking spice, which is a member of the mint family.

The presence of sage and another common plant here, western wheatgrass, is a typical mix in those sections of the American prairie marked by colder temperatures and fairly dry conditions (12 to 14 inches of moisture per year). Head west from here and, very generally speaking, you'll encounter more sage and less grass; head east and the opposite will be true. Sagebrush does yield to grasses for several years after a fire goes through, but in some areas of Wyoming there is hardly enough grass to sustain a major fire.

About 100 yards down the road you'll also see needle and thread grass, and, a serious nonnative invader of the prairie, cheat grass. The former plant bears its pointed seeds on the end of long hanging "threads." These coiled threads actually twist every time there's a change in humidity—a trait that helps ensure germination by actually screwing the seed into the ground. Cheat grass is a relatively short grass with very blond, flag-shaped heads. It has taken over much of the Wyoming prairie and is of very little value of either domestic livestock or wild grazers. To a great degree this is the result of poor management practices, in particular allowing cattle to graze in one place for too long. An alternative management method, a lesson derived from the millions of bison that once roamed here, is simply to keep the cattle moving as they gaze—a pattern allowing, and to some degree stimulating, the growth of more desirable native plants. Strangely, few ranchers seem interested in pursuing the solution.

While you may sense a "sameness" to this land the first time you find yourself on it, there is really no shortage of diversions. The beautiful pronghorn, able to subsist on a remarkable variety of plants from prickly pear to sagebrush, is very much at home here. In the winter they may be seen huddling in groups across the landscape, dining on the leaves of big sagebrush plants blown free of snow by the restless prairie winds. Cottontails also are here as is the beautiful sage grouse. Sage grouse, not nearly as numerous today as a hundred years ago, are known for their fascinating courtship rituals. Each spring, males return to established display grounds and begin complex dances. Feathers of the neck, tail, and wing are spread, and special air sacs in the breast are inflated, showing off the downy mat of creamy white plumage that surrounds them. Loud popping noises rise from the chest, audible across remarkably long distances. After some time females will begin walking through the display area, eventually coming to rest in front of the mate of their choice.

Into the walk 0.5 mile you'll come to a *playa*, which is a depression in the terrain, sometimes lined with an underground cap of clay that each spring fills with water. These shallow pockets remain wet well into summer, providing both cattle and wildlife with drinking water. Notice that the plant life here is quite different from that of the surrounding terrain. Most obvious is the absence of sagebrush, a gap you'll see in the prairie quilt wherever there are saturated soils.

Continue to walk south for another 0.25 mile or so, far enough away from the highway so that you can sense the complete lack of noise variety on the prairie, its one pervading sound being either a whisper or rush of tumbling prairie winds. Really stop and take a long look at these vast open spaces, the sheer magnitude of which goes far beyond what most of us are able or perhaps willing to consider.

SCHOOL CREEK

Distance: 1.75 miles
Location: From Wyoming State Highway 59, turn east onto Wyoming State Highway 450, toward Newcastle. Proceed for about 15 miles and turn right (south) onto School Creek Road. In approximately 0.5 mile, turn left (east) onto a two-track road. Park in about 0.2 mile, at the side of a small stream channel.

A stream corridor winding across the prairie can be a ribbon of magic, bringing an explosion of willow, cottonwood, rush, and cord grass to these long, yawning fields of grass and sage. Here in the thickets great congregations of birds may be seen, and hiding beneath a cloak of darkness, raccoons, badgers, long-tailed weasels, muskrat, coyotes, and occasionally ermine and mountain lion. After spending some time investigating the who and what of this riparian corridor, climb up past it toward the east to a small roadway running beside a small reservoir, and turn right. If you creep up on this reservoir slowly, you're likely to spot a group of mallards. These birds, with their green heads and beautiful chestnut breasts, are the most plentiful of all the North American ducks. They are the ancestors of our domestic ducks.

As you make your way long this small roadway, you'll pass through thick mats of cheat grass, as well as occasional clumps of plains prickly pear. As you walk south, to the left you'll see an escarpment covered with ponderosa pine. This long, broken ridge line runs north all the way into Montana, where it forms a portion of the famed Missouri Breaks. This ridge also marks one of the

Locoweed

largest coal seams in the West. The Black Thunder coal operation, which you passed coming east from Wyoming Highway 450, is just one of several mines operating on the 500,000 acres of Thunder Basin National Grassland. On the other side of the pine breaks is the town of Newcastle, a former hotbed for poker players, founded in search of coal in the late 1800s.

Into the walk 0.25 mile you'll reach a large flat covered with greasewood. The salty leaves of greasewood are quite edible in limited quantities and were a source of greens for many Indian tribes. In the animal world, jackrabbits are particularly fond of the plant. The greasewood has definitely expanded its territory on Thunder Basin and in other areas of the northern plains. Some researchers believe that over the years, through a complex altering of the environment due to overgrazing, the alkalinity of bottomland soils has increased, making the land much more appropriate to the growth of greasewood, and much less so to more traditional native plants.

In a short distance you'll come to our turnaround point at a T intersection. Rather than return by the same route, head cross-country to the School Creek drainage, visible 100 yards or so over your left shoulder (north) by a light peppering of cottonwoods. You can follow this back toward the reservoir you passed earlier in the walk. As you make your way across the landscape, keep your eyes out for badger holes, recognizable by their distinctive half-moon entrances, as well as the more rounded dens of fox and coyote. There are also prairie rattlesnakes here. Although they have no more interest in you than you may have in them, you should nevertheless be on the lookout.

The trees of this delightful meandering drainage are common perches for bald eagles who are often seen here from November through March. During periods of intense cold, they congregate in the tree-lined hummocks immediately to the north, in a section of the pine breaks known as the Rochelle Hills. Also in these hills are a herd of about 90 elk, a surprising occurrence, since these regal animals are usually found in much more extensive reaches of the high country.

As you make your way up through this braid of old stream channels, look for the tracks of raccoons in the jigsaw blocks of wet clay that often line this bottomland. These remarkable animals, which may weigh up to 25 pounds and live for a dozen years, are extremely agile and clever—two traits that allow them to escape death at the jaws of much larger and faster predators. Raccoons will eat almost anything, but in this area their diet consists mostly of small animals, fruits, birds' eggs, and carrion. True to the tales we all grew up with, raccoons do wash much of their food before eating it, a fact reflected in their Latin species name, *lotor*, or "washer."

Earlier I suggested that changes in the environment due to overgrazing have increased the alkalinity of certain bottomland soils. But over the past 75 years, overgrazing has brought about an even more devastating change to these riparian corridors. Because the lushest grass cover of the prairie is found along its streams and rivers, it is no surprise that cattle have always made their way to these areas first. By staying along the banks for long periods of time, completely devouring some plants and trampling others, the protective cover of vegetation is eventually destroyed. This allows the stream to cut deeper and deeper into its banks.

Rather than drifting across the floodplain in the usual series of oxbows and meanders, over the decades the stream begins to channelize itself, cutting down instead of across. Unfortunately, the beautiful wide bands of cottonwoods that line the bottomlands

Red Fox

Badger

of the western prairies, important both for their control of erosion and as wildlife habitat, are completely dependent on the normal drifts of stream channels for their propagation. The flooded silts along a drifting stream channel are what allow cottonwood seeds, only viable for a few weeks, to take hold and grow. A patch of trees located far from the stream got their start as a group, at a time when the stream channel was closer to that location. This is why you'll see cottonwoods that are essentially the same age growing in groups.

All this means that the wide prairie belts of cottonwoods, such as those near Little Thunder Creek along Wyoming Highway 450, are on the way out. As these trees die off—and most here are nearing the end of their life cycle—they will not be replaced by others. Eventually there will be only a narrow ribbon of cottonwoods along the immediate stream channel. Although this situation is to an extent correctable with proper land management, few people in either the government or the private sector seem willing

Blue Grama

266

to pursue the matter. Cattle continue to graze the stream bottoms very heavily and the land continues to suffer.

On the way back, take a closer look at the escarpment off to the east—sedimentary rocks topped with a layer of brick red scoria. Scoria is created when the heat from burning underground coal seams actually bakes the layers of shale above them, much as a clay pot is fired in a kiln. (Coal seams can ignite by a number of methods including spontaneous combustion.) You are, in fact, walking near an extremely large underground coal seam, 70 to 100 feet thick.

ROCHELLE HILLS

Distance: 1.4 miles
Location: Take Wyoming Highway 59 out of Douglas for approximately 35 miles, and at a place where the highway veers to the northwest, leave it to head north on the Steinle Road. In just over 5.5 miles, the Steinle Road turns east, and continues for another 6 miles to the Dull Center Road. Turn left (north). In just under 10 miles you'll turn left onto the Rochelle Hills Road. Continue north and then west on this road for 11.4 miles, to a small dirt road taking off to the north. Park here and begin your walk northward along this route.
Note: These roads can become slick after a good rain.

The Rochelle Hills are a complete surprise in a land that appears to be a place of only subtle cuts and swells from Wyoming Highway 59, a slightly crumpled blanket of wheatgrass, cheat grass, and sage. But this small road will take you into a very different place, one cool and thick with ponderosa, with high, sheer escarpments that make dizzy plunges toward the prairie below. There is no shortage of quiet, wooded pockets for sitting and daydreaming, or of high perches from which to watch prairie falcons, golden eagles, and Swainson's, ferruginous, and red-tailed hawks hanging high on the winds above the Thunder Basin.

This walk begins in a large meadow of cheat, bluebunch wheat, blue grama, June and little bluestem grasses, surrounded by a thick wall of ponderosa pine. Blue grama, the plant with curled flag-shaped heads and a low, matted base, is the most common short grass on this prairie, as well as the most nutritious for grazing animals. It tends to form thick mats of tough sod that are very resistant to erosion. It's interesting to consider how the grasses of the prairie are grazed in such a manner as to allow wild and domestic grazers alike to store up the maximum amount of energy possible. In spring or early summer blue grama is the main entree. As this becomes limited later on, the animals move over to buffalo grass, or to the tops of needle and thread grass. It was through such cyclical grazing that at one time millions and millions of bison were able to sustain themselves on the fare of the Great Plains.

Of course the ponderosa, lending such stature and beauty to this high escarpment, deserves some honorable mention here. This is the most widely distributed pine on the continent and is an extremely important source of commercial wood products. The nuts of the ponderosa were collected and eaten by various Indian peoples, and still provide a good food source for chipmunks, jays, and squirrels. Another animal that seems fond of this pine is the porcupine; look for sections on these trees where the tasty bark has been peeled away. Porcupines are rather solitary animals but will huddle (carefully!) together during extremely cold weather. As you might guess, porcupines have few enemies. Some clever, hungry coyotes, however, have developed the ability to roll the porcupine over and attack its soft belly. But woe to those who miss their mark! A mouth full of these tough, barbed quills has caused many a predator to starve to death because it became too painful to ingest food.

Even with these ponderosa breaks, you may notice more than a little wind up on this escarpment. While such constant blowing is not relished by most humans, for the pronghorn who live here it is a vital link to life. Unlike deer and elk, pronghorn have almost no body fat. As a result, there is no option to wait out a bad winter storm; they must eat virtually every day of their lives. Were it not for the winds blowing the big sagebrush you see here free of snow, the pronghorn would most certainly not be able to survive.

In 0.7 mile you'll reach our turnaround point, at a high perch offering tremendous views of the prairie lands to the west, north, and east. According to geologists, much of the region lying before you was once the same height as these pine breaks. The escarpment is simply capped with a protective layer of scoria, or clinker, which kept wind and water from eroding it away. Basically, scoria is a layer of shale that the heat from a burning underground coal seam hardened into rock. (This process still goes on in some areas today.) This brick-colored stone lies in pieces all along the top of the pine breaks.

On a clear day, you can look to the northeast and easily see all the way into the Black Hills of South Dakota. It was hostilities in this region that led to some of the last, bloodiest encounters in the Western Indian wars. Despite the fact that the Black Hills had been made a part of the Great Sioux Reservation by the Treaty of 1868, in 1874 General George Armstrong Custer led a wagon train of soldiers into the region and found gold. Predictably, in no time at all miners were pouring into the area, totally unconcerned that they were storming Indian lands. This invasion, combined with strong efforts the following year to prohibit native peoples from roaming unsettled territory, sent an unprecedented number of reservation Indians packing. They joined spring hunting parties to the west in great numbers along the streams south of the Yellowstone River. It was one such congregation of perhaps 10,000 Blackfoot, Oglala, Sioux, and Cheyenne, along the Greasy Grass (Little Bighorn River), that Custer found that fateful June day in 1876 when he and 215 men came to their deaths on a windswept Montana prairie.

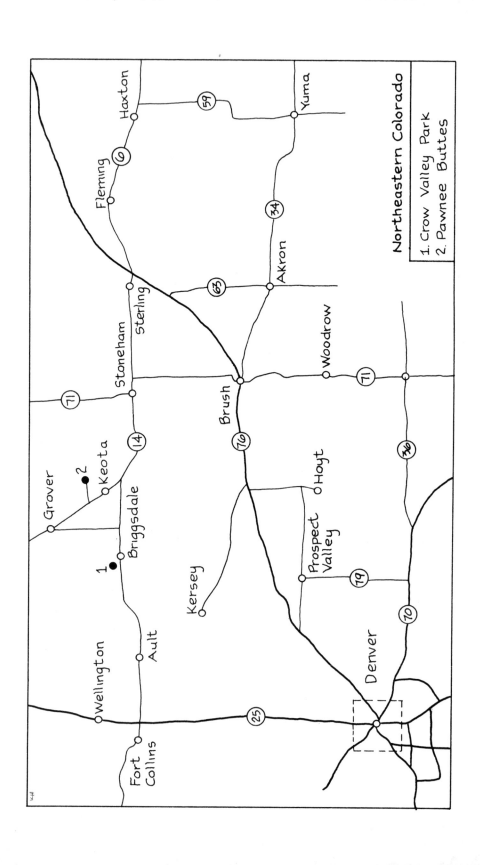

Northeastern Colorado

1. Crow Valley Park
2. Pawnee Buttes

Northeastern Colorado

CROW VALLEY PARK

Distance: 0.1 mile
Location: Heading east on Colorado State Highway 14, turn
north just outside the small town of Briggsdale. Follow signs
for Crow Valley Park, which turns off to the left about 0.2 mile
north of Colorado State Highway 14. Head west through the
park into the campground; our walk takes off beside camping
unit 4.

This quiet little park is one of those pleasant jewels that drifting
vacationers hope to find but almost never do along the main thor-
oughfares of travel. While much of it is nicely manicured—the
"state park" look—a tiny slice of moist prairie thrives directly west
of the campground, thanks in large measure to the nurturing waters
of Crow Creek. Make no mistake: There are more than a few
introduced plants mixed in with the natives. Yet this shortest of all
our walks will provide you with a good opportunity to learn a few
of the plants that you'll see on other, more remote forays in the
Pawnee Grasslands. (See the Pawnee Buttes walk, page 275.)

The Pawnee Indians, for which this grassland is named,
were among the first Indians of the past 300 years to establish
themselves on the grasslands. They came at a time when bison and
pronghorn thundered across this gentle landscape by the millions,
and great flocks of migratory birds darkened the skies each autumn.
Besides the food, tools, clothing, and ceremonial objects that these
creatures provided, the plants of the shortgrass prairie also were an
important ingredient for their survival.

Threats of this delicate balance between the Pawnee and
their homeland did not come from other tribes (Sioux poured
through these lands early in the nineteenth century, pushed out of

271

Minnesota by the Chippewa) but rather from the storms of Europeans who decided to go west. Hundreds of thousands of pioneers
rumbled through this country in wagon trains bound for the Pacific
coast in the 1850s and 1860s, wiping out a good share of Pawnee
grass, game, and timber in the process. Much later came those
looking to be farmers, each determined with the help of their
government to put this land into more productive use. Watching
his former hunting grounds being bitten into by the blades of
plows, one dismayed Pawnee chief said "grass no good upside
down." This was a rather prophetic comment, considering that just
a few decades later the great drought arrived, turning these tended
fields into nothing but barren sand and blowing dust.

Our short stroll takes off from behind camping unit 4. Once
past a couple of beautiful willows, the path drops down off a small
bench into a congregation of young cottonwoods, thistle, and curly
dock. This latter plant is one of the most common in the entire
world, easily identifiable by its curly leaf edges. Curly dock (sometimes called yellow dock) has had a rather long history as a medicinal plant, primarily for the treatment of indigestion and
constipation, but occasionally in the treatment of acne as well.
Before more modern therapies came along, it was also used to treat
intestinal cancer.

On the left 30 to 40 yards you'll see a collection of Rocky
Mountain juniper and Siberian elm as well as a fairly lush carpet of
smooth brome grass. Both the elm and the brome grass were
brought into the plains area long ago as part of the effort to retard
soil erosion. Even today, brome, with its ability to form sod quickly,
is one of several species used in seed form by highway departments
to stabilize disturbed road corridors.

As the trail makes a turn to the left, you'll be walking
through a mixture of western and crested wheatgrasses, the latter
being another nonnative species, brought in from Asia to stabilize
soils abused by farming and overgrazing. Further down the path are
the very delicate fronds of switchgrass, and the distinctive low,
curly mat leaves belonging to blue grama.

In a short distance the trail will make another turn to the
left, heading back toward the campground. The small depression
on your left contains willow, curly dock, and the beautiful evening

primrose. Once the beautiful blooms have withered away on the primrose, the seeds of the plants provide an important source of food. Also here is the milkweed, which certainly deserves special attention for its amazing attributes. The beautiful monarch butterfly depends entirely on milkweed leaves for its sustenance. Thomas Edison used the sap to make a primitive form of rubber.

But perhaps the most astounding use of the milkweed plant occurred during World War II. Up until the early 1940s, the United States used tremendous amounts of a fibery seed from the silk cotton tree, which grew on the East Indian islands, to fill life vests for fighting Navy men. But in 1942, these islands were captured by the Japanese, leaving us in a major pinch for flotation material. Milkweed to the rescue! It was found that less than two pounds of milkweed floss could keep a 150 pound man afloat for two days. Prodded into action by the Department of Agriculture, thousands of school children and Boy Scout troops set out across the American countryside, filling onion sacks with pods and sending them off for processing to a plant in Petosky, Michigan. Before they were finished, these young pickers had harvested 25 million pounds of pods—enough for more than a million life vests. As a result, many lives were saved by this humble, often overlooked plant.

As you continue along this depression, keep your eyes open for western kingbirds, horned larks, shrikes, western meadowlarks, vesper, and lark sparrows, as well as the beautiful lemon-colored plumage of the American goldfinch. The path will pass near a cluster of old elm trees on your right, and then exit adjacent to camping unit 5.

Western Kingbird

Western Meadowlark

PAWNEE BUTTES

Distance: 4.2 miles
Location: Head east out of Briggsdale on Colorado State Highway 14. At the point where this highway veers to the southeast,
turn left (north) onto Weld County Road 390. Proceed for 14.2
miles, then turn right (east) onto Weld County Road 112. In
6.6 miles you'll come to a T intersection; turn right onto Weld
County 107. In 2.1 miles you'll take a left (north) onto a signed
road for Pawnee Buttes Trail. After this turn, 1.1 miles, make
one last left turn at a windmill; the parking area for the trail is
down this road 50 yards on the right.

It's little wonder that the director of the movie version of James
Michener's *Centennial* chose this place to film wagons rolling into
the wild frontier. This is still a remarkably uncluttered slice of
Colorado prairie. The songs of early America seem fresh and crisp
here, and they riffle through your hair and past your ears, carried in
the strong arms of the western wind. Though they rise only 250
feet above the grassy valleys below, the Pawnee Buttes must have
seemed like giants to those who jostled in their wagons across half
a continent. To some they were warm portals of welcome; to
others, troublesome reminders that not far beyond were the ramparts of the Rockies.

Our walk begins with a gentle descent to the east down a
shallow ravine peppered with yucca, western wheatgrass, and cheat
grass. While the first two of these plants are natives, cheat grass was
introduced more than a century ago, and with its remarkable ability
to take over abused soils, it is absolutely flourishing on the overgrazed prairies of the West. Unfortunately for the cattle industry,
which has inadvertently brought about the rapid spread of cheat
grass, the plant has very little value as forage.

Down the trail 0.2 mile you'll come to a beautiful flat plain
rich with blue grama, an important sod builder and valuable forage
plant on the prairies of the West, now the state grass of Colorado.
From this plateau the view is indeed a grand one, the great plains
tumbling off to the east for mile after mile, finally lost to vision in
a melt of summer sky. It was on the distant shore of this great sea
of grass that in 1853 a bizarre event took place in Westport, Missouri, the jumping-off place for the Santa Fe Trail.

275

Living at the edge of the frontier provided the citizens of Westport with more than their share of excitement. Yet no one was ready for the stir that a former seafaring captain named Zeb Thomas caused when he came rolling down Main Street that sunny spring morning on a wagon powered by sails rather than horses. His intention, as he revealed to a full house of curious residents at a local tavern, was to launch an entire fleet of these prairie clippers on the rolling grasslands between Westport and Sante Fe. With their great speed and no need for fuel, windwagons would make the road to riches one smooth sail. All he needed to get started was a few partners—a few partners with money, that is.

"Windwagon Thomas" didn't wait for the hoots and hollers of laughter to die down. He stormed out of the tavern, climbed aboard his prairie schooner, and announced that he was off to Council Grove, Kansas. When he returned from the 300-mile trip six days later, armed with a letter from a prominent resident of the city as proof of the trip, suddenly there was a shortage of laughter and an abundance of investors. Showered with all the money he could use, Thomas wasted no time in getting down to the business of building the first freight-hauling windwagon. And what a vessel it was, measuring 25 feet long and 7 feet wide, sporting wheels twice the height of a man. As

Deer Mouse

the partners stood by, grinning at the thought of how much cargo a fleet of these clippers could carry, Admiral Thomas prepared the sleek craft for its maiden voyage.

Things started off well enough. But then the wind picked up a little. And then it picked up a little more. Soon Thomas and his rather inept crew of landlubbers began cruising at a much higher speed than they had ever intended. And then, as luck would have it, there was that blasted dip in the prairie. Unable to get the boom down in time, the windwagon drove hard into the side of the ravine, pivoting it into the air and smashing it on its side in a flurry of splinters. Admiral Thomas was tossed onto his head in the process. With a blue streak of curses that only a New England sailor could muster, Thomas got up and stomped away. Later that evening he loaded a few belongings into his smaller, still intact windwagon, and sailed out of sight, never to be heard from again.

Shortly after passing a fence at 0.5 mile, the trail begins a descent through a lovely huddle of miniature shale pillars, framed on either side by large, buff-colored sandstone buttes. Look for creepers here, sinking their roots deep into this dry ground. As wind and water carry away the surrounding soil, the patches protected by these plants are left standing as sandy pillars, looking from a distance like huddles of green stumps. (A larger feat of erosion, conducted by great rivers of glacial melt water that coursed through the area following the last ice age, is what left the Pawnee Buttes standing far above the surrounding landscape.) Watch along this stretch for little bluestem grass, whose seeds provide an important source of food for wintering birds. Speaking of birds, the rock spires around you form an important nesting area for several raptors; turn your eyes skyward occasionally and you may glimpse a soaring prairie falcon or golden eagle.

The path continues into a ravine with squawbush and Rocky Mountain juniper, then climbs back up onto a flat dappled with needle and thread grass. After passing a large butte on the left, at 1.5 miles you'll come out on a road with a view of a teapot-shaped butte ahead and slightly to your left. Follow the road to our turn-around point at the base of this massive monument. Sit for a few

Swainson's Hawk

minutes with your back against these warm brown walls, letting the
prairie winds blow this airy, silent scene into your consciousness—
the stroke of grass, the wash of rock and sky. While I was here I had
the distinct feeling that in some small measure this was still the old
West—a priceless launching pad for the spirits of yet another gen-
eration.